From the library of

*Rfn J.F. Flint*

## Palgrave Studies in European Union Politics

Edited by: **Michelle Egan**, American University, USA; **Neill Nugent**, Manchester Metropolitan University, UK; and **William Paterson OBE**, University of Aston, UK.

Editorial Board: **Christopher Hill**, Cambridge, UK; **Simon Hix**, London School of Economics, UK; **Mark Pollack**, Temple University, USA; **Kalypso Nicolaïdis**, Oxford, UK; **Morten Egeberg**, University of Oslo, Norway; **Amy Verdun**, University of Victoria, Canada; **Claudio M. Radaelli**, University of Exeter, UK; and **Frank Schimmelfennig**, Swiss Federal Institute of Technology, Switzerland

Following on the sustained success of the acclaimed *European Union Series*, which essentially publishes research-based textbooks, *Palgrave Studies in European Union Politics* publishes cutting-edge, research-driven monographs.

The remit of the series is broadly defined, in terms of both subject and academic discipline. All topics of significance concerning the nature and operation of the European Union potentially fall within the scope of the series, which is multidisciplinary to reflect the growing importance of the European Union as a political, economic and social phenomenon.

*Titles include*:

Jens Blom-Hansen
THE EU COMITOLOGY SYSTEM IN THEORY AND PRACTICE
Keeping an Eye on the Commission?

Oriol Costa and Knud Erik Jørgensen (*editors*)
THE INFLUENCE OF INTERNATIONAL INSTITUTIONS ON THE EU
When Multilateralism Hits Brussels

Falk Daviter
POLICY FRAMING IN THE EUROPEAN UNION

Renaud Dehousse (*editor*)
THE 'COMMUNITY METHOD'
Obstinate or Obsolete?

Kenneth Dyson and Angelos Sepos (*editors*)
WHICH EUROPE?
The Politics of Differentiated Integration

Michelle Egan, Neill Nugent and William E. Paterson (*editors*)
RESEARCH AGENDAS IN EU STUDIES
Stalking the Elephant

Theofanis Exadaktylos and Claudio M. Radaelli (*editors*)
RESEARCH DESIGN IN EUROPEAN STUDIES
Establishing Causality in Europeanization

Kevin Featherstone and Dimitris Papadimitriou
THE LIMITS OF EUROPEANIZATION
Reform Capacity and Policy Conflict in Greece

David J. Galbreath and Joanne McEvoy
THE EUROPEAN MINORITY RIGHTS REGIME
Towards a Theory of Regime Effectiveness

Roy H. Ginsberg and Susan E. Penska
THE EUROPEAN UNION IN GLOBAL SECURITY
The Politics of Impact

Eva Gross
THE EUROPEANIZATION OF NATIONAL FOREIGN POLICY
Continuity and Change in European Crisis Management

Adrienne Héritier and Martin Rhodes (*editors*)
NEW MODES OF GOVERNANCE IN EUROPE
Governing in the Shadow of Hierarchy

Wolfram Kaiser, Brigitte Leucht and Michael Gehler
TRANSNATIONAL NETWORKS IN REGIONAL INTEGRATION
Governing Europe 1945–83

Hussein Kassim and Handley Stevens
AIR TRANSPORT AND THE EUROPEAN UNION
Europeanization and Its Limits

Robert Kissack
PURSUING EFFECTIVE MULTILATERALISM
The European Union, International Organizations and the Politics of Decision Making

Xymena Kurowska and Fabian Breuer (*editors*)
EXPLAINING THE EU's COMMON SECURITY AND DEFENCE POLICY
Theory in Action

Karl-Oskar Lindgren and Thomas Persson
PARTICIPATORY GOVERNANCE IN THE EU
Enhancing or Endangering Democracy and Efficiency?

Philomena Murray (*editor*)
EUROPE AND ASIA
Regions in Flux

Daniel Naurin and Helen Wallace (*editors*)
UNVEILING THE COUNCIL OF THE EUROPEAN UNION
Games Governments Play in Brussels

Sebastiaan Princen
AGENDA-SETTING IN THE EUROPEAN UNION

Emmanuelle Schon-Quinlivan
REFORMING THE EUROPEAN COMMISSION

Roger Scully and Richard Wyn Jones (*editors*)
EUROPE, REGIONS AND EUROPEAN REGIONALISM

Mitchell P. Smith (*editor*)
EUROPE AND NATIONAL ECONOMIC TRANSFORMATION
The EU after the Lisbon Decade

Asle Toje
AFTER THE POST-COLD WAR
The European Union as a Small Power

Richard G. Whitman and Stefan Wolff (*editors*)
THE EUROPEAN NEIGHBOURHOOD POLICY IN PERSPECTIVE
Context, Implementation and Impact

Richard G. Whitman (*editor*)
NORMATIVE POWER EUROPE
Empirical and Theoretical Perspectives

Sarah Wolff
THE MEDITERRANEAN DIMENSION OF THE EUROPEAN UNION'S INTERNAL SECURITY

Jan Wouters, Hans Bruyninckx, Sudeshna Basu and Simon Schunz (*editors*)
THE EUROPEAN UNION AND MULTILATERAL GOVERNANCE
Assessing EU Participation in United Nations Human Rights and Environmental Fora

**Palgrave Studies in European Union Politics**
**Series Standing Order ISBN 978–1–4039–9511–7 (hardback)**
**and ISBN 978–1–4039–9512–4 (paperback)**
(*outside North America only*)

You can receive future titles in this series as they are published by placing a standing order. Please contact your bookseller or, in case of difficulty, write to us at the address below with your name and address, the title of the series and one of the ISBNs quoted above.

Customer Services Department, Macmillan Distribution Ltd, Houndmills, Basingstoke, Hampshire RG21 6XS, England

# Research Design in European Studies

## Establishing Causality in Europeanization

Edited by

Theofanis Exadaktylos
*Lecturer in European Politics, University of Surrey, UK*

and

Claudio M. Radaelli
*Professor of Political Science, University of Exeter, UK*

First published 2012 by
PALGRAVE MACMILLAN

Palgrave Macmillan in the UK is an imprint of Macmillan Publishers Limited, registered in England, company number 785998, of Houndmills, Basingstoke, Hampshire RG21 6XS.

Palgrave Macmillan in the US is a division of St Martin's Press LLC, 175 Fifth Avenue, New York, NY 10010.

Palgrave Macmillan is the global academic imprint of the above companies and has companies and representatives throughout the world.

Palgrave® and Macmillan® are registered trademarks in the United States, the United Kingdom, Europe and other countries.

ISBN 978–0–230–28531–6

This book is printed on paper suitable for recycling and made from fully managed and sustained forest sources. Logging, pulping and manufacturing processes are expected to conform to the environmental regulations of the country of origin.

A catalogue record for this book is available from the British Library.

A catalog record for this book is available from the Library of Congress.

10   9   8   7   6   5   4   3   2   1
21  20  19  18  17  16  15  14  13  12

Printed and bound in Great Britain by
CPI Antony Rowe, Chippenham and Eastbourne

*To*
*Vakis and Katerina*
*Fausto and Luisa*

# Contents

# Tables, Figures and Boxes

## Tables

## Figures

## Boxes

# Preface

The expansion of academic work on Europeanization is continued evidence of the vibrancy of research on European studies. This timely edited collection brings together scholars interested in understanding causality in European integration, drawing on the fields of international relations and comparative politics. The concept of Europeanization has gone through several 'waves' of research, from the early work on institutional adaptation to membership, to the 'second wave' of research on structural changes to domestic political systems that can be attributed to European integration, to the more recent 'third wave' of research that does not focus on Europeanization only in terms of administrative and institutional adaptation. This final wave also draws on the burgeoning research on civil society, parties and enlargement to processes that link Europeanization with transnationalism, partisan politics and party cleavages, as well as good governance and conditionality. It moves beyond concepts and definitions to more self reflection on how the language that is used shapes theoretical debates, and to understand how discourse, ideas and socialization shape the process of Europeanization. It has also been more conscious of the political contestation that affects Europeanization as well as the contestation and oppositional responses to Europeanization which constrain the role and actions of the European Union (EU). And it recognizes the politics of non decision-making, where negotiated outcomes are either deferred or shelved, or where structural barriers or veto points within the institutions themselves shape the dynamics of Europeanization. Preferences and meaning develop when new tasks are taken on board and new participants become involved, leading to the development of new choices which affect causality in Europeanization. Research on Europeanization is thus confronted with ambiguity, temporality, cross-pressures and conflicts that produce a more nuanced view of how to deal with such research problems. The logic of method and methodology are not mutually exclusive, as the editors point out, and the range of methods available – from statistical modelling to ethnographic approaches – are broad.

While different perspectives address causality in European integration, this volume takes stock of the research agenda in this area and tries to tease out the appropriate research design to understand domestic political and social changes that involve adaptation and resistance to Europeanization. The focus on Europeanization brings to the fore the relationship between the international system and the domestic one, as the authors focus on the characteristics of the 'top down' approach to understanding how the regional level has become a factor in explaining domestic developments and how the international system has become a cause and not a consequence of the way states operate in Europe. Member states – as well as applicant states – more than ever derive some of their domestic organizational operations, their political mobilization and their different institutional configurations from the exigencies of EU governance. Many of the characteristics of the current system, such as economic interdependence and the role of trade, transnational actors' political mobilization and contentious politics, have placed pressure on sovereignty, have been amplified by European integration and have been discussed widely in the international political economy and international relations literature.

The impact of Europeanization goes beyond this, to influencing specific decisions and policies, coalition and ideological patterns, and the processes and procedures of decision-making, which constitute important effects on domestic outcomes. And while structural features are often those that elicit the most visible changes, such as referendums, elections, privatization and constitutional amendments, the authors here look for systematic, diachronic relationships between the domestic and international. While strategic decisions – such as those states accepted into the euro, an applicant state accepted for membership or an agreement on border controls – impact both territoriality and governance, they are often not the beginning or end point of Europeanization, raising questions regarding the measurement, observation and impact of the temporal dimension in studies of Europeanization, which involve developing models in terms of causality, instrumentation and evaluation. Although there is still a great deal that needs to be done in terms of causation, there is an extant body of knowledge about instruments and outcomes.

The contributors grapple with this issue through detailed case studies that allow them to take account of variation in domestic political systems, organizational setting and different instruments which may foster Europeanization. These include both litigation and formal mechanisms of compliance, as well as the provision of information, advocacy and persuasion, economic incentives and disincentives, and regulation. Key considerations are the degree to which incentives or coercion are used and formal versus informal mechanisms of governance in shaping policy outcomes. In looking at what contextual and policy factors impact Europeanization, the authors are conscious of trying to understand what is attributable to the process of Europeanization and what is the result of other mediating factors. In their efforts to transcend the initial concerns about concept definition, to focus on the differential as well as incidental impacts of Europeanization and to expand spatially to include both the internal and external dynamics of European discourse, identity and policy framing, shaping and promoting to include non-EU member states, the editors have put together a team of researchers who illustrate the complexity and multiple configurations of Europeanization.

Covering a range of topics and theoretical approaches related to European integration, this book is a major contribution to that 'third wave' of work on Europeanization, focusing not just on policy outputs but also on changes in identities in terms of norms and values and of institutions in terms of bureaucratic culture and political organization. This new wave of research is much more attuned to structure and agency, and the question of temporality is also important as the authors do not use a time series where they observe events at different uniform intervals and assume that there is a natural ordering and sequence to events. They are much less mechanistic, using discourse analysis, critical realism, cross-national variation, process tracing and single case studies – in sum, a mixed methods approach.

For some of the authors, values, ideas and options derive from past events, performance or action; hence Europeanization is not built on a *tabula rasa* but reflects the importance of path dependency. For other authors, the outcomes of Europeanization are determined by the nature and constraints being built into the policymaking process or institutional outcome so that a new set of incentives or actions can change behaviours. In all these cases, the process of Europeanization may be incremental and thus the time horizon for identifying substantive change or resistance is one the authors must grapple with. Nor should the process be just 'top down' regulative; it can also be normative and cognitive in effect.

Clearly the editors believe it is important to bring to the table the conceptual, ontological, spatial and sectoral effects of Europeanization and to see the interactive effects between the domestic and international levels. In this way, Europeanization unifies and separates, creating similarities and differences across states, which provides for mechanisms of adjustment and adaptation as well as of circumvention, opposition and differentiation. The first few chapters provide readers with a statistical overview of research on Europeanization – both a critical realist and discursive view – before turning to case studies in the remainder of the book linked by the ideas of Europeanization as process rather than outcome.

This is an innovative text in that it tries to apply systematic procedures for conducting research on Europeanization, recognizing that different approaches rest on diverse ontological and epistemological assumptions. The authors are rigorous in applying a process tracing methodology but do so using diverse theoretical approaches. The book does not use large-scale quantitative studies but rather frames the process of Europeanization through discourse, relational, power and network approaches. Pushing the boundaries of research on Europeanization requires us to focus on the logic of inquiry – the relationship between theory and method – so that we have much more rigour in the nature of conceptualization and measurement of the phenomena. This new volume, with contributors taking their cues from the editors' first two framing chapters, takes up this challenge.

This edited collection should raise additional questions and debates about the relative contribution of philosophical and methodological considerations for research on European integration. It reflects on current knowledge in the subfield of Europeanization and demonstrates the different ways in which Europeanization can be used as a tool to look at broader issues of implementation and compliance, political conditionality and the external impact of Europeanization on non-member states. Areas that had traditionally been viewed as less subject to EU influence are also considered, such as parties and cities, as well as health care and social service provision. These debates in European studies reflect the increasing conceptual pluralism in the field, and this book reflects concerns about methodology – the logical structure and procedures of understanding causality – which allow for reflexivity in understanding the notion of Europeanization.

Professor Michelle Egan
Associate Professor,
School of International Service, American University,
Washington, D.C.

# Acknowledgements

The idea of a volume on causality in Europeanization research originated within a team of researchers at the Centre for European Governance of the University of Exeter, UK, which was involved in different
ways in the study of Europeanization. Over the last three years or
so, Susan Banducci, Nicole Bolleyer, Dario Castiglione, Samuele Dossi,
Claire Dunlop, Theofanis Exadaktylos, Oliver Fritsch, Alison Harcourt,
Claudio Radaelli, Duncan Russel, Stephen Wilks, Georgios Xezonakis,
Eleni Xiarchogiannopoulou and others have written articles, dissertations and research reports on Europeanization in different sectors and
contexts, including public opinion, political theory and public policy.
It was therefore almost a natural progression for us to move above our
substantive concerns and address broader issues of causality. To do that,
we felt we needed a team of scholars from different traditions and gen-
erations. This was the motivation behind our first workshop in February
2010, followed by a second workshop on 20 and 21 September 2010,
soon after having agreed the contract with the publisher.

The editors are grateful to the participants of the two workshops
at the University of Exeter, UK, where we discussed drafts of our
chapters. We are particularly grateful to our discussants, Alison Harcourt,
Francesco Stolfi and Stephen Wilks, and also to Roberto Di Quirico
for his invaluable contributions to both workshops and the historian's
insights he kindly offered to our project. Susan Banducci and Georgios
Xezonakis contributed a research paper to the first workshop, and they
also provided comments on individual chapters.

The Centre for European Governance at Exeter, UK, generously contributed to the cost of the workshops with the Jean Monnet Centre of
Excellence Award of the European Commission. The Palgrave Macmillan
series editors, and especially Professor Michelle Egan, assisted us in the
transition from the workshops to the manuscript with helpful comments and invaluable suggestions at different crucial stages of the
project.

Finally, the editors and contributors wish to show their appreciation
to the editorial team at Palgrave Macmillan, Amber Stone-Galilee and Liz
Holwell, for having encouraged and supported our project throughout.

# Abbreviations and Acronyms

| | |
|---|---|
| BSEC | Black Sea Economic Cooperation Organization |
| BSS | Black Sea Synergy |
| CDU/CSU | Christian Democratic Union/Christian Social Union (Germany) |
| CEECs | Central and Eastern European Countries |
| CFSP | Common Foreign and Security Policy |
| COREPER | Council of Permanent Representatives |
| CR | critical realism |
| DEFRA | Department for Environment, Food and Rural Affairs |
| DG | Directorate General |
| DGB | German Trade Union Federation |
| EaP | Eastern Partnership |
| ECA | European Court of Auditors |
| ECB | European Central Bank |
| ECJ | European Court of Justice |
| ECT | European Community Treaty |
| EMU | Economic and Monetary Union |
| ENP | European Neighbourhood Policy |
| ENPI | European Neighbourhood and Partners Instrument |
| EP | European Parliament |
| ERDF | European Regional Development Fund |
| ESDP | European Security and Defence Policy |
| EU | European Union |
| HI | historical institutionalism |
| ICBSS | International Centre for Black Sea Studies |
| IG Bau | Construction Union (Germany) |
| IGC | intergovernmental conference |
| IMF | International Monetary Fund |
| MAFF | Ministry of Agriculture, Forestry and Fisheries |
| MEPs | Members of European Parliament |
| MLG | multi-level governance |
| MPs | Members of Parliament |
| NGOs | non-governmental organizations |
| NHS | National Health System |
| NPM | new public management |

| | |
|---|---|
| NVZ | Nitrate-Vulnerable Zones |
| OECD | Organization for Economic Co-Operation and Development |
| OMC | Open Method of Coordination |
| PASOK | Pan-Hellenic Socialist Movement (Greece) |
| PCA | Partnership and Cooperation Agreement |
| QCA | qualitative comparative analysis |
| RI | rational institutionalism |
| SGP | Stability and Growth Pact |
| SI | sociological institutionalism |
| SIGMA | Support for Improvement in Governance and Management |
| SMEs | small and medium enterprises |
| SPD | Social Democratic Party (Germany) |
| TACIS | Technical Assistance to the Commonwealth of Independent States |
| TFEU | Treaty on the Functioning of the European Union |
| UN | United Nations |
| UNDP | United Nations Development Programme |
| UNEP | United Nations Environment Programme |
| USAID | United States Agency for International Development |

# Notes on Contributors

## Editors

**Theofanis Exadaktylos** is Lecturer in European Politics at the University of Surrey, UK. His research focuses on the Europeanization of national foreign policy and the impact of enlargement on the foreign policies of Greece and Germany. Prior to his current position, he was based at the University of Exeter, UK, where he contributed to several research projects on modes of governance and quality of legislation, as well as to international conferences and workshops. He was the *European Journal of Political Research* editorial office manager until July 2011.

**Claudio M. Radaelli** is Professor of Political Science, Director of the Centre for European Governance and Jean Monnet Chair in EU Policy Analysis at the University of Exeter, UK, and co-editor of the *European Journal of Political Research*. He has carried out several projects on Europeanization, international taxation, discourse and the politics of expertise, and also on regulatory impact assessment in comparative perspective. He is currently directing a four-year project on 'Analysis of Learning in Regulatory Governance', funded by the European Research Council.

## Contributors

**Ian Bache** is Professor of Politics at the University of Sheffield, UK. His publications include *Cohesion Policy and Multi-level Governance in South East Europe* (Routledge 2011, co-editor); *Europeanization and Multilevel Governance: Cohesion Policy in the European Union and Britain* (Rowman and Littlefield, 2008); *The Europeanization of British Politics* (Palgrave, 2006; co-editor). He is currently conducting research on the politics of wellbeing.

**Simon Bulmer** is Professor and Head of the Department of Politics at the University of Sheffield, UK. His publications include many significant books and articles on issues of Europeanization and the EU member states. His principal research interests are EU–member state relations (especially the EU's relations with Germany and the UK), EU governance and new institutionalism.

**Samuele Dossi** is a PhD candidate in politics at the University of Exeter, UK. His doctoral thesis aims to analyse the process of Europeanization as it applies to cities and urban areas in the EU.

**Defne Gunay** is a PhD candidate at the University of Sheffield, UK. Her research interests focus on Europeanization, EU–Turkey relations and foreign policy analysis.

**Stella Ladi** is Lecturer in Public Policy at Panteion University in Athens, Greece. Her research interests include processes of policy transfer, global governance, comparative public policy, the relationship between Europeanization and globalization and their impact upon domestic public policy, and the role of non-governmental organizations and experts in the policy process.

**Robert Ladrech** is Professor of European Politics at Keele University, UK. His research focuses on the relationship between party politics and European integration. He recently completed a British Academy-funded project on social democratic parties and climate change, and is expanding the scope of this project to include centre-right parties. He is also a visiting professor at the College of Europe, Bruges, Belgium.

**Kennet Lynggaard** is Associate Professor in the Department of Society and Globalization, Roskilde University, Denmark. His research focuses on the relationship between Europeanization and globalization, and decision-making in the EU from the perspective of new-institutionalism and discourse analysis.

**Dorte Sindbjerg Martinsen** is Associate Professor in the Department of Political Science at the University of Copenhagen, Denmark. Her research focuses on issues of European integration and the effects thereof, with special interest in EU social policy and the EU's influence on national welfare policies – primarily health care.

**Kyriakos Moumoutzis** has recently completed his PhD thesis on Greece's external relations within the context of the EU, with the title 'Explaining change in Greek policy on EU-Turkey relations 1996–1999:

The prime minister's leadership style and the formulation of the Helsinki Strategy' at the London School of Economics, UK.

**Diana Panke** is Lecturer in Politics at University College Dublin, Ireland. Her research interests focus, broadly speaking, on governance beyond the nation state. She works on small states in international negotiations, on the role of capacities for the shaping of law beyond the nation state, on the development and degeneration of international norms, and on compliance and legalization.

**Sabine Saurugger** is Professor of Political Science at Sciences Po Grenoble, France. She has published extensively in many English and French journals of political science. Her research interests include Europeanization and institutional transfer, non-state actors and interest groups, and sociological approaches to theories of European integration.

**Annette Elisabeth Töller** is Professor of Political Science at the Fern-Universität in Hagen, Germany. Her publications include both German and English articles and books. Her research interests focus on public policy in general and, in particular, the Europeanization of public policies and its measuring.

# 1
# Europeanization: The Challenge of Establishing Causality

*Claudio M. Radaelli*

The field of Europeanization is well established in political science and more generally in the social sciences. Broadly speaking, it is a process of change affecting domestic institutions, politics and public policy. Change occurs when political behaviour at the European Union (EU) level has a transformative effect on domestic political behaviour. As we shall see shortly, sometimes Europeanization is treated as outcome rather than process, especially with reference to the condition of a policy sector or a country, seen as more or less 'Europeanized'.

In turn, the notion of 'EU behaviour' covers a wide range of phenomena. The classic case is the so-called 'community method' through which the EU produces legislation (Dehousse, 2011). Often EU legislation provides a template (e.g., the obligation to set up a national regulatory authority with certain characteristics) and prescribes behaviour at the level of the member states (e.g., quality standards for water). Fiscal coordination and Economic and Monetary Union are two sectors where the binding and constraining power of the EU on the member states goes beyond the effects of a single piece of legislation. In these cases the EU is trying to transfer an institutional framework (based on an independent European Central Bank in charge of a common currency, the euro) and a governance architecture concerning budgets and, arguably, a culture of responsibility in fiscal policy.

But one can also think of EU-level fora of discussion that do not produce legislation and, unlike the complex architectures of the Eurozone and bail-out plans, are not technically binding on the recipients. The EU is indeed a political platform for working parties, consultation processes, non-binding recommendations and horizon-scanning high-level groups that consolidate shared benchmarks of public policy, political beliefs and, perhaps, identities (Radaelli, 2000). Nevertheless, there is more than technical activity in working parties and EU committees. Prime ministers and heads of state use the EU summits to make declarations about global politics, perhaps gradually embedding a definition of what is distinctive about the European identity and the 'others'. In turn (more or less), solemn declarations, benchmarks, beliefs and identities may become embedded in domestic political behaviour, thus generating Europeanization effects.

Alongside the community method, the EU also has its own process of facilitated or 'open' coordination of public policy. This open method of coordination is based on the identification of goals and targets for public policy at the EU level, which are then implemented by the member states as they see fit, allowing for greater flexibility than in the case of EU legislation.

There is yet another distinction to consider. Sometimes the EU origin of change is a single decision, like the creation of a new piece of legislation. It can, however, also be a long process of discussion and deliberation, a chain of decisions or, at the other extreme, a series of meetings and bargaining sessions that over the years do not end up with a final agreement, yet they may change at least some opinions in some countries through socialization of national delegates (Radaelli, 1997). These long policy processes are often characterized by the activism of the Courts and specialized bureaucracies of the EU; for example, the European Court of Justice, the European Court of Auditors and the EU regulatory agencies.

Given this full range of ways in which the EU can affect domestic politics, the process of Europeanization may take place via the constraining power of legislation, ideational and learning processes of socialization and convergence around shared paradigms of public policy, the re-calibration of identities and material resources (including budgets, financial constraints and bail-out plans). We can see already the problem of causality. The EU may or may not produce domestic effects in many different ways. It is easy to compile a long list of ways in which this can theoretically happen, but it is difficult to pin down the exact conditions under which Europeanization occurs, and its mechanisms.

Add to this complexity the fact that Europeanization also occurs from below. In fact, social and political contestation can affect Europeanization; for example, by muting some effects on domestic policy. By resisting and opposing Europe, social and political collective actors define and constrain the role of the EU in policy and politics in their countries. Public opinion sentiments about the EU lead political parties to re-calibrate their position on European integration.

Sometimes these processes are transnational, creating waves of public opinion in a group of member states, anti-European sentiments and moods for or (more often) against liberalization, competition or military intervention. These moods may be echoed by parliamentarians and ministers. Indirectly, they may even affect the EU attitude in worldwide regulatory fora, as shown by the controversies on international tax competition, offshore finance, foodstuff regulation and genetically modified organisms. Contestation of EU policy may be social but also more bureaucratic-technical and less visible: national bureaucracies and their political masters have learned a number of tricks of the trade about how not to implement EU legislation correctly and on time, or to adapt commitments to domestic needs and goals.

At its most basic, however, Europeanization concerns a relationship between a cause located at the EU level and change at the domestic level, be it national, regional or even at the level of cities and territorial policy systems; for example, territorially based sectors like the wine industry. In studies of candidate countries or those that are recipients of EU aid or democracy-promotion initiatives, the 'effect' is located outside the EU, but the essential causal dilemma is the same: how do we know that the EU cause is having (or not having) an impact? How do we measure this impact without bias or at least while keeping bias under control?

This is why the problem of establishing causality in Europeanization has become the most interesting issue in this field of research (Haverland, 2007). Although research projects on Europeanization typically have a substantive focus on a given policy, a type of political party, a country or a group of cities, at the deeper level of research design the issue with which they have to grapple is establishing causality.

This issue affects the components of research design. Because of this, causality defines the field of Europeanization and provides the major challenge for studies making causal claims about how Europe is having a transformative effect on the member states, or how the nation state is reasserting its autonomy from EU governance. Surely, this problem is not unique to Europeanization. All studies of how international governance affects domestic politics and policy seek to get to grips with the same problems of causality. Indeed, the whole literature on Europeanization has taken off by re-elaborating classic research designs of how international politics affects national political systems (for a review of the early stages of the debate, see Featherstone and Radaelli, 2003). Diffusion studies are inspirational because they raise the possibility that rather than the EU affecting domestic policy, spatial interdependence and cross-country learning generate domestic change (Dobbin et al., 2007; Meseguer, 2009). Before we get into the definition of causes and the components of research design, let us consider an example. Suppose that we observe a change in tax policy in a given member state; for example, a trend towards lower corporate taxes levied by central government. Note that in this case we try to establish causality starting from the effect; that is, domestic change. What do we make of this domestic change? Is it evidence of Europeanization? The following dilemmas arise.

The change can be the result of a legal impulse coming from the EU. The European Court of Justice may have taken important decisions over the last ten years concerning some corporate tax regimes in our member state that are not compatible with the treaties and the single market of the EU. The impulse can be ideational rather than legal. We can reason that the EU has provided a policy space for the consolidation of ideas about competitiveness and growth. Since high corporate taxes contrast with this paradigm of competitiveness, our argument would carry on, the member state has decreased its taxes on corporation because of ideational alignment with the EU paradigm, even in the absence of corporate tax directives prescribing lower corporate taxes. However, the fact that we find the same idea both at the EU level and in the country with which we are concerned does not necessarily mean that there has been a causal effect of the EU on the government of our country. In fact, the decision to reduce corporate taxes may be the outcome of a wider and deeper process of diffusion, perhaps originating in major policy changes in economic superpowers such as the United States of America, as diffusion scholars would most probably point out.

Further, learning mechanisms involving communities of experts and ideational brokers active in organizations such as the Organisation for Economic Co-operation and Development (OECD) may cause the trend in domestic taxes. The OECD, acting as a club of countries with similar policy beliefs, may have transformed domestic policy. In yet another conjecture, the domestic outcome may be the result of domestic corporations threatening 'exit': they may be lobbying the government, showing that they could leave the country unless taxes are lowered. Finally, domestic change may be the result of economic rather than political pressure: the presence of tax havens in the world is sufficient to trigger a downward trend in corporate taxation, given that national economic systems are interdependent. For the researcher engaged in establishing causality, these alternative options provide serious challenges of research design, compounded by the fact that more than one 'cause' may be operating at the same time. For example, it is reasonable to make the assumption that court decisions, economic pressure from tax havens and domestic corporate lobbying simultaneously impinge on domestic policymakers, who are at the same time involved in international organizations such as the OECD and listen to their ideational brokers. Hence, we do not know whether the hypotheses are rival alternatives (i.e., mutually exclusive) or complementary.

We said we would track down causality starting from the effect, but the problems are equally daunting if one follows the causal path from the origin down to the effect. First, there is the risk of prejudging the importance of the cause and reducing the peripheral vision of the researcher (Dyson, 2002; Radaelli and Pasquier, 2007). This happens if we think in a narrow chain-of-command mode that connects the EU and the domestic level. The chain-of-command thinking hinders explanation when there are untheorized intervening variables. It may also be the case that statistically we manage to find EU causes that are significant, but with small coefficients alerting us to the possible presence of factors that are not captured by our chain of command. Second, there is the problem that by simply relating a frequently remote change at the EU level to change at the domestic level, we establish not causality but correlation. In large data sets it is easy to find bivariate correlation among many different variables, and without theoretical conjectures about causation we cannot proceed further. In small-$n$ studies, the fact that the EU cause precedes temporally is not sufficient to exclude bias. It seems logical to think that if there is a directive at time $t_0$ and a change in country X at time $t_1$ (and the EU directive and change are correlated), the cause has produced the effect, but there are several reasons – well known to everyone who has studied causality – why this may not be the case. By contrast, when we start from the effect at the domestic level, it is easier to control for explanations different from the EU – it has been argued that there are fewer pitfalls of causal reasoning (Radaelli and Pasquier, 2007). Third, unless we say something about how exactly the EU is affecting the domestic political system, we do not know anything about the causal path that connects cause and effect.

Given this complexity, it is useful to look at the different components of research design. There are various definitions of research design. John Gerring, in his authoritative *Social Science Methodology*, differentiates among three levels: general criteria, methods and strategies (Gerring, 2001). His general criteria for research design are:

- plenitude (i.e., how many cases do we need to produce evidence?);
- coherence of the population;
- comparability;
- independence of the cases with respect to the factors that affect the relationship between cause and effect, or just the effect;
- representativeness;
- variation in the cases or within a single case (controlling for collinearity);
- theoretical-analytical utility of the sample;
- replicability of the research design, mechanisms and causal comparison (i.e., does the chosen design allow the researcher to test rival hypotheses?).

The methods can be divided in classic fashion between the single case study, the small-*n* methods and the statistical methods. Over the last 20 years a number of research projects have also used medium-*n* methods, such as qualitative comparative analysis. Equally popular are experimental methods in political science (see Gerring, 2001: 202 on a typology of methods). Methods can be used synchronically or across time. The single case study comes in different types, such as 'extreme', 'typical', 'crucial' or 'counterfactual'.

All methods can be scored against Gerring's general criteria to assess their strengths and limitations. Some draw on probabilistic logic, such as econometrics and statistical modelling. Others are deterministic, such as the most different and most similar cases in small-*n* designs. Finally, the strategies can be exploratory or confirmatory. In a field like Europeanization, researchers may wish to explore causality before they move to confirmatory strategies; hence the two strategies are not mutually exclusive in a given field.

It would take a much larger volume to reflect on each element of Gerring's approach to research design. To simplify things, the purpose of research design is to reduce bias. Some researchers may be concerned with bias in drawing inferences from data, others in testing hypotheses deductively constructed. Yet another group may conceive of bias as violation to canons of interpretation; for example, a genuine narrative account provided by ethnographic fieldwork may be distorted in the 'scientific' final results of the project, as when oral sources are turned into an article submitted to a journal.

Within this broad approach to research design, our project singles out the following elements:

- concept formation;
- the notion of cause and causality;
- the relationship between variables;
- the mechanisms;
- the methods.

This book also covers more abstract issues of ontology and theoretical lenses on causality, as we shall see shortly.

Concept formation is somewhat foundational for any research project. All too often, researchers suffer from a sort of data-induced alteration of the conceptual aims of their project. Since data are available only for some phenomena but not for others, we take the data as crude proxies of concepts we cannot measure. This may be acceptable in some cases, but it is often a source of bias, especially when researchers start from mindless data-mining rather than first considering their concepts and how they can be measured. Thus, it is useful to reiterate that concept formation occurs prior to measurement (Brady and Collier, 2004). Put differently, concept formation comes first.

As mentioned, there are two approaches to concept formation. Some researchers treat Europeanization as *outcome*. It follows that we can talk of Europeanization as a quantity using ordinal categories such as 'more' or 'less' or cardinal measures. To illustrate, a project anchored to Europeanization as outcome can conclude that social policy is more Europeanized in Denmark than in Sweden. Others, including the editors of this volume, prefer to handle Europeanization as a *process* that affects domestic politics, public policy and institutions. This choice has wide-ranging consequences. Europeanization as outcome is not the same as Europeanization as process, and empirically the two concepts lead to different strategies. There is no reason to debate which notion is superior since they are both legitimate and useful, but obviously one has to be clear and explicit about the initial choice, be it outcome or process.

Let us now turn to the motivation that got our project off the ground. At the outset, the editors and contributors to this volume were concerned with causality. What is a cause in Europeanization? Do we have a common, widely shared idea of causality or are we proceeding from very different, perhaps incommensurable ontological and epistemological assumptions about causality? Do we stick to probabilistic or deterministic causality? How do we handle counterfactuals in our field? Can we be eclectic in handling research traditions to address a substantive research question?

Causation is a relationship between an event (the cause) and its effect. In the social sciences, it is customary to stick to the Rubin–Holland concept of causal effect (Sekhon, 2008). Donald Rubin thought of the causal effect of a given treatment, E, over another, C, for a particular unit in a period of time from $t_1$ to $t_2$. For Rubin, this causal effect is the difference between what would have happened at time $t_2$ if the unit had been exposed to E initiated at $t_1$ and what would have happened at $t_2$ if the unit had been exposed to C initiated at $t_1$. To exemplify, the causal effect of taking an aspirin is the difference between how my head would have felt in case E (taking the aspirin) and case C (not taking it). If the headache would disappear in E but would not change in C, then the causal effect of the aspirin is headache relief.

There are three main approaches to causality: regularity, probability and counterfactuals. Regularity approaches are based on constant coincidence between a cause and its effect. This is a deterministic approach, although in empirical research coincidence is never perfect, so one should think that an event leads 'almost always' to a given effect. The classic example concerns the causes of social revolutions in France, China and Russia (Skocpol, 1979).

In probabilistic approaches, the basic idea is 'that the cause should raise the probability of the effect' (Dupré, 1984: 170; cited by Gerring, 2001: 134–135). Gerring then goes on to observe that:

> Although deterministic claims are more useful where we have reason to believe that causal relationships are in fact deterministic, most social science research is based on the more flexible parameters of probabilistic causation.
>
> (Gerring, 2001: 134)

In counterfactual reasoning, a cause is a condition *sine qua non* for the effect to materialize. The classic counterfactual conditional is that if A had not occurred, Z would not have occurred (Levy, 2008).

Turning to Europeanization, if we are examining the provision in the second energy liberalization package of the EU for the establishment of national regulatory authorities in the member states, we can handle the question deterministically: we can say that in year x, the member states a, b and c complied with the provision while the others did not. For each member state in a given year, we can answer *yes or no* deterministically. We can also answer deterministically about which *countries have adopted independent regulatory authorities in key policy sectors, and which countries have not done so (Thatcher, 2002). But if we are concerned with measuring how long it takes on average* in the member states to implement the body of EU rules concerning energy, a probabilistic notion of causation is more adequate. In counterfactual terms, a research question in this field would sound like: had the EU energy provision for national regulatory authorities on energy not existed, would a country like Italy have created something like the Italian Regulatory Authority for Electricity and Gas?

Further, we have to consider that scholars engaged with Europeanization, like other social scientists, make use of both X-oriented and Y-oriented designs. Granted that at the most basic level we can conceive of causation as a Y = f(X) relationship, there are two approaches. The former focuses on X – or the cause: what are the possible effects of a cause? To illustrate, if a project is dealing with the role of veto players in Europeanization, it will seek to answer the question: what are the many ways in which the cause 'veto player' plays a role in Europeanization as process/or outcome' (Haverland, 2007)? The latter approach is interested in Y – the effect. We observe convergence in the adoption of competition policy authorities across Europe, and we raise the question as to whether this effect is determined by Europeanization (Wilks, 2005; Zahariadis, 2004). And actually, there are also projects interested in the 'f' or the relationship between X and Y. An example is Radaelli's study of how ideational factors shape the relationship between EU policy and domestic change in two member states (Radaelli, 1997). In any case, the 'f' does not have to be linear: one important element that must be established is whether the relationship is linear, curvilinear or quadratic – predictive models have to take this point seriously (Taagepera, 2008). There may be turning points or irreversible changes that make causality differ in a major way across time (Pierson, 2004).

Early research on Europeanization has also established that causality is not simply a matter of X affecting Y (Börzel and Risse, 2003): there are several intervening or mediating variables. We also need to establish counterfactuals and consider both EU cases as well as those outside the EU in order to make valid conjectures (Haverland, 2007).

As in other domains of social science research, it is theory that provides inspiration for the choice of control cases and intervening variables. With regard to the latter, following Börzel and Risse (2003), Europeanization scholars often draw on either rational choice or social constructivism to identify mediating factors. Various blends of institutional analysis are concerned with this strategy. One implication of entering intervening variables is that the causal chain becomes longer: some degrees of proximity between X and Y are necessarily lost (on the importance of proximity, see Gerring, 2001). We increase theoretical leverage but empirically we may encounter new sources of bias if the intervening variables are not measured correctly.

Interdependence adds its own sources of complexity: if X represents the EU and Y the member states, how can we measure the causal effect of X on Y if our Ys are interdependent (Franzese and Hays, 2008), possibly involved in dense networks of diffusion and emulation? Yet another source of complexity is the very special nature of some approaches. Scholars involved in discourse analysis have argued that discourse is not simply like all other Xs. Discourse, it has been argued, does not cause policy directly. Most often it has transformative effects on key variables affecting policy, such as the definition of policy problems and how actors interpret the nature of strategic interaction between the EU and the government (Schmidt and Radaelli, 2004). This transformative power of discourse is hard to measure in causal terms. Among other things it is difficult to specify *ex ante* the evidence that would be sufficient to show that discourse is *not* transformative (for an effort in this direction, see Xiarchogiannopoulou, 2011). The discursive research tradition in public policy tends to be biased towards studies which find that 'discourse matters' and says little about why and when discourse does not matter; for example, because it tracks down material interests pretty closely.

Research traditions and paradigms make a difference to how we handle causality. In critical realism, causes violate the classic Humean canons of causation (Kurki, 2006). Interpretivists consider social representations rather than 'variables' and 'data' (Yanow and Schwartz-Shea, 2006), yet for neo-positivists social representations can also be measured quite accurately. An example is the recent contribution of Jones and McBeth (2010) concerned with measuring and testing hypotheses about policy narratives.

At the deeper level, there is the issue of whether phenomena that are ontologically socially constructed can be studied with objective epistemology. The socially constructed nature of most political science phenomena is not a hindrance to objective epistemologies. We know that party competition is not an object that exists out there but a social representation created by our language; yet there are plenty of indicators of party competition. In economics, we know that money is a piece of paper that only via our language acquires value beyond the paper, yet we can certainly measure money quite accurately, and all economists would know the difference between indicators like $M_2$ or $M_3$ to measure the quantity of money in a given system. Then there is the problem of showing exactly how X and Y are linked. This is the domain of mechanisms. There is now a vast literature on social mechanisms (Falleti and Lynch, 2009; Gerring, 2010; Hedström, 2005). There is no shortage of mechanisms in sociology, economics and political science. Indeed, the risk with mechanisms of Europeanization is one of ending up with a long, and perhaps useless, shopping list. One way forward is to use theory to group mechanisms. One can theorize that certain mechanisms of Europeanization rely on incentives and responses to incentives within the logic of choice, others are triggered by logic of appropriateness, while yet another group may be encased in categories of learning, provided that we can single out a sort of 'learner–teacher' relationship (Dunlop and Radaelli, 2011). With their goodness of fit model, Börzel and Risse (2003) have prepared the ground for the examination of a wide range of adaptational mechanisms, or responses to EU pressure more generally.

Another way is to relate mechanisms and context. Falleti and Lynch argue that 'unless causal mechanisms are appropriately contextualized, we run the risk of making faulty causal inferences'. Accordingly, 'causal effects depend on the interaction with aspects of the context within which these mechanisms operate' (Falleti and Lynch, 2009: 1144). To produce valid results, we need different units of analysis to be equivalent in aspects that are likely to be causally relevant. This is often *not* the case with the EU and national contexts. Elections at the EU level are contextually different from national elections. In statistical models, multilevel analysis takes care of this problem; in qualitative studies, the strategy is to associate mechanisms and context (Falleti and Lynch, 2009).

This brings us to the choice of methods, our final item on the research design list introduced above. The traditional choice of distinguishing between qualitative and quantitative methods is nowadays a limitation. To begin with, complex causality issues can be fruitfully addressed by drawing on multi-method research design approaches. One can start from statistical analysis, identify patterns and then turn to qualitative analysis to explore outliers or mechanisms underlying the patterns. Second, qualitative approaches are a broad category including ethnography, interpretive policy analysis and critical approaches, as well as small-*n* controlled comparisons and discursive methods. More importantly still, the various types of qualitative approach do not share the same ontological assumptions and follow different epistemologies. As such, they cannot be put into a single box.

With regard to Europeanization, especially in those projects that consider it to be a process rather than an outcome, tracking down events across time has become a necessity. There are two strategies we have already mentioned above. On the one hand, a researcher can choose an X at the EU level and track it down to the Y in domestic policy or politics. For example, one can take the directive on the liberalization of services and trace the process leading to adaptation, change or lack of change in the member states. On the other, projects may start from liberalization of services in a member state or group of member states and address the question: was this change caused by the EU, domestic variables or by diffusion and interdependence? This second strategy has been associated with the notion of so-called 'bottom-up' research designs (Radaelli, 2003; Radaelli and Pasquier, 2007).

Over the years, no matter whether the strategy is top-down or bottom-up, whether we deal with national or even sub-national change, process tracing has become prominent in Europeanization studies. Yet process tracing should be taken with its own set of caveats and, so to speak, handled with care. One goal in this volume is to examine different methods and to look at process tracing critically and reflexively.

## The structure of this book

To summarize, the main research questions addressed here are:

- What are the notions of causal explanation adopted by Europeanization scholars? How do they relate to different concepts of Europeanization? How can they be critically appraised?
- How do different research traditions handle causality in this field?
- What are the research design issues arising out of different strategies, from large-$n$ statistical analysis to the single case study, with emphasis on mechanisms, variables and intervening factors?
- What is the proper role of process-tracing techniques?
- How do individual case studies handle explanation? How do they generate the variation that is indispensable to addressing causal explanation?

This volume continues with an original attempt to review the literature by interrogating a sample of articles with the aid of meta-analysis. Exadaktylos and Radaelli (Chapter 2), after having coded their sample, show how research design issues affect the findings, and reflect on mechanisms and variables in causal explanation.

We then turn to causal explanation by providing different theoretical and ontological lenses on this issue. Töller (Chapter 3) addresses the dilemma of the large-*n* approach by considering the important case of Europeanization of legislation. In the political discussion, references are often made to EU legislation being quantitatively more important than national legislation; it has been argued that 80 per cent of national laws are of EU origin. How can a social scientific approach control this proposition? What are the tools available for this enterprise and what does the evidence show? Töller discusses different strategies and concludes that the 80 per cent figure is a myth.

In the following chapter we look at causality from a much more abstract perspective. Bache, Bulmer and Gunay (Chapter 4) introduce the concept of meta-theory. They reflect on the ontological assumptions behind various approaches to casual explanation. They then move on to the insights of critical realism and suggest how a critical realist perspective would handle causality and explanation. Lynggaard (Chapter 5) looks at causality from a different research tradition; that is, discourse analysis. Discourse-analytical approaches are themselves a very mixed bag in terms of ontology. Moreover, discourse traditions are not always and not exactly concerned with causal explanation. Lynggaard digs inside the strands of discourse analysis to provide a unique set of insights into how discourse may have causal effects on domestic politics and policy. By doing so, he also shows how different notions of causality should be handled.

As mentioned, Europeanization also involves contestation, resistance and lack of change. This is typically the case when member states do not comply with legislation or more broadly do not implement EU public policy. Saurugger (Chapter 6) takes a broad perspective on the issue of how to study lack of compliance causally. While most of the literature refers to compliance with legal norms, she deals with a wider range of non-compliant behaviour and seeks to explain it by blending structural factors with actor-based variables.

Since one of the research questions concerns process tracing, Panke (Chapter 7) offers a political science approach to testing multiple hypotheses with a small number of cases. *Prima facie*, this looks like the quintessential mission impossible, given degrees of freedom problems. But since process tracing can generate within-case variation in both dependent and independent variables, this can be done. Her chapter combines a methodological reflection with substantive issues of compliance, thus complementing Saurugger's analysis of non-compliance.

In the next chapter, Martinsen (Chapter 8) addresses the least likely case of health-care policy. Since this is not the most typical case where one would expect Europeanization to occur, research design considerations about processes and factors require a different, original strategy. Another case that does not look typical at all is the Europeanization of cities. Granted that, after some experiences in the past, like the URBAN initiative, there are practically no formal EU policies specifically targeting urban governance, there is a vibrant discussion about 'European cities' and the role of cities in Europe. Can we scientifically get to grips with the concept of Europeanization of cities? To answer this question, Dossi (Chapter 9) takes issue with the tendency to examine EU policies from a formal or legalistic perspective. In the past, scholars have looked only at initiatives of the European Commission that targeted the city level – as he says, they had 'cities written on the tin'. From a theory-driven perspective, however, there are several modes of governance and processes through which Europeanization effects on cities can be theorized. Thus, Dossi claims, we need to switch from formal approaches to theory-driven research questions.

Turning to party politics, Ladrech (Chapter 10) observes that a political party as such does not have regular channels of communication with the EU institutions. Neither has European integration become a new cleavage in European politics. Thus, the question arises: what can 'Europeanization of political parties' possibly mean? In his contribution, Ladrech airs the conceptual and methodological issues in this field of research. In a way, that is similar to Dossi's intuition in that we cannot possibly limit our search to categories that have 'EU policy for parties' written on the tin. In consequence, Ladrech turns to more subtle and sophisticated ways to causally explain what the EU has 'done' to the parties and offers some testable hypotheses.

Exadaktylos (Chapter 11) combines process tracing and theoretical policy analysis to provide a solution to a causal puzzle: granted that the Common Foreign and Security Policy (CFSP) is already a difficult test for causal explanations concerning Europeanization, how can we appraise changes that are originated by the involvement of a member state with this policy but fall outside the policy? The research weaponry suggested in his contribution yet again combines process tracing and a precise segmentation of policy-level variables, such as actors, instruments, decision-making procedures and beliefs. Ladi (Chapter 12) considers an equally challenging task when she examines how the EU effects on the Black Sea can be causally appraised. One way to make progress, she argues convincingly, is to generate rival alternative hypotheses including the null hypothesis of non-Europeanization (or change caused by factors other than the EU). In contrast, Moumoutzis (Chapter 13) is puzzled with a problem at the micro level. Specifically, he takes a historical decision affecting the relationship between Greece and Turkey and raises the question of establishing causality. While it is customary to look at long periods of policymaking to establish causality, he shows that Europeanization can be established (and, if necessary, refuted) also in the context of decisions. Finally, in the concluding chapter, the editors refer back to the motivation and questions of the volume and provide their answers, acknowledge the limitations of the project and discuss options for future research.

## References

Börzel, T.A. and Risse, T. (2003). Conceptualizing the domestic impact. In K. Featherstone and C. Radaelli (Eds.), *The Politics of Europeanization* (pp. 57–80). Oxford: Oxford University Press.

Brady, H.E. and Collier, D. (Eds.) (2004). *Rethinking Social Inquiry: Diverse Tools, Shared Standards*. Lanham, MD: Rowman and Littlefield.

Dehousse, R. (2011). *The 'Community Method': Obstinate or Obsolete?* Basingstoke: Palgrave Macmillan.

Dobbin, F., Simmons, F. and Garrett, G. (2007). The global diffusion of public policies: Social construction, coercion, competition or learning? *Annual Review of Sociology*, 33(2), 449–472.

Dunlop, C. and Radaelli, C.M. (2011). Systematizing policy learning. *Paper Delivered to ECPR Joint Sessions of Workshops*, University of St. Gallen, Switzerland, 12–17 April 2011.

Dupré, J. (1984). Probabilistic causality emancipated. In P.A. French, T.E. Uehling Jr and H.K. Wettstein (Eds.), *Midwest Studies in Philosophy, Vol. IX: Causation and Causal Theories*. Minneapolis, MN: University of Minnesota Press.

Dyson, K. (Ed.) (2002). *The European State and the Euro*. Oxford: Oxford University Press.

Falleti, T.G. and Lynch, J.F. (2009). Context and causal mechanisms in political analysis. *Comparative Political Studies*, 42(9), 1143–1166.

Featherstone, K. and Radaelli, C.M. (Eds.) (2003). *The Politics of Europeanisation*. Oxford: Oxford University Press.

Franzese, R.J. and Hays, J.C. (2008). Interdependence in comparative politics. *Comparative Political Studies*, 41(4–5), 742–780.

Gerring, J. (2001). *Social Science Methodology: A Criterial Framework*. Cambridge and New York: Cambridge University Press.

Gerring, J. (2010). Causal mechanisms: Yes, but... *Comparative Political Studies*, 43(11), 1499–1526.

Haverland, M. (2007). Methodology. In P. Graziano and M.P. Vink (Eds.), *Europeanization: New Research Agendas* (pp. 59–70). London: Palgrave Macmillan.

Hedström, P. (2005). *Dissecting the Social. On the Principles of Analytical Sociology.* Cambridge: Cambridge University Press.

Jones, M.D. and McBeth, M.K. (2010). A narrative policy framework: Clear enough to be wrong? *Policy Studies Journal*, 38(2), 329–353.

Kurki, M. (2006). Causes of a divided discipline: Rethinking the concept of cause in International Relations theory. *Review of International Studies*, 32, 189–216.

Levy, J.S. (2008). Counterfactual and case studies. In J.M. Box-Steffensmeier, H.E. Brady and D. Collier (Eds.), *The Oxford Handbook of Political Methodology* (pp. 627–644). Oxford: Oxford University Press.

Meseguer, C. (2009). *Learning, Public Policy and Market Reform.* New York and Cambridge: Cambridge University Press.

Pierson, P. (2004). *Politics in Time: History, Institutions and Social Analysis.* Princeton, NJ: Princeton University Press.

Radaelli, C.M. (1997). How does Europeanization produce policy change? Corporate tax policy in Italy and the UK. *Comparative Political Studies*, 30(5), 553–575.

Radaelli, C.M. (2000). Policy transfer in the European Union: Institutional isomorphism as a source of legitimacy. *Governance*, 13(1), 25–43.

Radaelli, C.M. (2003). The Europeanization of public policy. In K. Featherstone and C.M. Radaelli (Eds.), *The Politics of Europeanization* (pp. 27–56). Oxford: Oxford University Press.

Radaelli, C.M. and Pasquier, R. (2007). Conceptual issues. In M.P. Vink and P. Graziano (Eds.), *Europeanization: New Research Agendas* (pp. 35–45). Basingstoke: Palgrave Macmillan.

Schmidt, V.A. and Radaelli, C.M. (2004). Policy change and discourse in Europe: Conceptual and methodological issues. *West European Politics*, 27(2), 183–210.

Sekhon, J.S. (2008). The Neyman-Rubin model of causal inference and estimation via matching methods. In J.M. Box-Steffensmeier, H.E. Brady and D. Collier (Eds.), *The Oxford Handbook of Political Methodology* (pp. 271–299). Oxford: Oxford University Press.

Skocpol, T. (1979). *States and Social Revolutions.* Cambridge: Cambridge University Press.

Taagepera, R. (2008). *Making Social Sciences More Scientific. The Need for Predictive Models.* Oxford: Oxford University Press.

Thatcher, M. (2002). Regulation after delegation: Independent regulatory agencies in Europe. *Journal of European Public Policy*, 9(6), 954–972.

Wilks, S. (2005). Agency escape: Decentralization or dominance of the European Commission in the modernization of competition policy? *Governance*, 18(3), 431–452.

Xiarchogiannopoulou, E. (2011). Discursive institutionalism and pension reform in Greece 1990–2002: Appraising Europeanization from the 'bottom-up'. University of Exeter, PhD thesis.

Yanow, D. and Schwartz-Shea, P. (Eds.) (2006). *Interpretation and Method: Empirical Research Methods and the Interpretive Turn.* Armonk, NY: M.E. Sharpe.

Zahariadis, N. (2004). European markets and national regulation: Conflict and cooperation in British competition policy. *Journal of Public Policy*, 24, 49–73.

# 2
# Looking for Causality in the Literature on Europeanization

*Theofanis Exadaktylos and Claudio M. Radaelli*

## Introduction

Europeanization is like one of those bumblebees that seem to defy the laws of aerodynamics, yet they fly. In 2002, Johan Olsen was lamenting that, several years after his seminal paper on *Europeanization and Nation State Dynamics* (Olsen, 1995), political scientists were still debating about concepts and definitions (Olsen, 2002). Each author, he argued, appeared to go on with their own concepts and frameworks in mind, and merrily ignore more substantive questions concerning how exactly Europeanization is changing politics and policy at the domestic level. Hussein Kassim (cited by Olsen, 2002) had concluded in 2000 that such an unwieldy field did not deserve too much attention, suggesting the futility of the whole exercise. In the end, Olsen reasoned, Europeanization may be nothing but an attention-directing device.

Some years later, in the third edition of J.J. Richardson's *European Union* textbook, Andrea Lenschow discussed the methods used by different authors to disentangle 'Europe as pressure' and 'Europe as usage' without being able to find how all this work could lead to 'concrete hypotheses about when and to what extent Europe affects the domestic level' (Lenschow, 2005: 67). Yet this question – that is, how European Union (EU) policy and politics affect the domestic level – is one of the defining questions for this field of research, as mentioned by Radaelli in Chapter 1 of this volume.

In the meantime, the academic enthusiasm for Europeanization has remained stable, practically undeterred by these fundamental doubts, as shown by the growing number of articles, books and doctoral dissertations on this topic, in different European languages. The bumblebee is flying, indeed. Other authors have produced more optimistic appraisals of the field. Peter Mair for example, in a short review piece (Mair, 2004: 346), praised the freshness of this field, contrasting it with the dull and a-theoretical work that dominated the field of EU politics until recently. Radaelli and Exadaktylos (2009: 208) also come to qualify Lenschow's conclusion, arguing that the field is ready to move towards the exploration of 'more ambitious questions, such as: what does Europeanization tell us about the politics of integration, power and legitimacy?' So, not only does Europeanization have the task of explaining the effects of the EU on the domestic level, but it should also engage with questions that have defined the whole academic struggle to understand the politics of integration. Has the bumblebee turned into a modern aircraft?

Amidst pessimistic and optimistic assessments lies the question of establishing causality. Perhaps this is only a modest question when compared with the grandiose plan to address power and the politics of integration. Perhaps it is not as exciting as engaging with definitions and concepts, but it is on this terrain that this field of research should either take off or admit its futility. To get close to causality, however, one has to take some distance. Causality, in fact, is a component of research design (see Chapter 1). It can be studied by different methods and with research strategies that may criss-cross the qualitative–quantitative divide. It may focus on mechanisms, cases or variables. It can also raise ontological questions, as we are reminded in Chapter 4, and by Peter Hall's argument about the alignment of ontology and methodology (2003), or produce questions about the usefulness of a meta-theory in EU studies – a field that experiences an increasing fragmentation or specialization (Jupille, 2005; Chapter 4 in this volume).

In this chapter we examine the issue of causality by looking at different aspects, including variables and mechanisms, as well as case selection and other features of research design. The chapter is organized as follows. In the following section we introduce the research questions, the methodological approach and the data used in the chapter. We then present our results, followed by the discussion. The last section provides a brief conclusion.

## Research questions, methods and data

The classic question we often hear from our students is: When we talk about 'findings' in this literature, do we mean 'more' or 'less' Europeanization? Yet for us as well as for many other political scientists, Europeanization is a process, not an outcome variable (see Chapter 1 on the difference between the two concepts). Most authors define Europeanization as a process with some specific properties. They measure the dependent variable *not* as 'Europeanization' but in terms of political change, alterations in the constellation of actors at the domestic level or variation in certain elements of policy (ideas, instruments or procedures). This means that questions about the findings raise some issues, in terms of both process and outcome variables. As will become clear in the remainder of the chapter, there are many different operationalizations of the dependent variable.

With this caveat in mind, we can turn to specific research questions. We address the following questions:

RQ1 – Are the findings about Europeanization correlated to research design features of the studies in the sample we examined, such as 'case selection' (type of countries examined), the choice to examine policy or politics, the presence or absence of clearly articulated hypotheses, the preference for one or another lever of change (such as path-dependency or opportunity structure)? We do not have any strong prior expectations about RQ1, although we suspect that the more rigorous the design, the more difficult it is to find Europeanization. This is because authors such as Dyson (2000) and Radaelli and Pasquier (2007) have argued that in this type of research it is easy to prejudge the role of the EU in domestic change (see also Chapter 1). Consequently, only by using thoughtful designs to examine complex temporal causal sentences can one avoid this type of bias. Findings may also be related to the dimensions considered. Broadly speaking, some authors are concerned with politics, some (more) with public policy while a few work on the 'polity' dimension (Börzel and Risse, 2003).

RQ2 – Granted that for most of the authors Europeanization is a process rather than an outcome, is there a common pattern in the identification of the dependent variable? The question is whether the studies talk past each other because they are using different operationalizations of the dependent variable, or vice versa. Our prior expectation here is that there are very different definitions of the dependent variable, since there is no consensus on what exactly researchers are trying to measure (Lenschow, 2005; Raunio and Wiberg, 2010: 76).

RQ3 – Authors working on the *politics* dimension of Europeanization are typically informed by comparative politics, whilst the authors dealing with the *policy* dimension draw on policy analysis or neo-institutionalism (Featherstone and Radaelli, 2003). This is a broad categorization, but it leads us to the question: To what extent does the choice to look at either politics or policy make a difference, and precisely in relation to what?

RQ4 – Given that explanation (at least in this field) revolves around both variables and mechanisms, what are the mechanisms used to explain Europeanization? Particularly in this field of research, but not just in this field, causal explanations tend to go beyond correlational analysis between a set of independent variables and a dependent variable. Most authors engage with mechanisms, no matter how contested a mechanism-based approach to explanation may be (Gerring, 2010; see also Chapter 1 in this volume and Falleti and Lynch, 2009, on mechanisms and context). Some mechanisms have been tailor-made to suit the specific questions of this field of research, while others are more general mechanisms well known in the literature on social interaction and causal explanation (Hedström, 2005). In the more general social sciences literature, the categories of mechanisms are much broader, covering for example relational (i.e., mechanisms triggered by the interaction between one social actor and another, such as collective action problems and heresthetics), behavioural (cognition, learning, positive feedback, individual emotional responses to perceptions of threat) and environmental mechanisms (pressure and opportunities arising out of factors exogenous to the system under examination).

Within Europeanization as a field of research, Vivien Schmidt highlights the mechanisms of coordinative and communicative discourse to explain the dependent variable of domestic policy change (Schmidt, 2002). Knill and Lehmkuhl (2002) draw attention to the mechanisms of competition, hierarchy and framing. In later work, Knill and Lenschow (2005) look at Europeanization through the lenses of governance theory. They point to three mechanisms: coercion, competition and communication. Thus the question we address here is whether we can find patterns in the choice of explanatory mechanisms. We expect to find mechanisms that have been suggested by the Europeanization literature, such as competition, hierarchy and framing (Bulmer and Radaelli, 2005). We expect to find that mechanisms featuring in the more general political science-sociology literature (Hedström, 2005) are less explored. Mechanisms suggested by critical realist theories are examined in Chapter 4 of this volume.

To answer these questions, we used meta-analysis of the articles (for various approaches to this technique, see Newig and Fritsch, 2009).

We extracted a sample of highly cited articles from the social science citation index, searching for 'Europeani$ation' and filtering for political science. We cut the sample at the H-index point. The H-index is usually defined for individual researchers – a scholar with an H-index of five has published five papers each of which has been cited by others at least five times. We can, however, calculate the index for a given field, in our case Europeanization, to provide a synthetic number of the impact of the field. In our case, after having refined Europeanization by excluding papers from outside the field of political science, we end up with an H-index of 14. All the articles with at least 14 citations were published between 1997 and 2007. This left us with no recent articles in the sample.

To increase the number of observations, as well as to gather information from more recent trends, we added all the political science articles on Europeanization that have been published since January 2007 (up to September 2009) in the same journals where the articles with at least 14 citations had been published. We combined the two sets of articles and checked for statistical artefacts, that is, papers that had nothing to do with this field but accidentally included the word 'Europeanization' somewhere in either the abstract or the title. Eventually, this process produced a sample of 46 articles, with a balanced distribution between highly cited and more recent articles.

Twenty articles stick to one of the classic definitions of Europeanization, 4 provide their own original definition and 22 do not provide any definition – this is often because the authors take for granted that the field is rather mature and there is a common understanding of what Europeanization is. Some 21 articles work inside the conceptual-analytical framework of Europeanization as defined in previous studies, 10 use it in contrast with alternative analytical frameworks, and 15 criticize and significantly amend the framework. These 15 articles show that there is a lively debate on what Europeanization as conceptual framework is. There is no correlation between definition or its absence and the use of the Europeanization framework as the main drive for the research.

We designed a scorecard to measure 15 variables for each article. Coding was carried out by a team of three doctoral students and the two authors. We piloted the scorecard on test articles, redefined the measurement of some variables and proceeded to code the whole sample. Each article was coded independently by two researchers.

Later, we confronted the scorecard results and discussed in bilateral meetings in order to find agreement on the values of the variables. When no agreement was possible, we left the value of that specific

*Table 2.1* Sample

| ID | Author(s) | Journal | Year | Citations (N) |
|----|-----------|---------|------|---------------|
| 1 | Anderson | *AmBeSc* | 2002 | 16 |
| 2 | Barbe et al. | *JEPP* | 2009 | 2 |
| 3 | Benz and Eberlein | *JEPP* | 1999 | 33 |
| 4 | Beyers and Trondal | *WEP* | 2004 | 14 |
| 5 | Blavoukos and Pagoulatos | *WEP* | 2008 | 2 |
| 6 | Börzel | *JCMS* | 1999 | 43 |
| 7 | Börzel | *JCMS* | 2000 | 36 |
| 8 | Bursens | *Scandinavian Pol Studies* | 2002 | 18 |
| 9 | Cole and Drake | *JEPP* | 2000 | 20 |
| 10 | Dardanelli | *Party Politics* | 2009 | 0 |
| 11 | Dimitrova | *WEP* | 2002 | 26 |
| 12 | Dimitrova and Toshkov | *WEP* | 2007 | 1 |
| 13 | Dyson | *JCMS* | 2000 | 14 |
| 14 | Esmark | *PA* | 2008 | 0 |
| 15 | Gilardi | *Annals* | 2005 | 23 |
| 16 | Grabbe | *JEPP* | 2001 | 57 |
| 17 | Harmsen | *Governance* | 1999 | 19 |
| 18 | Hauray and Urfalino | *JEPP* | 2009 | 0 |
| 19 | Kern and Bulkeley | *JCMS* | 2009 | 1 |
| 20 | Knill and Lehmkuhl | *EJPR* | 2002 | 40 |
| 21 | Knill and Tosun | *JEPP* | 2009 | 1 |
| 22 | Knill et al. | *PA* | 2009 | 0 |
| 23 | Ladrech | *Party Politics* | 2002 | 26 |
| 24 | Ladrech | *WEP* | 2007 | 3 |
| 25 | Lavenex | *JCMS* | 2001 | 16 |
| 26 | Levi-Faur | *CPS* | 2004 | 14 |
| 27 | Lippert et al. | *JEPP* | 2001 | 19 |
| 28 | Marcussen et al. | *JEPP* | 1999 | 27 |
| 29 | Martinsen and Vrangbaek | *PA* | 2008 | 0 |
| 30 | Michelsen | *JEPP* | 2008 | 1 |
| 31 | Noutcheva | *JEPP* | 2009 | 0 |
| 32 | Parau | *WEP* | 2009 | 0 |
| 33 | Piana | *CPS* | 2009 | 0 |
| 34 | Quaglia | *JCMS* | 2009 | 5 |
| 35 | Radaelli | *CPS* | 1997 | 14 |
| 36 | Scharpf | *JEPP* | 1997 | 46 |
| 37 | Schimmelfennig and Sedelmeier | *JEPP* | 2004 | 31 |

| 38 | Schmidt | *JEPP* | 2002 | 19 |
| 39 | Schneider and Hage | *JEPP* | 2008 | 1 |
| 40 | Semetko et al. | *WEP* | 2000 | 14 |
| 41 | Sitter | *WEP* | 2001 | 14 |
| 42 | Stolfi | *JEPP* | 2008 | 0 |
| 43 | Tocci | *JCMS* | 2008 | 0 |
| 44 | Trampusch | *Governance* | 2009 | 0 |
| 45 | Warleigh | *JCMS* | 2001 | 17 |
| 46 | Wessels | *JEPP* | 1998 | 30 |

variable within a given article blank (missing value). The final results were then used as a data set for the analysis presented in the following section.

## Findings

In this section we present the results of our meta-analysis. Univariate analysis shows certain regularities and confirms prior expectations about the methods, the causal mechanisms and the research design. Bivariate analysis provides certain insights into the deeper implications of the use of various methodological tools. Logit and probit models test the expectations of how research design features (such as the choice to study politics or policy, mechanisms-based explanations, the presence or absence of causal hypotheses and so on) affect the findings.

### a. Univariate analysis

To begin with, let us first look at the two sub-samples, highly cited versus recent papers. Authors are more or less equally explicit about providing a section about research design, although awareness is slightly greater in the newer articles. Overall, the sample is split exactly into two on the presence or absence of a research design section. The motivation for case selection is greater for the highly cited.

Since this field of research is led by political scientists coming from the qualitative tradition it is not surprising to see a preference for qualitative methods – a strong preference indeed that has been a trend in EU studies in general (Jupille, 2005). Only three studies use explicitly proper quantitative methods (regression, econometrics, etc.). In terms of the hypotheses, the vast majority make an explicit reference to a causal hypothesis tested in the article (27 articles). Nevertheless, out of those, 15 do not offer a set of rival hypotheses, which adds to the 19

*Table 2.2* Aggregate data on design issues*

| Research design | Highly cited | New | Total |
|---|---|---|---|
| Yes, there is a section | 9 | 12 | 21 |
| No such section | 14 | 7 | 21 |
| Unclear | 3 | 1 | 4 |
| **Case selection** | | | |
| Justified | 11 | 8 | 19 |
| Not justified | 7 | 5 | 12 |
| Irrelevant | 8 | 7 | 15 |
| **Measurement method** | | | |
| Quantitative | 1 | 2 | 3 |
| Qualitative | 21 | 12 | 33 |
| Single case narrative | 4 | 5 | 9 |
| **Hypotheses** | | | |
| Yes, specific hypotheses | 8 | 4 | 12 |
| Yes, but no rival offered | 8 | 7 | 15 |
| No causal hypotheses | 10 | 9 | 19 |
| **Time as variable** | | | |
| Yes, specific period | 5 | 8 | 13 |
| Yes, vaguely specified | 13 | 7 | 20 |
| No or irrelevant | 8 | 5 | 13 |

*Note*: *Total of 45; one case was marked as missing as coding was not conclusive.

articles that did not include causal hypotheses at all. Finally, 33 make an explicit reference to time as a variable, with 13 specifying a time period. The following Table 2.2 provides an aggregate view of these findings.

In terms of the politics–policy choice, a dimension we introduced above with reference to RQ3, there is a preference for studying policy effects, thus revealing a bias (Table 2.3). Most of the papers fall within the categories of public administration, political economy and generic public policy analysis. In a sense, what Bulmer and Radaelli observed in 2005 – that, roughly speaking, there is more Europeanization of public policy than of politics – may be just an opinion, but there is definitively less intellectual appetite for appraising the politics dimension. This, however, stands in contrast to recent projects that have shown that the politics dimension is very important in this field. In particular, it has been argued that politics may be Europeanized in a subtle yet deep way – for example, via the EU-induced transformation of party organization and party politics (Poguntke et al., 2007; see also Chapter 10 in this volume).

*Table 2.3*  Field and framework for total and sub-samples

| Field and framework | Highly cited | New | Total |
|---|---|---|---|
| Policy analysis | 6 | 6 | 12 |
| Public administration | 6 | 4 | 10 |
| Parties, government, comparative politics | 6 | 2 | 8 |
| Political economy | 2 | 3 | 5 |
| International relations, identity | 2 | 3 | 5 |
| Elections, public opinion | 1 | 0 | 1 |
| Political theory | 1 | 0 | 1 |
| Impossible to find | 2 | 2 | 4 |

With regard to choice of countries, the so-called awkward partners like the UK (8 articles) and Denmark (5) receive a lot of attention. This is also explained by the high concentration of scholars publishing in English-speaking journals in these two countries. It is a well-known fact that the social science citation index discriminates against journals that use languages other than English. Overall, there is still much more interest in Europeanization effects in the former 12–15 member states of the EU (43) than in the new members (13). Non-EU countries such as Switzerland are examined in 9 cases. Overall, there is bias in country selection, in terms of the choice of both old or new member states, and even within the 6 founding members (e.g., Italy features in 4 articles and Belgium in 3, but there are 7 articles for France and 8 for Germany, and no articles dedicated explicitly to the Netherlands). The sample shows that the Commission and the Council or the Committee of Permanent Representatives (COREPER) are the main European-level actors. The national executive and the political parties are the most important at the domestic level. The scorecard question was 'Which of the following actors are found in the article?' Actors are defined as 'purposeful agents that participate in social interaction'.

Let us now look at what kinds of variables (politics-level and policy-level) are explained. The scorecard question was 'Does the article try to explain variation of any of the following variables?' In terms of policies, we found that, competition, the internal market, trade and regulation, both economic policies (fiscal and monetary) and environmental policies – which are directly controlled at the EU-level – are prominently featured. With regard to politics-level variables, the national executive and the political parties appear along with various interest groups. Table 2.4 summarizes these findings.

*Table 2.4* Actors and independent variables (total actors, $N = 183$; total variables, $N = 68$)

| Actors | Observations | Variables | Observations |
|---|---|---|---|
| Commission | 25 | Agricultural policy | 1 |
| European Parliament | 6 | Cohesion policy | 1 |
| ECJ | 4 | Competition, internal market, trade and regulation | 7 |
| Council/COREPER | 15 | Economic (monetary and fiscal) | 5 |
| Other EU actors | 3 | Environmental policy | 7 |
| National executive | 34 | Foreign and security policy | 3 |
| Political parties | 11 | Refugee, asylum and migration policy | 1 |
| National parliaments | 6 | Social, welfare and education policy | 3 |
| Domestic courts | 2 | Urban and regional policy | 2 |
| Other domestic actors | 22 | National elections | 2 |
| Public opinion | 9 | Political parties | 5 |
| EU business groups | 2 | National executive | 5 |
| Domestic business groups | 12 | Media | 1 |
| EU non-governmental organizations (NGOs) | 4 | Public opinion | 1 |
| Domestic NGOs | 6 | Interest or other groups | 4 |
| Media | 2 | Other political actors | 7 |
| Epistemic community | 6 | Other variables | 13 |
| Other actors | 14 | | |

We tracked down the explanatory factors, distinguishing between those that are simply 'controlled for' and those that are also found significant. We use these concepts in a non-statistical sense, given the high number of qualitative articles in the sample. Indeed, we found a strong emphasis on ideational explanations (in the sense of Stolfi, 2008), covering factors such as discourse, ideas and norms; socialization and identity; followed by the composition of the executive; bureaucracy;

*Table 2.5* Explanatory factors: Controlled-for (*N* = 200) and significant (*N* = 131)

| Explanatory factor | Controls for | Significance |
|---|---|---|
| Discourse, ideas, norms and frames | 30 | 22 |
| Socialization and identity | 24 | 13 |
| Executive, composition of government | 19 | 15 |
| Bureaucracy | 17 | 12 |
| Learning | 16 | 7 |
| Veto players and veto points | 14 | 9 |
| Type of political system | 13 | 8 |
| Transnational actors | 12 | 7 |
| Economic variables | 12 | 7 |
| Pressure groups/NGOs | 11 | 7 |
| Electoral competition | 8 | 7 |
| Legal system | 7 | 4 |
| Political parties | 6 | 3 |
| Media | 1 | 1 |
| Other | 10 | 9 |

and learning. Learning is frequently examined, but it is found significant only in a handful of cases. Table 2.5 summarizes the results.

## b. Bivariate analysis

One of our research questions is about the relationship between findings and research design choices made by the authors. We coded a variable 'Europeyes' with a value of 1 for papers that found Europeanization effects either qualitatively or quantitatively; and 0 for papers that found no effects (e.g., because rival alternative hypotheses were confirmed and Europeanization hypotheses falsified) or showed unclear results.

Simple cross-tabulation shows that whether or not the authors find Europeanization depends on the presence or absence mechanisms, time or normative issues. If authors address mechanisms or are clear about their time period, they increase the probability of finding Europeanization effects. Articles that address normative issues tend to find 'less' effects of Europeanization processes on their dependent variable – a finding not supported by any prior expectation since we did not assume that normative issues arise out of prejudging Europeanization in whatever way. There is no statistical significance for variables such as research design, case selection or causal hypotheses, although the tabulation reveals a certain bias in the expected direction (e.g., when no causal hypotheses are present there is a bias towards finding Europeanization).

## c. Logistic regression

We ran a simple logistic regression to explore statistical significance (see Pampel, 2000, on logistic regression) of the variables we used in cross-tabulation. We found significance in items (i), (ii) and (iii) of Table 2.6 with a greater emphasis on mechanisms and time (Table 2.7).

*Table 2.6* Cross-tabulation between Europeanization effects ('europeyes') and (i) time, (ii) causal mechanisms ('mechan') and (iii) normative issues ('norm'); all values are expressed as percentages

**(i) Europeyes × time cross-tabulation:** if time period is included, the likelihood of finding Europeanization effects is higher

|           |      | Time |      | Total |
|-----------|------|------|------|-------|
|           |      | 0.00 | 1.00 |       |
| Europeyes | 0.00 | 61.5 | 39.4 | 45.7  |
|           | 1.00 | 38.5 | 60.6 | 54.3  |
| Total     |      | 100.0| 100.0| 100.0 |

**(ii) Europeyes × mechan cross-tabulation:** if articles use causal mechanisms, the likelihood of finding Europeanization effects is higher

|           |      | Mechan |      | Total |
|-----------|------|--------|------|-------|
|           |      | 0.00   | 1.00 |       |
| Europeyes | 0.00 | 73.7   | 25.9 | 45.7  |
|           | 1.00 | 26.3   | 74.1 | 54.3  |
| Total     |      | 100.0  | 100.0| 100.0 |

**(iii) Europeyes × norm cross-tabulation:** if the articles discuss normative issues, the likelihood of finding Europeanization effects is lower

|           |      | Norm |      | Total |
|-----------|------|------|------|-------|
|           |      | 0.00 | 1.00 |       |
| Europeyes | 0.00 | 38.7 | 60.0 | 45.7  |
|           | 1.00 | 61.3 | 40.0 | 54.3  |
| Total     |      | 100.0| 100.0| 100.0 |

*Table 2.7*  Logistic regression: Time, mechanisms and normative issues

**(i) Variables in the Equation – Time**

|  |  | B | S.E. | Wald | df | Sig. | Exp(B) |
|---|---|---|---|---|---|---|---|
| Step 1(a) | time | 0.901 | 0.672 | 1.795 | 1 | **0.180** | 2.462 |
|  | Constant | −0.470 | 0.570 | 0.680 | 1 | 0.410 | 0.625 |

a Variable(s) entered on step 1: time.

**(ii) Variables in the Equation – Mechanisms**

|  |  | B | S.E. | Wald | df | Sig. | Exp(B) |
|---|---|---|---|---|---|---|---|
| Step 1(a) | mechan | 2.079 | 0.681 | 9.313 | 1 | **0.002** | 8.000 |
|  | Constant | −1.030 | 0.521 | 3.906 | 1 | 0.048 | 0.357 |

a Variable(s) entered on step 1: mechan.

**(iii) Variables in the Equation – Normative Issues**

|  |  | B | S.E. | Wald | df | Sig. | Exp(B) |
|---|---|---|---|---|---|---|---|
| Step 1(a) | norm | −0.865 | 0.643 | 1.808 | 1 | **0.179** | 0.421 |
|  | Constant | 0.460 | 0.369 | 1.553 | 1 | 0.213 | 1.583 |

a Variable(s) entered on step 1: norm.

Although the authors work on different dimensions of 'explanation', we scored the articles in relation to three main levers of change. One way to map explanations in political science is to distinguish between structuralist and ideational levers of change (Stolfi, 2008). Thus, our first lever is ideational. The second is structuralist – variations of the 'opportunity structure' type of explanation, including veto points and strategic reactions to changes in electoral laws, incentives, policy resources and so on. The third lever of change is based on a notion of causality that is intimately different from the ideational and structuralist explanations (following Hall, 2003) – we cover these approaches under the category of path-dependent levers of change. The results show that if the lever is ideational, then change is most likely to be triggered by a policy variable. If the lever of change is identified as opportunity structure, then it is most likely to have been triggered by a politics variable. Finally, if change is path-dependent, then change is likely to be triggered by a policy variable although this is not statistically significant. These results are further reinforced, at least for the ideational and opportunity structure levers that are statistically significant, by a simple logistic regression (Table 2.8):

*Table 2.8*  Logistic regression: Levers of change ('polpot' = policy/politics triggers)

**(i) Variables in the Equation – Ideational**

|          |          | B      | S.E.  | Wald  | df | Sig.  | Exp(B) |
|----------|----------|--------|-------|-------|----|-------|--------|
| Step 1(a) | polpot   | 2.079  | 1.167 | 3.174 | 1  | 0.075 | 8.000  |
|          | Constant | −2.773 | 1.031 | 7.235 | 1  | 0.007 | 0.063  |

a Variable(s) entered on step 1: polpot.

**(ii) Variables in the Equation – Opportunity structure**

|          |          | B      | S.E.  | Wald  | df | Sig.  | Exp(B) |
|----------|----------|--------|-------|-------|----|-------|--------|
| Step 1(a) | polpot   | −1.618 | 0.774 | 4.373 | 1  | 0.037 | 0.198  |
|          | Constant | 0.606  | 0.508 | 1.426 | 1  | 0.232 | 1.833  |

a Variable(s) entered on step 1: polpot.

**(iii) Variables in the Equation – Path-dependency**

|          |          | B      | S.E.  | Wald  | df | Sig.  | Exp(B) |
|----------|----------|--------|-------|-------|----|-------|--------|
| Step 1(a) | polpot   | 0.470  | 0.749 | 0.394 | 1  | 0.530 | 1.600  |
|          | Constant | −0.875 | 0.532 | 2.705 | 1  | 0.100 | 0.417  |

a Variable(s) entered on step 1: polpot.

Based on the results of the regression and cross-tabulation analysis, we ran a simple probit model reporting on the marginal effects (see the model in the Appendix). The results are indeed encouraging for our intuitive hypothesis on how research design and mechanisms affect Europeanization findings. The probit model shows that $\chi^2 = 0.0067$ and the results verify the importance of mechanisms and research design. Transforming this into an equation based on probit analysis we obtain the following: the constant is not statically significant; if mechanisms are part of the equation there is a 57.8 per cent increase in the probability of finding Europeanization; if normative issues are discussed the probability of finding Europeanization decreases by 37.9 per cent; and finally, if there is a research design section in the study the probability of finding Europeanization drops by 33.5 per cent.

## Discussion

In this section we answer our research questions and add more information drawn from a broader conceptual analysis of the sample.

The first research question concerned the role of research design in finding Europeanization effects (or lack thereof). Research design shows elements of bias, such as lack of justification of case selection and the lack of explicit causal hypotheses that can be tested rigorously. The presence of a clear time-period and the inclusion of mechanism are also significant for appraising the effects of Europeanization processes on the dependent variables of the sample. The role of normative issues is also statistically significant, although we found no explanation for this. Overall, these particular features of research design are not insignificant for the findings.

Let us now turn to RQ2 on the dependent variable. Do the papers in the sample exhibit a common understanding of the explanans? We found all sorts of Europeanization: as process, as context in which the study is situated, as outcome, and as *sui generis* an independent variable (i.e., Europeanization causing certain other outcomes). Clearly Europeanization as such is not the dependent variable. For most papers it is a process. There are also cases in which Europeanization as framework is problematized and criticized (Hauray and Urfalino, 2009; Trampusch, 2009). Discouragingly perhaps, almost each article has its own way of defining and operationalizing the dependent variable – arguably one of the features that, at least according to some critics, makes this field a clumsy bumblebee. However, there are at least some broad categories, based on the type of variables examined. The following categories are present:

- development and change of ideas or identities (9 articles);
- variation of policy, regulations, and implementation (19);
- governance-related variations, institutional development and building (10);
- change of processes or procedural change (7).

In category (a) we find articles that deal with a measurement of the impact of the EU on the development of certain ideas or the development of identities within member states or within institutions. They explore the impact on the strategic goals of parties in party competition and the exploitation of the idea of Europe as well as the development of Euro-scepticism as a political trend (ID numbers 9, 10, 23, 41 in Table 2.1). They deal with the development of the supranational identity of public officials within EU institutions (4) or at home within party elites (24). They also refer to the development of European identities in the member states (28) and how this is reflected on media coverage (40) or within the involvement of the civil society in European affairs (32).

In category (b) we encounter mainly articles problematizing issues of policy change or convergence (16, 34), initiation of regulation and implementation records of EU directives (8, 29, 35) or more generally rules (17, 21, 22, 31). Issues of policy convergence are discussed (2, 20), as well as domestic policy responses to European-wide policies such as economic and monetary policies (13, 38); more concrete creation of specific market rules (18, 26, 30); or even in non-classic Community areas like the welfare state or education and public procurement (36, 39, 44).

In category (c) papers the explanans lies in institution-building and development and issues of governance. Examples of this type would include hierarchical and power relations between institutions (1, 6, 27) as well as institutional framework creation and institutional capacity building (9, 11), coordination of markets (12) through independent authorities (15), issues of good governance (19) and institutional reform (7, 42).

Finally, in category (d), the explanans is process creation or procedural change. This includes territorial interaction and network building (3), deliberation with transnational interest groups and NGOs (5, 45) and procedural relations (14, 37), and judicial procedures at different levels (33, 46).

As for RQ3, we already mentioned the widespread impression (Bulmer and Radaelli, 2005) that there is more Europeanization of policy than on politics. This is confirmed by more authors studying the former rather than the latter – a possible source of bias in selecting the object of research. Interestingly, we found that if policy is the main concern of the paper, there is a tendency to use ideational explanations, whilst the politics-oriented papers draw on opportunity structure arguments.

RQ4 leads us to the discussion of mechanisms. Since most of the articles in the sample are qualitative, there is considerable work on mechanisms here. The majority of the papers seek to establish causality by drawing on mechanisms-oriented explanations. We concur with Gerring that, at least in our sample, the emphasis on mechanisms is 'not at variance with traditional practices in the social sciences, and thus hardly qualifies as a distinct approach to causal assessment' (Gerring, 2010: 1499); only a minority of articles draw on mechanisms to explore non-traditional approaches to causality (see Saurugger, 2009, on types of causality).

The trouble is that are almost as many names for mechanisms as the articles that utilize a mechanism-based approach. (Very) broadly speaking we found the classic Knill and Lehmkuhl triad of hierarchy, competition and framing effects. There are also traces of the (ideational and rational-choice theoretic) variations of the goodness of fit model that is the baseline model for Europeanization explanations (Caporaso, 2007 adds the notion of 'institutional' goodness of fit to the 'policy'-level goodness of fit). Some articles contain more than one key mechanism. However, a more precise categorization of the families of mechanisms is as follows.

- ideational and discursive mechanisms (11 articles);
- mechanisms of (mainly regulatory) compliance or competition (12);
- mechanisms of institutional change and goodness of fit (12);
- cognitive mechanisms: heresthetics, learning and diffusion (6).

The first category contains mechanisms that deal with the ideational pressures and the legitimacy of discourse arenas, including development of cultural norms and norms entrepreneurs (ID numbers 13, 32 in Table 2.1), socialization and networking (18, 21, 33, 43, 45, 46), acclimatization and diffusion of ideas (9, 16, 46).

The second category of mechanisms refers to those on (regulatory) compliance and competition such as policy-level pace-setting, foot-dragging and fence-sitting (7), policy conditionality (33, 37, 43) and horizontal emulation (15); market competition and cooperation (18, 21, 39), exit and voice (29), policy-level conflict (30) and policy compliance (22, 38).

The third category of mechanisms includes those that deal with adaptation of domestic institutions to EU pressures: institutional adaptation (including adaptation in anticipation of EU membership and conditionality) and goodness of fit mechanisms (5, 6, 11, 14, 15, 16, 20, 27, 32, 33), institutional coercion and mimesis (38), opportunity structure (42) or passive enforcement (43). Finally, the fourth category refers to mechanisms that frame expectations and beliefs of the member states and the public: for example, heresthetics (10); learning and lesson-drawing (37); diffusion and transfer of knowledge and best practices (5, 18, 20, 34). Overall, we found evidence of the mechanisms that have been theorized within the field, but also traces of the wider debate on social mechanisms.

## Conclusions

A decade from its inception, Europeanization is still a field of research that attracts considerable interest among political scientists. Both English-speaking and French/Italian textbooks include a chapter on this topic (Attinà and Natalicchi, 2007, Ch. 5; Cini and Perez-Solorzano Borragan, 2009, Ch. 25; Saurugger, 2009, Ch. 8). However, there are different opinions about the added value of looking at Europeanization. One crucial question concerns causality (see also Chapters 1 and 4).

In this chapter we have examined both highly cited papers and recent articles. We have found that research design features impact whether authors find Europeanization effects or not, the clearest result being that research design choices statistically alter the probability of finding Europeanization effects. Another result is that the choice of studying politics or public policy has important consequences for the logic of explanation. Country selection is not even, with some countries more systematically studied and others neglected.

Finally, we evaluated the role of mechanisms in causal explanations, showing that the field is slowly exploring some general categories of mechanisms, although there is still considerable interest in the mechanisms theorized within the field. Overall, ideational explanations are preferred to structural explanations. Ideational approaches lead to policy-level explanations, whilst structuralist approaches determine a preference for politics-level explanations. Qualitative modes prevail over quantitative approaches. Researchers could usefully spend some more time in quantitative analyses, possibly strengthening the link between this field and the contiguous field of quantitative analysis of legislation (Raunio and Wiberg, 2010; Töller, 2010, and her Chapter 3 in this volume), particularly because the latter has already explored ways to measure the scope and extent of Europeanization effects. It is striking that the quantitative analysis of legislation is not (as yet) represented in the highly cited articles on Europeanization.

There are several caveats that come with our results. We did not examine *every* paper on Europeanization included in the social science citation index. We did not code books, only articles, and we used a scorecard that, although validated by discussion and deliberation within a team of five researchers, may contain its own bias. Finally, in contrast to our previous research (Exadaktylos and Radaelli, 2009) we did not use a control group for our meta-analysis, since we did not think it could have helped us to answer the research questions that motivate this chapter.

Future research will probably have to dig deeper into the issue of causality, by examining ontological as well as methodological issues, and by exploring what is the exact role of mechanisms-based explanations in appraising and establishing causality (Gerring, 2010). The bumblebee is indeed clumsy, but so are several other fields of political science and this does not prevent them from flying high in the sky of the social sciences.

## Acknowledgements

Research for this chapter was funded by the Jean Monnet Excellence Award of the Centre for European Governance, University of Exeter. We wish to thank very warmly Samuele Dossi, Marie Christine Fontana and Marzio Menichetti for their valuable input to the design of the scorecard and for having coded the articles with us. We also would like to thank Dr Georgios Xezonakis for having advised us on the regression models and having shown unlimited patience each time we went back to his office with 'just another quick question'. Errors and omissions are our fault, of course.

## Appendix

We construct the following probit equation based on the rounded results of our probit model:

$$y_{(europeyes)} = -0.88\chi_{(resdes)} - 0.01\chi_{(hypoth)} + 0.4\chi_{(casejust)}$$
$$+ 0.54\chi_{(time)} + 1.61\chi_{(mechan)} - 0.99\chi_{(norm)}$$

The variable *europeyes* denotes the dependent of whether a study concludes positively on Europeanization; the independent variables are *resdes* on the presence of a clear research design section, *hypoth* on the presence of hypotheses or not, *casejust* on whether case selection is justified or is arbitrary, *time* on whether the study examines a certain time period, *mechanisms* on the use of mechanisms of Europeanization or not and, finally, *norm* on whether the study includes a discussion of normative issues.

```
. dprobit europeyes resdes casejust hypoth time mechan norm, r

Iteration 0:   log pseudolikelihood = -31.710637
Iteration 0:   log pseudolikelihood = -31.710637
Iteration 1:   log pseudolikelihood = -22.72568
Iteration 2:   log pseudolikelihood = -22.360938
Iteration 3:   log pseudolikelihood = -22.357651
Iteration 4:   log pseudolikelihood = -22.357651

Probit regression, reporting marginal effects      Number of obs  =      46
                                                    Wald chi2(6)   =   17.83
                                                    Prob > chi2    =  0.0067
                                                    Pseudo R2      =  0.2949
Log pseudolikelihood = -22.357651
```

| europe~s | dF/dx | Robust Std. Err. | z | P>\|z\| | x-bar | [95% C.I.] |
|---|---|---|---|---|---|---|
| resdes* | -.3384674 | .1817653 | -1.78 | 0.076*** | .456522 | -.694721   .017786 |
| casejust* | .1539839 | .1812729 | 0.84 | 0.402 | .413043 | -.201305   .509272 |
| hypoth* | -.0403576 | .1882311 | -0.21 | 0.831 | .586957 | -.409284   .328569 |
| time* | .2114302 | .1907444 | 1.09 | 0.276 | .717391 | -.162422   .585282 |
| mechan* | .5784436 | .1286762 | 3.63 | 0.000* | .586957 | .326243   .830644 |
| norm* | -.3792213 | .1727695 | -2.02 | 0.044** | .326087 | -.717843  -.040599 |

```
  obs. P| .5434783
 pred. P| .5655667  (at x-bar)
```

(*) dF/dx is for discrete change of dummy variable from 0 to 1
z and P>|z| correspond to the test of the underlying coefficient being 0

```
. probit europeyes casejust hypoth time mechan norm, r

Iteration 0: log pseudolikelihood = -31.710637
Iteration 1: log pseudolikelihood = -22.470998
Iteration 2: log pseudolikelihood = -22.357779
Iteration 3: log pseudolikelihood = -22.357651
Iteration 4: log pseudolikelihood = -22.357651

Probit regression                                Number of obs   =       46
                                                 Wald chi2(6)    =    17.83
                                                 Prob > chi2     =   0.0067
Log pseudolikelihood = -22.357651                Pseudo R2       =   0.2949
```

| europeyes | Coef. | Robust Std. Err. | z | P>\|z\| | [95% Conf. Interval] | |
|---|---|---|---|---|---|---|
| resdes | -.8826512 | .4970627 | -1.78 | 0.076*** | -1.856876 | .0915738 |
| casejust | .3962169 | .4732294 | 0.84 | 0.402 | -.5312957 | 1.32373 |
| hypoth | -.1027488 | .4809215 | -0.21 | 0.831 | -1.045338 | .8398401 |
| time | .5369642 | .4933409 | 1.09 | 0.276 | -.4299661 | 1.503895 |
| mechan | 1.607961 | .4429945 | 3.63 | 0.000* | .7397083 | 2.476215 |
| norm | -.9895183 | .4902442 | -2.02 | 0.044** | -1.950379 | -.0286574 |
| _cons | -.5416459 | .5780238 | -0.94 | 0.349 | -1.674552 | .5912599 |

```
.dprobit europeyes resdes casejust hypoth time median norm, r
Iteration 0: log pseudolikelihood = -31.710637
Iteration 1: log pseudolikelihood = -22.72568
Iteration 2: log pseudolikelihood = -22.360938
Iteration 3: log pseudolikelihood = -22.357651
Iteration 4: log pseudolikelihood = -22.357651
```

Probit regression, reporting marginal effects

| | |
|---|---|
| Number of obs | = 46 |
| Wald chi2(6) | = 17.83 |
| Prob > chi2 | = 0.0067 |
| Pseudo R2 | = 0.2949 |

Log pseudolikelihood = -22.357651

| europe~s | dF/dx | Robust Std. Err. | z | P>\|z\| | x-bar | [95% C.I.] |
|---|---|---|---|---|---|---|
| resdes* | -.3384674 | .1817653 | -1.78 | 0.076*** | .456522 | -.694721 .017786 |
| casejust* | .1539839 | .1812729 | 0.84 | 0.402 | .413043 | -.201305 .509272 |
| hypoth* | -.0403576 | .1882311 | -0.21 | 0.831 | .586957 | -.409284 .328569 |
| time* | .2114302 | .1907444 | 1.09 | 0.276 | .717391 | -.162422 .585282 |
| mechan* | .5784436 | .1286762 | 3.63 | 0.000* | .586957 | .326243 .830644 |
| norm* | -.3792213 | .1727695 | -2.02 | 0.044** | .326087 | -.717843 -.040599 |

```
-----------+---------------
obs. P  |  .5434783
pred. P |  .5655667   (at x-bar)
-----------+---------------
```

(*) dF/dx is for discrete change of dummy variable from 0 to 1

z and P>|z| correspond to the test of the underlying coefficient being 0

. probit europeyes resdes casejust hypoth time mechan norm, r

```
Iteration 0: log pseudolikelihood = -31.710637
Iteration 1: log pseudolikelihood = -22.470998
Iteration 2: log pseudolikelihood = -22.357779
Iteration 3: log pseudolikelihood = -22.357651
Iteration 4: log pseudolikelihood = -22.357651
```

Probit regression

```
Number of obs   =        46
Wald chi2(6)    =     17.83
```

# References

Anderson, M.S. (2002) 'Ecological modernization or subversion? The effect of Europeanization on Eastern Europe.' *American Behavioral Scientist* 45(9): 1394–1416.

Attinà, F. and G. Natalicchi (2007) *L'Unione Europea: Governo, Istituzioni, Politiche* (Bologna: Il Mulino).

Barbé, E., O. Costa, A. Herranz Surrallés and M. Natorski (2009) 'Which rules shape EU external governance? Patterns of rule selection in foreign and security policies.' *Journal of European Public Policy* 16(6): 834–852.

Benz, A. and B. Eberlein (1999) 'The Europeanization of regional policies: Patterns of multi-level governance.' *Journal of European Public Policy* 6(2): 329–348.

Beyers, J. and J. Trondal (2004) 'How nation states "hit" Europe: Ambiguity and representation in the European Union.' *West European Politics* 27(5): 919–942.

Blavoukos, S. and G. Pagoulatos (2008) ' "Enlargement Waves" and interest group participation in the EU policy-making system: Establishing a framework of analysis.' *West European Politics* 31(6): 1147–1165.

Börzel, T.A. (1999) 'Towards convergence in Europe? Institutional adaptation to Europeanization in Germany and Spain.' *Journal of Common Market Studies* 37(4): 573–596.

Börzel, T.A. (2002) 'Member state responses to Europeanization.' *Journal of Common Market Studies* 40(2): 193–214.

Börzel, T.A. and T. Risse (2003) 'Conceptualizing the domestic impact.' In Featherstone, K. and Radaelli, C. (Eds.) *The Politics of Europeanization* (Oxford: Oxford University Press).

Bulmer, S. and C. Radaelli (2005) 'The Europeanization of national policy.' In Bulmer, S. and Lequesne, C. (Eds.) *The Member States of the European Union* (Oxford: Oxford University Press).

Bursens, P. (2002) 'Why Denmark and Belgium have different implementation records: On transposition laggards and leaders in the EU.' *Scandinavian Political Studies* 25(2): 173–195.

Caporaso, J. (2007) 'The three worlds of regional integration theory.' In Graziano, P. and Vink, M. (Eds.) *Europeanization: New Research Agendas* (Basingstoke: Palgrave Macmillan).

Cini, M. and N. Perez-Solorzano Borragan (Eds.) (2009) *European Union Politics*, 3rd edition (Oxford: Oxford University Press).

Cole, A. and H. Drake (2000) 'The Europeanization of the French polity: Continuity, change and adaptation.' *Journal of European Public Policy* 7(1): 26–43.

Dardanelli, P. (2009) 'Europeanization as heresthetics: Party competition over Self-Government for Scotland, 1974–97.' *Party Politics* 15(1): 49–68.

Dimitrova, A. (2002) 'Enlargement, institution-building and the EU's administrative capacity requirement.' *West European Politics* 25(4): 171–190.

Dimitrova, A. and D. Toshkov (2007) 'The dynamics of domestic coordination of EU policy in the new member states: Impossible to lock in?' *West European Politics* 30(5): 961–986.

Dyson, K. (2000) 'EMU as Europeanization: Convergence, diversity and contingency.' *Journal of Common Market Studies* 38(4): 645–666.

Esmark, A. (2008) 'Tracing the national mandate: Administrative Europeanization made in Denmark.' *Public Administration* 86(1): 243–257.

Exadaktylos, T. and C.M. Radaelli (2009) 'Research design in European studies: The case of Europeanization.' *Journal of Common Market Studies* 47(3): 507–530.

Falleti, T.G. and J.F. Lynch (2009) 'Context and causal mechanisms in political analysis.' *Comparative Political Studies* 42(9): 1143–1166.

Featherstone, K. and C. Radaelli (Eds.) (2003) *The Politics of Europeanization* (Oxford: Oxford University Press).

Gerring, J. (2010) 'Causal mechanisms: yes, but ...' *Comparative Political Studies* 43(11): 1499–1526.

Gilardi, F. (2005) 'The institutional foundations of regulatory capitalism: The diffusion of independent regulatory agencies in western Europe.' *Annals of the American Academy of Political and Social Science* 598: 84–101.

Grabbe, H. (2001) 'How does Europeanization affect CEE governance? Conditionality, diffusion and diversity.' *Journal of European Public Policy* 8(6): 1013–1031.

Hall, P.A. (2003) 'Aligning ontology and methodology in comparative research.' In Mahoney, J. and Rueschmeyer, D. (Eds.) *Comparative Historical Analysis in the Social Science* (Cambridge: Cambridge University Press).

Harmsen, R. (1999) 'The Europeanization of national administrations: A comparative study of France and the Netherlands.' *Governance* 12(1): 81–113.

Hauray, B. and P. Urfalino (2009) 'Mutual transformation and the development of European policy spaces. The case of medicines licensing.' *Journal of European Public Policy* 16(3): 431–449.

Hedström, P. (2005) *Dissecting the Social: On the Principles of Analytical Sociology* (Cambridge: Cambridge University Press).

Jupille, J. (2005) 'Knowing Europe: Metatheory and methodology in European Union studies.' In Cini, M. and Bourne, A.K. (Eds.) *Palgrave Advances in European Union Studies* (Basingstoke: Palgrave Macmillan).

Kern, K. and H. Bulkeley (2009) 'Cities, Europeanization and multi-level governance: Governing climate change through transnational municipal networks.' *Journal of Common Market Studies* 47(2): 309–332.

Knill, C. and D. Lehmkuhl (2002) 'The national impact of European Union regulatory policy: Three Europeanization mechanisms.' *European Journal of Political Research* 41(2): 255–280.

Knill, C. and J. Tosun (2009) 'Hierarchy, networks, or markets: How does the EU shape environmental policy adoptions within and beyond its borders?' *Journal of European Public Policy* 16(6): 873–894.

Knill, C., J. Tosun and M.W. Bauer (2009) 'Neglected faces of Europeanization: The differential impact of the EU on the dismantling and expansion of domestic policies.' *Public Administration* 87(3): 519–537.

Ladrech, R. (2002) 'Europeanization and political parties – Towards a framework for analysis.' *Party Politics* 8(4): 389–403.

Ladrech, R. (2007) 'National political parties and European governance: The consequences of "Missing in action".' *West European Politics* 30(5): 945–960.

Lavenex, S. (2001) 'The Europeanization of refugee policies: Normative challenges and institutional legacies.' *Journal of Common Market Studies* 39(5): 851–874.

Lenschow, A. (2005) 'Europeanization of public policy.' In Richardson, J.J. (Ed.) *European Union: Power and Policy-Making* (Abingdon: Routledge).

Levi-Faur, D. (2004) 'On the "net impact" of Europeanization – The EU's telecoms and electricity regimes between the global and the national.' *Comparative Political Studies* 37(1): 3–29.

Lippert, B., G. Umbach et al. (2001) 'Europeanization of CEE executives: EU membership negotiations as a shaping power.' *Journal of European Public Policy* 8(6): 980–1012.

Mair, P. (2004) 'The Europeanization dimension.' *Journal of European Public Policy* 11(2): 337–348.

Marcussen, M., T. Risse et al. (1999) 'Constructing Europe? The evolution of French, British and German nation state identities.' *Journal of European Public Policy* 6(4): 614–633.

Martinsen, D.S. and K. Vrangbaek (2008) 'The Europeanization of health care governance: Implementing the market imperatives of Europe.' *Public Administration* 86(1): 169–184.

Michelsen, J. (2008) 'A Europeanization deficit? The impact of EU organic agriculture regulations on new member states.' *Journal of European Public Policy* 15(1): 117–134.

Newig, J. and O. Fritsch (2009) The case survey method and applications to political science, *Paper Delivered to the Annual Meeting of the American Political Science Association.* Toronto, 3–6 September 2009.

Noutcheva, G. (2009) 'Fake, partial and imposed compliance: The limits of the EU's normative power in the Western Balkans.' *Journal of European Public Policy* 16(7): 1065–1084.

Olsen, J.P. (1995) *Europeanization and Nation-state Dynamics.* Oslo: ARENA, Vol. Working Paper No. 9.

Olsen, J.P. (2002) 'The many faces of Europeanization.' *Journal of Common Market Studies* 40(5): 921–952.

Pampel, F. (2000) *Logistic Regression: A Primer* (London: Sage).

Parau, C.E. (2009) 'Impaling Dracula: How EU Accession empowered civil society in Romania.' *West European Politics* 32(1): 119–141.

Piana, D. (2009) 'The power knocks at the courts' back door two waves of postcommunist judicial reforms.' *Comparative Political Studies* 42(6): 816–840.

Poguntke, T., N. Aylott, R. Ladrech and K.R. Luther (2007) 'The Europeanization of national party organisations: A conceptual analysis.' *European Journal of Political Research* 46(6): 747–771.

Quaglia, L. (2009) 'The "British Plan" as a pace-setter: The Europeanization of banking rescue plans in the EU?' *Journal of Common Market Studies* 47(5): 1063–1083.

Radaelli, C.M. (1997) 'How does Europeanization produce domestic policy change? Corporate tax policy in Italy and the United Kingdom.' *Comparative Political Studies* 30(5): 553–575.

Radaelli, C.M. and T. Exadaktylos (2009) 'New directions in Europeanization research.' In Egan, M., Nugent, N. and Paterson, W.E. (Eds.) *Research Agendas in EU Studies: Stalking the Elephant* (Basingstoke: Palgrave Macmillan).

Radaelli, C. and R. Pasquier (2007) 'Conceptual issues.' In Vink, M.P. and Graziano, P. (Eds.) *Europeanization: New Research Agendas* (Basingstoke: Palgrave Macmillan).

Raunio, T. and M. Wiberg (2010) 'How to measure the Europeanization of a national legislature?' *Scandinavian Political Studies* 33(1): 74–92.

Saurugger, S. (2009) *Théories et concepts de l'intégration européenne* (Paris: Presses de Sciences Po).

Scharpf, F.W. (1997) 'Economic integration democracy and the welfare state.' *Journal of European Public Policy* 4(1): 18–36.

Schimmelfennig, F. and U. Sedelmeier (2004) 'Governance by conditionality: EU rule transfer to the candidate countries of Central and Eastern Europe.' *Journal of European Public Policy* 11(4): 661–679.

Schmidt, V.A. (2002) 'Europeanization and the mechanics of economic policy adjustment.' *Journal of European Public Policy* 9(6), 894–912.

Schneider, V. and F.M. Hage (2008) 'Europeanization and the retreat of the state.' *Journal of European Public Policy* 15(1): 1–19.

Semetko, H.A., C.H. de Vreese et al. (2000) 'Europeanised politics – Europeanised media? European integration and political communication.' *West European Politics* 23(4): 121–141.

Sitter, N. (2001) 'The politics of opposition and European integration in Scandinavia: Is Euro-scepticism a government-opposition dynamic?' *West European Politics* 24(4): 22–39.

Stolfi, F. (2008) 'The Europeanization of Italy's budget institutions in the 1990s.' *Journal of European Public Policy* 15(4): 550–566.

Tocci, N. (2008) 'The EU and conflict resolution in Turkey and Georgia: Hindering EU potential through the political management of contractual relations.' *Journal of Common Market Studies* 46(4): 875–897.

Töller, A.E. (2010) 'Measuring and comparing the Europeanization of national legislation: A research note.' *Journal of Common Market Studies* 48(2): 417–444.

Trampusch, C. (2009) 'Europeanization and institutional change in vocational education and training in Austria and Germany.' *Governance* 22(3): 369–395.

Warleigh, A. (2001) '"Europeanizing" civil society: NGOs as agents of political socialization.' *Journal of Common Market Studies* 39(4): 619–639.

Wessels, W. (1998) 'Comitology: Fusion in action. Politico-administrative trends in the EU system.' *Journal of European Public Policy* 5(2): 209–234.

# 3
# Causality in Quantitative Approaches

*Annette Elisabeth Töller*

## Introduction

If Europeanization is about the 'domestic consequences of the process of European integration' (Radaelli, 2004: 2), then what are the 'quantitative approaches to Europeanization'? The term can refer to two kinds of research: studies that use quantitative methods to establish causal links in the field of Europeanization, and studies that try to quantify Europeanization.[1] This chapter deals with the second kind of studies, in particular those studies that aim at quantitatively measuring the scope and the extent of the Europeanization of national legislation.[2]

These approaches have been developed somewhat independently from each other in several EU member states. They started as rather technical exercises in the 1990s (see Page, 1998; Töller, 1995) and over the following decade acquired methodological sophistication, variation and political awareness (Asser Institute, 2007; Bovens and Yesilkagit, 2010; Brouard et al., 2007; Christensen, 2010a; Jenny and Müller, 2010; König and Mäder, 2008; Raunio and Wiberg, 2010; Töller, 2008, 2010).

These studies have been motivated by both political and scholarly considerations. Stemming from the 80 per cent prophecy made by Jacques Delors in 1988,[3] political discussions in member states on the overall impact of European integration on national policymaking have increasingly focused on the extent and the areas in which national legislators have lost their policymaking autonomy. While in some countries the debate has focused on European integration as such (e.g., in Denmark, see Christensen, 2010a; in Austria, see Jenny and Müller, 2010), in others it concerns rather the limits of ongoing political and legal integration (e.g., BVErfGE 89, 155; Conseil d'État, 1993; Douma,

2009). In most debates the 80 per cent myth has been the starting point for both serious attempts to illuminate the issue and attempts to demonize the European Union (e.g., Herzog et al., 2010), turning a prophecy into a rather dubious diagnosis. Some researchers believe they should be able to put the whole debate on a more rational footing (Christensen, 2010b; Jenny and Müller, 2010; Müller et al., 2010; Plehwe, 2008; Töller, 2008, 2010).

As for the scholarly debate, the first generation of Europeanization studies mostly dealt with the mechanisms and effects of Europeanization. Yet the highly specific contexts for which these studies could provide results eventually prompted certain scholars to analyse Europeanization from a broader perspective (Christensen, 2010b; Franchino, 2005: 251; Vink and Graziano, 2007: 176), allowing for more general insights. Moreover, the *institutional dimension* of Europeanization, particularly the role of national parliaments, can be approached adequately only if we establish the sphere of autonomous decision-making that such institutions enjoy (O'Brennan and Raunio, 2007). In this context we need to know 'what is left for national policy' (Bulmer and Radaelli, 2005) and what is left for national legislators in particular (Müller et al., 2010). Finally, since qualitative Europeanization studies have demonstrated how greatly the effects of Europeanization can *differ* across policy sectors and across countries, comparative and comparable findings on the (different) degrees of Europeanization could be a starting point for systematic comparative analysis, explaining variations by reference to, for example, institutional or agency factors.

The core objective of all these studies is to quantify *how much national legislation is influenced by European policies* in a broader sense. As will be demonstrated in the following section, although these studies approach quantification in different ways, they all seek to identify and quantify the European impact on national legislation as a *relative* parameter *compared* with other factors (mostly national, sometimes international)[4] that also affect this legislation.

The chapter proceeds as follows. The first section provides a brief overview of the most important studies measuring the Europeanization of national legislation in quantitative terms. The second section analyses how these different studies address causality and what must be considered adequate and problematic ways of doing so. It deals first with national legislation as the dependent variable and then with Europe as the independent variable. The third section discusses the problems that arise from organizing these complex interrelations in terms of dependent and independent variables. It attempts to demonstrate the limits of such an approach and discusses some conceptual and methodological measures to improve our notion of causality, and lead to conclusions.

## Overview: Measuring Europeanization

This section discusses causality in quantitative studies of Europeanization basically by reference to eight studies that seek to quantify the European impact on national legislation: the study by Page (1998) of the UK; two studies with a similar research design – one that Bovens and Yesilkagit (2010) presented (first in 2004) for the Netherlands and another that Blom-Hansen and Christensen presented for Denmark (Christensen, 2010a); a pilot monitor by the Asser Institute (2007) on the Netherlands; a slightly different study of Austria by Jenny and Müller (2010); a study of France by Brouard, Costa and Kerrouche (2007); a study of Germany by Töller (2008) and, most recently, a study of Finland by Raunio and Wiberg (2010). Most of these studies have already been discussed elsewhere in more detail (Töller, 2010: 412–425). For the purpose of this section it is sufficient to present an overview that focuses on the points that will be discussed below and a comparison based on this overview (see Table 3.1).

In summary, the various studies that have been presented so far approach the measurement task in quite different ways and consequently come up with rather different overall national shares of Europeanized laws, which range from 6 to 81 per cent of national totals. Based on this finding two points need to be made. First, the data cited are obviously by no means *comparable*, because each study measures different things (see Töller, 2010). Second, the data are highly *contextual*, as researchers in this field are well aware. The data that they produce reflect two kinds of factors. One category of factors is 'real': legal traditions and routines in the broadest sense that have an impact on the data – for example, whether laws tend to be many and short or few and long; whether directives tend to be implemented mainly by secondary legislation or in the first instance by parliamentary legislation; and whether this is affected by legislative acts dedicated solely to the task or is integrated into routine legislation. The other category of factors is of a methodological nature; as demonstrated in Table 3.1, the data are highly dependent on how the dependent and independent variables are operationalized and what we think connects them. This is what I discuss in the subsequent sections.

*Table 3.1* Studies measuring the Europeanization of national legislation

| Study/ Author | Country | Operationalized dependent variable | Operationalized independent variable | Values (all policy fields) | Highest Europeanization values | Time frame |
|---|---|---|---|---|---|---|
| Page (1998) | UK | Statutory instruments (secondary legislation only) | Directives | 15.5% average all years | Agriculture: 51.1%; trade and industry: 28.6% | Annual values (1987–1997) |
| Christensen (2010a) | Denmark | Primary and secondary legislation | Directives | 14% | Agriculture: 27.3%; labour: 22.4%; economy: 21.8% | Accumulated legislation to 2003 |
| Bovens and Yesilkagit (2010) | Netherlands | Primary and secondary legislation | Directives | 12.6% | Agriculture: 21.9%; health: 20.6%; economy: 19.8% | Accumulated legislation to 2003 |
| Asser Institute (2007) | Netherlands | Primary and secondary legislation and European regulations | Directives, regulations, Court decisions | Environment: 66.6% Education: 6% | Environment: 66.6%. | Accumulated legislation to 2005 |
| Jenny and Müller (2010) | Austria | Primary and secondary legislation | Directives, European regulations, decisions, treaties, etc. | Laws: 10.6% Decrees: 14.1% | Agriculture/health/ environment: 36.9%; transport/technology: 27.4% | All legal acts to 2001 |

*Table 3.1* (Continued)

| Study/ Author | Country | Operationalized dependent variable | Operationalized independent variable | Values (all policy fields) | Highest Europeanization values | Time frame |
|---|---|---|---|---|---|---|
| Brouard et al. (2007) | France | Primary legislation only | International treaties, directives, regulations, Court decisions | Between 3 and 27%. | Science/technology: 39%; banking/finance/ trade: 28%; family/ health: 42.3% | Annual values (1986–2006) |
| Töller (1995, 2008) | Germany | Primary legislation only | *European Impulses*: directives, Council decisions, Court decisions, partly on regulations | 15th election period (2002–2005): 39.1% | Environment: 81.3%; agriculture 75% | Values acc. to election periods (1983–2005) |
| Raunio and Wiberg (2010) | Finland | Primary legislation only | Finlex reference to EC, EEC, O.J., etc. | Between 1 and 24% | No data | Annual values (1992–2007) |

## Concepts of causality

Following the summary of the most important studies entailing different approaches to measuring the Europeanization of national legislation, we now turn to the concepts of causality and related problems that underlie them.

To be clear, in this context Europeanization is neither the dependent nor the independent variable, neither explanandum nor explanans (see Radaelli, 2004: 5). Rather, it describes the (possible) causal connection between a European measure and a national measure.

There has been some debate in the Europeanization literature on what the *dependent variable* of Europeanization studies actually is. A dominant group equates Europeanization with *changes* in national policies or laws resulting from European policies (Radaelli, 2004: 4; Vink and Graziano, 2007: 9; Saurugger, Chapter 6 in this volume). Other authors argue that Europeanization can also result in the continuation of policies that would, most probably, have changed without the 'European factor' (Roederer-Rynning, 2007: 23). The dependent variable in the quantitative Europeanization studies is the European *impact* either on a particular piece of legislation or on a group of legal acts (e.g., Christensen, 2010b; Jenny and Müller, 2010; Page, 1998). This impact can bring about a *change* in a former policy, the *continuation* of an existing policy or the *introduction* of a new policy.

To use a rather simple concept of causality,[5] there is variable $y$ that is in a certain condition caused by variable $x_1$, $x_2$ or $x_3$. The $y$ of all the studies mentioned above is a group of legal acts (e.g., in a specific policy sector and over a specific period of time, such as a legislative period). We look for legal acts whose legislative substance has been influenced by a European impulse as distinct from those measures that are the product purely of national factors or international factors. Thus, European policies in a wider sense are $x_1$, namely, one factor that may explain the content of one legal act in particular and a share of all legal acts of a certain group. Let us call $x_2$ national factors and $x_3$ transnational or international factors.

The connection between $y$ and $x$ is constructed via mechanisms of *how x* impacts on $y$ (see below).

This section first deals with the *dependent variable* and how it can be constructed. It then analyses how 'Europe' as the *independent variable* is being operationalized.

## The dependent variable: National legislation

To discuss how the quantitative studies construct the dependent variable, namely, the body of national legislation (divided into policy sectors and/or time units) that European policies are expected to affect, three major issues need to be addressed. First, how true is it that legislation is the backbone of a policy (so that the analysis makes any sense at all) and that within such legislation European influence can be traced? Second, does our dependent variable, 'national legislation', have to contain only parliamentary legislation, or only secondary legislation, or both? Third, over what time period do we need to bundle our legislation?

On the first issue, all the attempts to measure the European impact on national legislation are based on two assumptions that unfortunately do not apply under all circumstances. In fact, we are primarily interested in *policies*, and we treat legislation as a proxy for policies. This is adequate for those policy sectors in which most policy is shaped by legislation, such as regulatory policies governing the environment and finance and also areas such as justice and agriculture. In contrast, policy in foreign affairs, defence and foreign aid is not shaped by legislation. Moreover, if our analysis is to make sense, European *effects* must be traceable to the laws enacted in a particular sector.

Further details on possible sources of Europeanization are presented below. But it should be noted here that there are *policy sectors* in which Europeanization does occur but cannot be identified in laws. One of the most important areas in focus is *budgetary policy*. Clearly, the EU's Stability and Growth Pact (SGP) has a major impact on national budgetary policies, but this impact cannot be traced in national budget acts. Yet it would be misleading to argue that the fact that German budget acts, for example, do not display any overt 'European' influence is evidence that such influence is absent. Again, but in a different vein, *competition policy* is not a suitable area in which to measure Europeanization in national legislation. This is basically because the Community does not need to legislate in this area, but the European Commission, based directly on its powers derived from the Treaty, takes decisions that do not usually find their way into national legislation (with the possible exception of state aid policy). Similarly, it is doubtful whether in the area of tax policy the European impact could be measured adequately in national legislation. In this area we might end up trying to calculate the share of tax revenue that is raised in compliance with European rules[6] in order to measure the European impact.

The analysis here is therefore restricted to those policy sectors that are *shaped* to a relevant degree by law and where a European impact would be *identifiable* in law. Second, we need to discuss whether 'national legislation' is adequately encompassed by parliamentary legislation alone (as it is in the approach of this author and that of Brouard et al.) or by secondary legislation alone (as in Page's study) or whether both need to be included (as in the studies by Bovens and Yesilkagit, Christensen, and Jenny and Müller). A point in favour of the approach of this last group of authors is that in many countries a large share of transposing directives is enacted by secondary legislation while the balance between primary and secondary legislation in transposing directives not only differs between countries but may even vary between portfolios within a given country (Bovens and Yesilkagit, 2004; Müller et al., 2010). Thus, Page's focus on secondary legislation makes sense in an analysis of the UK, but from a comparative perspective we might need to see data for primary legislation, too. The author's approach (Töller, 2008) is problematic, therefore, since *Rechtsverordnungen* (pieces of secondary legislation) are not included in the GESTA database and are thus excluded from the analysis. The same criticism applies to the French study, while the problem here is more acute since much more transposition is done by executive law-making as a consequence of constitutional requirements.

The third issue is the unit of analysis in terms of time with which the studies work. Some studies analyse the share of Europeanized acts in a cumulative way, that is, the total number of laws that have been adopted over the years up to a certain point in time. This is the case in the studies by Bovens and Yesilkagit and by Blom-Hansen and Christensen. Others, such as Page and Töller, choose as the unit of analysis the legal acts adopted in a certain period of time, a year in Page's study, a legislative period in Töller's study. The studies of Brouard et al. and König and Mäder include both. It is a clear advantage to work with a defined time series because this allows for the identification of developments over time that are not evident from cumulative numbers. This is especially important since the legislative output of the Community displays clear variation: an increase since the 1960s and in particular since the mid-1980s, and a decrease since the mid-1990s (Christensen, 2010b: 23). It is all but trivial to find out whether this variation is reflected in changing shares of Europeanized legislation.

Thus, ideally our dependent variable $y$ consists of groups of (primary and secondary) legal acts for particular policy sectors for specific periods of time.[7] What we want to find out is *whether* and *how much* their substance has been influenced by European policies ($x_1$) as distinct from by purely national factors ($x_2$) or international factors ($x_3$).

## The independent variable: The European impact

How do the aforementioned studies operationalize the European impact ($x_1$)? We noted above that it is actually European policies in a broader sense that affect national legislation. Nevertheless, as with many qualitative studies, most quantifying studies equate Europeanization with the transposition of directives into national law. They tend to combine at least two ways of identifying whether a law transposes a European directive. First, they look for such a reference in national legislation, either in databases or in the text of the legal act itself. Second, they look at lists of legislative acts that national governments communicate to the European Commission as evidence that European directives have been transposed into national laws (e.g., Christensen, 2010a). Most studies also cite as a third source the references in CELEX/EurLex, which indicates the national legislation in which directives are implemented (e.g., Jenny and Müller, 2010: 11). All studies that combine two or three methods conclude that these lists are far from congruent: some laws which refer to European directives are not listed in communications to the Commission, while some such lists contain legal acts whose texts make no reference to any European directive (e.g., Jenny and Müller, 2010; König and Mäder, 2008). Yet, even though these data are far from perfect, they provide the basis on which most of the studies operationalize the European impact, and there are good reasons for this: they are somehow manageable.

However, it is all too obvious that this is far *too narrow* a way to operationalize the European impact. If we restrict Europeanization to the transposition of directives it does not come as a surprise to learn that the national shares of Europeanized legislation turn out to be rather low, as we can see from the two studies on Denmark and the Netherlands. One major way in which European policies are injected into national legal systems is through *regulations*. The methodological problem lies in the well-known fact that regulations are directly applicable and thus, unlike directives, do not need to be transposed into national legislation. Sometimes national legislation needs to be adapted to the context of European regulations, but usually the potential influence of regulations on the national legal order is not traceable in national law because they bypass existing national legislation and possibly prevent the adoption of new national legislation. Thus, measuring Europeanization without accommodating the role of regulations appears highly problematic. This is the case because, as European regulations form a major (though varying and, overall, declining) component of policy-shaping rules (Christensen, 2010b), the exclusion of regulations produces misleadingly low values of Europeanization. In addition, including directives and excluding regulations distorts comparative results between policy fields because directives and regulations are applied differently in different policy fields (e.g., agriculture is dominated by regulations whereas environmental policy is dominated by directives). Yet, if we want to include regulations in our calculations, we have to redefine our dependent variable: we cannot restrict the dependent variable to *national legislation* in the sense of legislation that has been adopted in the national institutional system, but have to extend it to *legislation that is applicable in the national context*. This will have to include European regulations, a step which has so far been taken only by the Asser Institute (2007).[8]

Of course, there is much more under the European sun than directives and regulations that has the potential to affect national legislation, such as decisions of the Council, the European Court of Justice (ECJ), the Court of First Instance and even the Treaty itself. Certainly, scholars engaged in quantifying work are aware of the entire field of soft law (Christensen, 2010b; see Saurugger, Chapter 6 in this volume). Yet, when dealing with the quantification of the European impact on national legislation, there is broad agreement that we can deal only with *law* as the source of Europeanization (cf. Müller et al., 2010). Yet even this is less straightforward than one might think. Being inspired by qualitative work on Europeanization, one has to realize in particular how important the Single Market rules are for national legislation (see Schmidt, 2008; Töller, 2011).

One way to operationalize our dependent variable in a more comprehensive way is to work with the concept of the 'European impulse' as defined in the German DIP Database[9] including, as mentioned above, not only directives (roughly about 50 per cent of the impulses) but also regulations if they require adaptation of national legislation, Council decisions, decisions of the Courts and so on. It does not come as a surprise to learn that such a broad way of operationalizing European influence produces higher national shares of Europeanized legislation. The major problem is that these data are available only for Germany and thus cannot be analysed on a comparative basis.

## Problems with causality

While organizing complex relations by means of dependent and independent variables is always a convenient way to make life seem easy, the reality behind these variables is much more complicated. This means that the construction of causality (the value of the dependent variable is determined by variable $x_1 =$ European policy), as undertaken here, is problematic for a number of reasons.

### Problems with the construction of variables

The core problem is that, no matter how narrowly or broadly we operationalize our $x_1$, our construction of a causal link follows a purely formal argument: If we establish that a national legal act (and a certain share of all legal acts in a certain unit) serves to transpose a directive or to adapt a national law to a European regulation or a decision by the ECJ, it is *probable* that these European measures will have an *impact* on the content of the national measure, but such an impact is in no way a proven fact and remains nothing more than a *plausible assumption*.

Moreover, this plausible assumption only allows for the claim that the national measure is *somehow related* to a European measure. We can make no claims regarding the *relevance* or *intensity* of this relation – for example, whether with this legal act a fully new policy has been introduced or whether the European influence on this act has been at best marginal,[10] perhaps because the law already contained what was proposed by the directive (Douma, 2009: 3; Jenny and Müller, 2010: 9). Facing exactly this problem, Jenny and Müller (2010) introduce the three categories of 'impact' mentioned above. The argument that we have made no valid claims regarding the *relevance* or *intensity* of the relation between a European measure and national legislation applies to both individual legal acts and entire policy sectors: a national policy sector can be fundamentally transformed by one European directive, while five other directives yield only minor changes (as demonstrated by Plehwe for the Europeanization of German transport policy; see Plehwe, 2008).

Finally, this way of constructing a European legal act as an independent variable (and thus as something that comes from a different planet) ignores the fact that, within a multi-level system, this European measure itself can be seen as a dependent variable that has been influenced by the very member state whose national legislation it affects (cf. Saurugger and Radaelli, 2008: 213). Now, if a directive has been strongly influenced by the British government, for example, is the impact on the national legislation to be measured differently than if this was not the case? I am afraid that in terms of numbers we cannot tell.

Another problem is that we somehow neglect other independent variables ($x_2$, $x_3$) by not systematically identifying and testing them. Rather, we define and test them *ex negativo*: if there is no European measure affecting a piece of national legislation, we suppose that the national legislation is shaped purely by national or international factors.

## Causal mechanisms connecting our variables

In view of the criticism made above that an impact of a European measure is a plausible assumption but not a proven fact, it is helpful to elaborate on the *causal mechanisms*[11] that connect dependent and independent variables.

To draw on institutionalist arguments, the mechanism that is usually seen at work in Europeanization is *adaptation to coercive pressure* (see di Maggio and Powell, 1983: 150): European law enjoys legal primacy and requires member states to adapt their laws to it and individuals to comply with it. Yet, even here patterns of adaptation are more complex than simple reactions (Radaelli, 2004: 4). Coercion tends to be strongest with regulations because they leave little room for national choice, but, as mentioned, they are not usually embodied in national legislation. In the case of directives, it is well known that pressure to adapt does not result only from the degree of 'fit' or 'non-fit' – conceptually and empirically there is much room for both under-compliance and over-compliance, which can be determined by national institutions, party politics and other factors (Falkner et al., 2002; Radaelli, 2004: 7; but see Thomson, 2009). Notwithstanding these qualifications, *adaptation to legal coercion* is the core mechanism on which the entire idea of measuring Europeanization is based: European law puts member states under pressure to formulate their policies in accordance with European stipulations while leaving them more room for manoeuvre in some cases than others. At the other extreme, possible mechanisms include *shaping of discourses, learning* and *socialization* (see Radaelli, 2004: 4, 8; Töller, 2004); types of normative pressures (di Maggio and Powell, 1983: 152) are so soft that it is difficult to detect their hard effect on national legislation.

Yet there are other possible mechanisms, one of which is *prevention*. Faced with the requirement of the free movement of goods in particular, it is rather the rule than the exception that member states refrain from a planned trade measure because – rightly or wrongly – they fear this could be attacked by the Commission as a barrier to trade (Schmidt, 2008). Similar patterns can be observed in the field of state aid, where measures might be changed or elements omitted because they could be considered as amounting to direct or indirect state aid (Cini and McGowan, 2009). Thus, when constructing the dependent variable of national legislation one would also have to look for measures *not* adopted as a result of European stipulations, particularly the Treaty – a variety of non-decisions, as it were – or for *elements* of a measure that are not adopted. In some cases member states adopt strategies to *evade* these restrictions; for example, in the 1980s and 1990s the German government resorted to voluntary agreements when an outright national ban on hazardous substances seemed impossible (Töller, 2011).

Another mechanism is *instrumentalization*. This mechanism has been emphasized particularly in the field of liberalization policies. Some policies emanating from Brussels change national opportunity structures and help some national actors strengthen their position vis-à-vis other actors (e.g., Knill and Lehmkuhl, 2002; Thatcher, 2004). Sometimes governments use European policies to justify decisions already taken at the national level (Saurugger and Radaelli, 2008: 213).

While the mechanism of prevention only reminds us that we could miss relevant aspects if we have only adaptation to coercion in mind, the mechanism of instrumentalization is a more fundamental challenge to our enterprise. As long as we work with data that are produced by national governments we always run the risk that such data are biased by strategic instrumentalization. For instance, if we look at the rather high shares of Europeanized legislation in German environmental policy, we might conclude that environmental legislation betrays strong European influence – only 20 per cent of it can be defined without European stipulations. Yet we could also question this finding by suggesting that the rather weak Federal Ministry for the Environment instrumentalizes European stipulations in order to pursue projects that it would not have been able to in the purely national context.

### Solutions

Even if we take all these considerations seriously and design our dependent and independent variables with great care, the construction of causality is faced with serious challenges. Two modifications in research design and methods can help to deal with these challenges.

In dealing first with the problem of how to identify the 'if' of European impacts on legal acts in a reliable way, we should rely neither on European lists nor on nationally defined 'European impulses'. Rather, we should (and will) apply computerized methods of content analysis that have so far been applied in, for example, the field of manifesto research (see Laver and Benoit, 2003) in order to scan complete legislative texts for references to European legislation or other measures such as Court decisions. This will make us more independent of any strategic use of European measures by national ministries.

This will, however, only improve our ability accurately to measure the *scope* of Europeanization – which is a necessary if a relatively superficial exercise. If we want to learn something about *how much* the single piece of legislation and the sum of legislation in a given policy sector or portfolio (our $y$) has been influenced by the European factor ($x_1$), we have to analyse the *extent* of Europeanization. To do so we have to complement quantitative analysis with qualitative analysis, as Jenny and Müller (2010) do. I suggest applying a two-dimensional matrix that for each Europeanized law displays:

- the *breadth of a regulation*, by allowing, for example, for the claim that of the five regulatory aspects that a piece of legislation includes, three have been Europeanized whereas two have not;
- the *depth of a regulation*, by applying a modified version of the categories developed by Peter Hall (1993).[12] With this tool we could analyse what part of the national legislation has been subject to (how much) Europeanization:

  - the regulatory *level* (e.g., whether the emission limit for cars is 130 or 110 mg/km);
  - the *instruments* of regulation (whether bans, licence systems or quota certificate systems are required);
  - overall *objectives* (without necessarily touching upon instruments);
  - all three elements: level, instruments and objectives.

This matrix could be applied to each single law in a policy sector, and data could be aggregated for the sum of legislation in a sector over a period of time, for example stating that in the sector *a* over a specific period of time almost all aspects of legislation have been influenced by European policy, yet that this influence has touched questions of instruments but not of overall objectives; while in policy sector *b* only two very specific aspects have come under European influence but that here the entire policy (level, instruments and objectives) has been shaped according to European stipulations. How exactly this can be translated into numbers remains a major challenge.

With this approach we could also try to compensate for the neglect of rival independent variables by testing in a more systematic way whether particular elements were introduced because of European ($x_1$) national ($x_2$) or international ($x_3$) forces (Haverland, 2005; Saurugger and Radaelli, 2008: 214; Vink and Graziano, 2007: 116). Yet this approach, even if we use it to go beyond a purely formal (and thus superficial) identification of a European impact, also runs the risk of finding Europeanization as a result of case selection bias (Haverland, 2005: 2; Levi-Faur, 2004). Thus, working with a 'counterfactual scenario' (Haverland, 2005: 3–6) should be part of the exercise just mentioned: What would have happened *without* the European directive that is said to be the cause of 80 per cent of the legislative substance of a national law?

We are also considering whether the computerized programs of text analysis that we apply for identifying *if* there is a European impact or not (see above) are also able to measure *the degree of substantial overlap* between a national legal act and a European directive.

## Conclusion

The purpose of this chapter has been to analyse the concepts of causality adopted in studies that quantitatively measure the Europeanization of national legislation. Proceeding from a short explanation of why these studies were developed at all, the chapter first presented a brief overview on the most relevant studies and how, and with what results, they measure the Europeanization of national legislation. These studies share a common concept of causality in that they all seek to identify the *scope* of the European impact on national legislation in quantitative terms as a relative parameter and as compared with other (mostly national, sometimes international) factors that also affect this legislation. In addition, the chapter analysed how these studies (differently) construct their dependent variables and their independent variables and what needs to be considered in doing so. Finally, the last section addressed the problems that arise from attempts to organize complex realities with the help of simple categories, with regard to both the construction of the variables and the causal mechanisms that we imagine connect dependent and independent variables. A number of measures were proposed on which to base future attempts to construct a more elaborate concept of causality.

Most of the studies analysed here fail to provide a complete account of the *scope* and do not even try to measure the *extent* of the Europeanization of national legislation. This is because they display major shortcomings, both in the way they operationalize the dependent variable or the independent variables and (in part) with regard to the causal mechanisms that they assume to operate between the variables.

Thus, improvement is needed, both with regard to reliably identifying *whether* there has been a European impact on a national legal act (scope) and *how much* European policy has influenced national legislation (extent). Including European regulations and applying computerized programs of content analysis to analyse the texts of the legal acts could help researchers to construct a sound database on the *scope* of Europeanization. Complementing quantitative analysis with structured qualitative analysis could help also to determine the *extent* of Europeanization.

No matter how aware scholars may be that many more things emanate from Brussels than directives, regulations and Court decisions alone, their approaches to quantifying Europeanization are basically restricted to legally binding measures. To do this in a reliable way is hard enough; we should not try to accommodate all sorts of 'soft' measures which undeniably also Europeanize national legislation but which cannot be captured for quantitative purposes – this would overstretch our method. By focusing on the Europeanizing effects of legally bringing measures, we can identify a 'hard core' of Europeanized legislation that will be particularly useful if we manage to do so over time and across member states.

## Notes

1. I would like to thank Renate Reiter, the editors and the co-authors of this volume for very helpful comments on a previous draft of this chapter.
2. Contributions that do not seek to analyse Europeanization in quantitative terms use the term 'measuring Europeanization' in the context of the methodological challenge to establish the causal link between a domestic change and 'the European factor' (e.g., Vink and Graziano, 2007: 15–17; see also Exadaktylos and Radaelli, 2009). This is not the approach adopted in this chapter.
3. Jacques Delors, the former President of the European Commission, speaking before the European Parliament, said: 'In ten years 80 per cent of the legislation related to economics, maybe also to taxes and social affairs, will be of Community origin' (Bulletin No- 2-367/157, 6 July 1988).
4. Even though much of the debate that tries to relativize Europeanization vis-à-vis other factors cites 'globalization' as a second major driving force

(e.g., Haverland, 2005: 2; Radaelli, 2004: 9; Saurugger and Radaelli, 2008: 215), I prefer to speak of 'internationalization'. This is because European and international factors are mutually exclusive, whereas with 'globalization' there is much dispute over whether it is exemplified by 'Europeanization' or whether Europeanization is rather a counter movement to globalization (see, for example, Anderson, 2003; Ladi, Chapter 12 in this volume).

5. We are already getting into difficulties here with rather simple ideas of causality, and hence it would serve no purpose to go into the details of complex notions of causality such as, for example, multiple causation, critical junctures, mutual interference and reciprocal causation (see Hall, 2003: 383–387).

6. As suggested by Susanne Uhl at our Berlin Workshop in 2009, see http://www.aei-ecsa.de/tagung_measuring-europeanization.html#download

7. I do not want to discuss here the fairly problematic assumption on which, to date, all studies are based: that portfolios are adequate proxies for policy sectors (see Töller, 2010). Yet this is not of relevance with regard to the concept of causality.

8. Since the Asser Institute proceeded with this quite successfully it is disputable whether it is 'impossible to just add them to either the directives or the national rules transposing the directives' (Christensen, 2010b).

9. For more information: http://dip.bundestag.de/

10. The analysis of such difference would have to reflect the fact that cultures and traditions of legislation differ a great deal between member states, as do the ways of transposing European law into national law: Whereas some member states tend to integrate the requirements of European law into regular legislation, others pass separate laws for the purpose (e.g., Sweden) or, like Italy, adopt one legal act to transpose all European Directives in one move.

11. A causal mechanism is 'a causal process connection between an *explanans* and an *explanandum*' (Kittel, 2006: 655), a 'processes whereby those variables are thought to secure such an impact' (Hall, 2008: 309, 312).

12. It is a *modified* version of Hall's categories because Hall (and policy analysis following Hall) uses these categories in order to analyse policy change, whereas what we want to analyse here is not policy *change* but *impact* on policy substance. Moreover, we need one more category. Hall (1993: 278) presents three kinds of policy change (first-order change with regard to levels of regulation, second-order change with regard to instruments and third-order change, which covers overall political objectives but at the same time instruments and levels of regulation). For the specific context of analysing the influence that European law and policies exert on national policies, we need a fourth category in which policy objectives are influenced but regulatory levels or instruments are not.

## References

Anderson, J.J. (2003) 'Europeanization in Context: Concept and Theory' in K. Dyson and K. Goetz (eds) *Germany, Europe and the Politics of Constraint* (Oxford: Oxford University Press), pp. 3–35.

Asser Institute (2007) *Pilot-Monitor EU Involved* (Den Haag: Asser Institute).

Bovens, M. and Yesilkagit, K. (2010) 'The EU as Lawmaker: The Impact of EC-directives on National Regulation in the Netherlands', *Public Administration*, 88(1), pp. 57–74.

Brouard, S., Costa, O. and Kerrouche, E. (2007) 'The Europeanization of French Lawmaking: Levels, Modes and Institutional Impact'. Paper presented at APSA Conference, Chicago.

Bulmer, S.J. and Radaelli, C.M. (2005) 'The Europeanization of Public Policy' in S. Bulmer and C. Lequesne (Eds.) *The Member States of the European Union* (Oxford: Oxford University Press), pp. 338–359.

Christensen, J.G. (2010a) 'Keeping in Control: The Modest Impact of EU on Danish Legislation', *Public Administration*, 88(1), pp. 18–35.

Christensen, J.G. (2010b) 'Uncertain Steps towards a European Public Policy', *Public Administration*, 88(1), pp. 3–17.

Cini, M. and McGowan, L. (2009) *Competition Policy in the European Union* (Houndmills/New York: Palgrave Macmillan).

Conseil d'État (1993) *Rapport publique 1992*. Etudes & Documents No. 44 (Paris: La Documentation Française).

Di Maggio, P.J. and Powell, W.W. (1983) 'The Iron Cage Revisited: Institutional Isomorphism and Collective Rationality in Organizational Fields', *American Sociological Review*, 48(2), pp. 147–160.

Douma, W. (2009) 'Measuring the Influence of Europe on Legislation in the Netherlands'. Paper for the WZB-Workshop 'Measuring the Europeanization of Public Policies Beyond the 80% Myth', Berlin, 27–28 February.

Exadaktylos, T. and Radaelli, C. (2009) 'Research Design in European Studies: The Case of Europeanization', *Journal of Common Market Studies*, 47(5), pp. 507–530.

Falkner, G., Hartlapp, M., Leiber, S. and Treib, O. (2002) 'Transforming Social Policy in Europe? The AEC's Parental Leave Directive and Misfit in 15 Member States'. MPIfG Working Paper 02/11, October. Available online at: «http://www.mpi-fg-koeln.mpg.de/pu/workpap/wp02-11/wp02-11.html».

Franchino, F. (2005) 'The Study of EU Public Policy: Results of a Survey', *European Union Politics*, 6(2), 243–252.

Hall, P.A. (1993) 'Policy Paradigms, Social Learning, and the State: The Case of Economic Policymaking in Britain', *Comparative Politics*, 25(3), pp. 275–296.

Hall, P.A. (2003) 'Aligning Ontology and Methodology in Comparative Research' in J. Mahoney und D. Rueschenmeyer (Eds.) *Comparative Historical Analysis in The Social Sciences* (Cambridge: Cambridge University Press), pp. 373–404.

Hall, P.A. (2008) 'Systematic Process Analysis: When and How to Use It', *European Political Science*, 7(3), pp. 304–317.

Haverland, M. (2005) 'Does the EU Cause Domestic Developments? The Problem of Case Selection in Europeanization Research.' *EIoP* 9(2). Available online at: «http://www.eiop.or.at/eiop/pdf/2005-002.pdf».

Herzog, R., Gerken, L. and Boltkestein, F. (2010) 'Die EU schadet der Europa-Idee.' FAZ, 15 January. Available online at: «http://www.faz.net/s/RubDDBDABB9457A437BAA85A49C26FB23A0/Doc~EC34E29B107D74E889C DBF2E9E184CED0~ATpl~Ecommon~Scontent.html».

Jenny, M. and Müller, W. (2010) 'From the Europeanization of Law-Making to the Europeanization of National Legal Orders: The Case of Austria', *Public Administration*, 88(1), pp. 36–56.

Kittel, B. (2006) 'A Crazy Methodology? On the Limits of Macro-Quantitative Social Science Research', *International Sociology*, 21, pp. 647–677.

Knill, C. and Lehmkuhl, D. (2002) 'The National Impact of European Union Regulatory Policy: Three Europeanization Mechanisms', *European Journal of Political Research*, 41, pp. 255–280.

König, T. and Mäder, L. (2008) 'Das Regieren jenseits des Nationalstaates und der Mythos einer 80-Prozent-Europäisierung in Deutschland', *Politische Vierteljahresschrift*, 49, pp. 438–463.

Laver, M. and Benoit, K. (2003) 'Extracting Policy Positions from Political Texts Using Words as Data', *American Political Science Review*, 97, pp. 311–331.

Levi-Faur, D. (2004) 'On the "Net Impact" of Europeanization: The EU's Telecoms and Electricity Regimes between the Global and the National', *Comparative Political Studies*, 37(1), pp. 3–29.

Müller, W., Bovens, M., Christensen, J.G., Jenny, M. and Yesilkagit, K. (2010) 'Legal Europeanization: Comparative Perspectives', *Public Administration*, 88(1): 75-87.

O'Brennan, J. and Raunio, T. (2007) 'Introduction: Deparliamentarization and European Integration' in J. O'Brennan and T. Raunio (Eds.) *National Parliaments within the Enlarged European Union* (Abingdon: Routledge), pp. 1–26.

Page, E. (1998) 'The Impact of European Legislation on British Public Policy Making: A Research Note', *Public Administration*, 76, pp. 803–809.

Plehwe, D. (2008) 'Transformation europäischer Governance im Bereich Verkehrspolitik', *Integration*, 31(3), pp. 290–306.

Radaelli, C. (2004) 'Europeanization: Solution or Problem?' *EIoP* 8(16). Available online at: «http://www.eiop.or.at/eiop/pdf/2004-016.pdf».

Raunio, T. and Wiberg, M. (2010) 'How to Measure the Europeanisation of a National Legislature?', *Scandinavian Political Studies*, 33(1), pp. 74–92.

Roederer-Rynning, C. (2007) 'Agricultural Policy' in P. Graziano and M. Vink (Eds.) *Europeanization: New Research Agendas* (Basingstoke/NewYork: Palgrave Macmillan), pp. 212–225.

Saurugger, S. and Radaelli, C. (2008) 'The Europeanization of Public Policies: Introduction', *Journal of Comparative Policy Analysis*, 10(3), pp. 211–217.

Schmidt, S.K. (2008) 'Beyond Compliance: The Europeanization of Member States through Negative Integration and Legal Uncertainty', *Journal of Comparative Policy Analysis*, 10(3), pp. 297–306.

Thatcher, M. (2004) 'Winners and Losers in Europeanisation: Reforming the National Regulation of Telecommunications', *West European Politics*, 27(2), pp. 284–309.

Thomson, R. (2009) 'Same Effects in Different Worlds: The Transposition of EU Directives', *Journal of European Public Policy*, 16(1), pp. 1–18.

Töller, A.E. (1995) *Europapolitik im Bundestag* (Franfurt a. M: Peter Lang).

Töller, A.E. (2004) 'The Europeanization of Public Policies – Understanding Mechanisms and Contingent Results', *EIoP* 8(9). Available online at: «http:///eiop.or.at/eiop/texte/2004-000.htm».

Töller, A.E. (2008) 'Mythen und Methoden. Zur Messung der Europäisierung der Gesetzgebung des Deutschen Bundestages jenseits des 80%-Mythos', *Zeitschrift für Parlamentsfragen*, 39(1), pp. 3–17.

Töller, A.E. (2010) 'Measuring and Comparing the Europeanization of National Legislation – A Research Note', *Journal of Common Market Studies*, 48, pp. 413–440.

Töller, A.E. (2011) *Warum kooperiert der Staat? Kooperative Umweltpolitik im Schatten der Hierarchie. Schriftenreihe Staatslehre und politische Verwaltung* (Baden-Baden: Nomos).

Vink, M. and Graziano, P. (2007) 'Challenges of a New Research Agenda' in P. Graziano and M. Vink (Eds.) *Europeanization: New Research Agendas* (Basingstoke/New York: Palgrave Macmillan), pp. 3–20.

# 4
# Europeanization: A Critical Realist Perspective

*Ian Bache, Simon Bulmer and Defne Gunay*

## Introduction

Establishing causality in Europeanization research has been at the centre of methodological issues surrounding Europeanization literature (Exadaktylos and Radaelli, Chapter 2 in this volume). However, methodology is organically intertwined with the ontological and epistemological assumptions of the researcher (Hay, 2007: 117–118). Therefore, this chapter takes a deeper approach to the issue of establishing causality by acknowledging the meta-theoretical underpinnings of methodology by outlining a critical realist approach.

In broad terms, reflection on meta-theory involves identifying and foregrounding the social scientific roots on which research stands. It holds the promise of understanding more about the potential and limitations of our research and of promoting greater dialogue between scholars who might otherwise talk past each other. However, we note the dangers inherent in 'showing one's working' noted by Hay but also agree with his conclusion (2009: 897) that to do this is 'surely preferable to foreclosing all theoretical and conceptual debate by burying the theoretical inspiration for the analytical insights one's work presents'.

The remainder of the chapter is divided into four main sections. In the first section we briefly consider meta-theory and map our understanding of the terms ontology, epistemology and methodology. In Section 2 we outline the most common ontological positions and methodological practices in Europeanization literature. In Section 3 we discuss a critical realist perspective on causality in Europeanization research. In Section 4, a critical realist approach is discussed as a way of ameliorating and addressing the methodological problems that are found in Europeanization literature. We suggest that some of the most important methodological dilemmas of the Europeanization literature can be better understood from a perspective of critical realism (CR), namely the ontology (the role of structure and agency), temporality and methodology.

## Meta-theory: The context

Meta-theory reveals theories' assumptions about the nature of the social world: what exists (ontology), what we can know (epistemology) and what are the proper ways of acquiring knowledge (methodology). As such, meta-theory 'sets forth the basic architecture and requirements of scientific research, both guiding it and providing standards by which it can be assessed by a scholarly community' (Jupille, 2006: 210). We cannot do justice here to the subtleties of the components of meta-theory or to the intense debates that surround them, but simply set out how we understand them in developing our discussion of a critical realist approach to Europeanization.[1]

Ontology (see Box 4.1) is taken here to refer to the assumptions that a particular approach makes as to 'what exists, what it looks like, what units make it up and how these units interact with one another' (Blaikie, 2003: 6). Specifically, it answers questions such as what exists in the social realm and what is the relationship between those things that exist. It covers assumptions on the relationship between structure and agency, ideas and the material world as well as space and time. Ontological assumptions are not refutable by empirical evidence. They direct the researcher where to look for causes of political outcomes, regulate the concepts employed and frame the boundaries of the empirical part of study.

---

**Box 4.1 Ontology**

- What exists in the social realm (i.e., Is there an invisible structure that orders agents' behaviour? Do ideas exert causal influence?)
- What is the relationship between those things that exist (i.e., What is the relationship between structure and agency? What is the relationship between the material and the ideational? What is the rationale behind the agents' actions?)
- Does reality reveal itself as it is, or is there a discrepancy between reality and appearance (Hay, 2002)?

---

Epistemology (see Box 4.2) is broadly defined as the philosophy of knowledge. It problematizes how and what we can know about the world and what (if anything) counts as 'knowledge'. Epistemology seeks to answer questions in relation to the sources and criteria of knowledge; the degree to which knowledge is certain; and the relationship between the known and the knower (Wight, 2002: 35).

---

**Box 4.2   Epistemology**

Two traditions can be identified in social sciences: explaining and understanding.

- Explaining seeks to 'locate *causes* and *laws* of behaviour' (Hollis and Smith, 1991: 45). This tradition harbours an account of the social world that is governed by unobservable laws of causality.
- Understanding entails a rejection of explaining the social world by revealing causal laws underlying it. Instead, the basic assumption is that 'action must always be understood from within' (Hollis and Smith, 1991: 72). In this view social behaviour has subjective meaning.

---

Overton's (1998) definition of methodology as 'a set of interlocking rules, principles, or a story, that describes and prescribes the means of observational exploration in a scientific discipline' is useful for our purposes (quoted in Jupille, 2006: 214). There are several broad categories of methodology (see Box 4.3).

---

**Box 4.3   Methodology**

– Quantitative–qualitative methods

- Quantitative methods include statistical methods such as correlational analysis, regression analysis and formal methods such as game theory, decision theory, computational models and so on.
- Qualitative methods include document analysis, discourse analysis, individual or group interviews, ethnomethodology and so on.

---

- Historical methodology

  - Synchronic historical analysis explores a snapshot view of political reality.
  - Comparative statics compare more than one snapshot view of political reality.
  - Diachronic analysis traces the process of change: incremental or revolutionary (Hay, 2002: 144–150).

- Logics of inference

  - Induction moves from empirical observation to theory; deduction moves from hypothesis to empirical observation.

- Levels of analysis.

The next section reviews the common practices and problems in Europeanization literature, with special reference to their ontological and methodological connections.[2]

## Europeanization: Concept, ontology and methodology

Europeanization has emerged as a key theme in European Union (EU) studies over the past decade or so. While early studies focused on the top-down flow of causality from the EU to the national level, the literature increasingly considered alongside this 'downloading' the 'bottom-up' process through which states sought to 'upload' to the EU level to minimize difficulties at the post-decision stage (Börzel, 2005). Moreover, the literature has also encompassed more horizontal forms of Europeanization through the transfer of ideas and practices across states, a process that may or may not involve the EU directly (sometimes described as 'crossloading'). The distinction between top-down, bottom-up and horizontal forms of Europeanization is now a highly stylized take on the body of research – much of which seeks to incorporate elements of multidimensional flows – but one that provides a helpful heuristic in relation to understanding the extant and potential contribution of critical realism.

The early literature on Europeanization devoted considerable attention to definitional issues (for reviews, see Bache and Jordan, 2006; Bulmer and Lequesne, 2005; Olsen, 2002; Radaelli and Pasquier, 2007). As Radaelli and Pasquier note (2007: 35), while some analysts argue for greater precision in the use of the concept, others take an alternative view that Europeanization 'is a set of contested discourses and narratives on domestic political change' and 'what political actors make of it'. On the other hand, Buller and Gamble questioned whether it is possible to start researching Europeanization without knowing what to look for (2002: 4). Definitions of Europeanization crystallize elements of the literature's ontological assumptions. An early and influential definition of Europeanization was as 'an incremental process reorienting the direction and shape of politics to the degree that EC political and economic dynamics become part of the organizational logic of national politics and policy-making' (Ladrech, 1994: 69). However, Ladrech was clear that this process did not lead to harmonization across states, but that there were important domestic factors at play in shaping the nature and extent of Europeanization. Thus, in their agenda-setting book, Cowles, Caporaso and Risse (2001) set out the importance of mediating institutions and actors at the domestic level in shaping the contours of Europeanization effects.

An oft-cited definition, which balances the top-down and bottom-up concerns, came from Radaelli, who proposed that Europeanization comprises:

> Processes of a) construction, b) diffusion and c) institutionalization of formal and informal rules, procedures, policy paradigms, styles, 'ways of doing things' and shared beliefs and norms which are first defined and consolidated in the EU policy process and then incorporated in the logic of domestic discourse, identities, political structures and public policies.
>
> (2003: 30)

A key point in this definition is that there must be EU policy processes before there can be an impact at the domestic level, which directs our attention to the pre-existence of structure to agency. As Radaelli and Pasquier have noted (2007: 37), this does not mean that the EU policy processes have to generate tangible output, such as legislation. Meetings in expert working groups may be sufficient to generate a socialization effect on member state officials.

Bulmer and Radaelli suggested that regulatory competition and learning served as alternative dynamics of domestic change, while other research has emphasized the discursive and constructed nature of the EU as a pressure or indeed resource in domestic politics (Bache and Jordan, 2006; Buller and Gamble, 2002; Hay and Rosamond, 2002; Radaelli,

2003). An interesting twist to this focus is to be found in Woll and Jacquot's work (2010) in which the EU is seen as something that 'can become a vector of change by providing new resources, references and policy frames, which national policy actors use strategically' (Woll and Jacqout, 2010: 113). This contribution explains strategic action within a sociological understanding of structure. This emphasis upon the 'usage' of Europe further underlines the growing emphasis upon causal mechanisms at the domestic level, while emphasizing agential rather than structural factors.

The importance of time to Europeanization research is crucial, especially in historical institutionalist (HI) studies. Yet, time is not the exclusive turf of HI, nor is all HI analysis concerned with the temporal (Bulmer, 2009). Indeed path-dependence is a prominent concern in the Europeanization literature, but its investigation is limited to path-dependence at the domestic level. Klaus Goetz (2009: 214) has argued that the impact of EU time on political time in the member states opens up discretionary opportunities, since member states are not just 'time-takers'. For example, the EU policy timescape might not be strategically viable to individual member states in all cases, making successful negotiations dependant on granting a derogation in order 'to create relative political time' (Jessop, 2008: 195). In the political domain of Europeanization the deferral of a referendum on a big EU issue until after domestic elections have been held is a way of synchronizing EU and domestic timescapes strategically.

There also have been debates around methodological issues surrounding the study of Europeanization, one of which relates to the level of analysis in establishing causality. Here it is important to distinguish between top-down and bottom-up conceptions of Europeanization analytically and top-down and bottom-up conceptions methodologically: a concern with explaining top-down dynamics does not necessitate a top-down approach methodologically, but this may have been a weakness of early studies that took this approach and may have privileged the EU's causality in doing so.

In essence, the methodological priority of top-down research design is to start with an EU decision and trace it through the domestic arena to explain the EU effect, while the methodological priority of bottom-up research is to explain developments defined from the bottom-up (by actors in the domestic arena) of which the EU may be only part of the explanation. The weakness of using a top-down approach alone is a privileging of the EU perspective to the relative neglect of the domestic; this remains the case where domestic factors exist in research design purely as factors that mediate EU effects. It is Europeanization research in this tradition that has been open to criticisms that those seeking Europeanization effects tend to find them (Bache, 2008; Cini, 2006).

Another methodological debate in the Europeanization literature is the issue of case selection. There is a bias towards choosing member states over candidate or associate states, older EU members over new member states and the so-called 'awkward' members over 'normal' members (Exadaktylos and Radaelli, Chapter 2 in this volume). The literature is also generally characterized by a lack of justification for case selection. Moreover, Haverland (2007: 64–67, 2005) cautioned scholars about the problem of having no variation in the selection of cases in the study of Europeanization. Instead, he suggested comparing the impact of the EU on both member and non-member states, where the inclusion of 'non-cases' might provide a valuable control, and advocated the use of counterfactual reasoning to consider whether change would have happened in the absence of the EU.

Interestingly, the literature seems to converge towards using qualitative methods within case studies. Even the rational choice-informed variants of Europeanization studies, which are not that many (Bulmer, 2007), tend towards using case studies and qualitative methods. As Exadaktylos and Radaelli point out, the literature might benefit from using more quantitative data (Exadaktylos and Radaelli, Chapter 2 in this volume). However, any combination of quantitative and qualitative methods would require some meta-theoretical reflection, on which we will offer a critical realist perspective later in the chapter.

Another common focal point of methodological debate within the literature is the issue of historical methodology (i.e., how to factor time into the research design). The literature is usually tilted towards implicitly or explicitly acknowledging domestic timescapes in research designs (i.e., time as part of the domestic context), especially in those studies that are informed by historical institutionalism and/or sociological institutionalism. However, studies that are based on rational choice institutionalism still remain largely attached to snapshot views of history and configuration of actors. In these instances, history is mostly used in an informative sense and, in some instances, time is used only as a variable in periodization (Exadaktylos and Radaelli, Chapter 2 in this volume) rather than as a causal factor.

These debates raise the question as to whether it is possible to define Europeanization so broadly as to encompass all these elements, thereby reaching some semblance of a consensus in the field. Can it be defined as impacting 'ideas, discourses, ways of doing things' as well as 'formal institutions, policies, politics'? Can it work (analytically) top-down and bottom-up; vertically and horizontally; and both structurally and agentially at the same time? Would it be plausible to argue that actors are motivated both by incentives (or sanctions) and norms, thereby combining the logic of consequences intrinsic to rational choice with the logic of appropriateness associated more with 'sociological' explanations? If yes, what sort of a research design is required to address such a broad understanding of Europeanization? Through which mechanisms do structure and agency 'cause' political realities?

These questions will be addressed in the next section from a critical realist framework. However, it is important to note here that critical realism is not a theory of Europeanization but a meta-theory that lays the basis for research design. As Checkel (2010) rightly observes, bridge-building between contending approaches without a consideration of meta-theoretical underpinnings could be counterproductive, and he advocates awareness of extreme meta-theoretical opposites that may not lend themselves easily to bridge-building. However, within the Europeanization literature, it could be observed that there is rather a call for synthesis of approaches (i.e., new institutionalisms) and some convergence on research design. Therefore, as the critical realist Bhaskar argued, even if language is a barrier between competing paradigms, the referent objects of those concepts/approaches are the same, which makes it possible for different paradigms to translate and understand each other (1998a: xi). Building on this understanding, a critical realist approach to causality and methodology will be outlined as a meta-theoretical basis for greater self-reflection and for theoretical plurality in Europeanization research.[3]

## Critical realist perspectives on causality in Europeanization research

As noted earlier, the main contribution of this volume to the Europeanization literature is in shedding light on the issues surrounding causality in Europeanization and suggesting ways forward in making causal statements in relation to Europeanization. From this starting point, this section outlines the critical realist conceptualization of causality, thereby touching upon some of the ontological premises of critical realism. Following on from this analysis, methodological insights will be drawn from critical realism in an attempt to demonstrate different ways of looking at and establishing causal relationships within Europeanization research.

Critical realism has many variants;[4] however, the main common denominator is their ontological realism (see Box 4.4). For critical realists reality comprises three strata: the real, the actual and the empirical (observable). The distinctive contribution of CR is its emphasis on the domain of the *real*. It is here that we find causal powers and causal mechanisms – whether they produce an event or not. Once a mechanism produces an event, it comes under the domain of the *actual*, whether it is observed or not. When such an event is experienced, it becomes an empirical fact and comes under the domain of the *empirical*. An example here might be of an EU mechanism (the real) that creates an opportunity for domestic actors (actual) that becomes empirical when it is perceived as such by domestic actors.

---

**Box 4.4   The real, the actual and the empirical**

- Real: generative structures or causal mechanisms;
- Actual: events resulting from various real tendencies and countertendencies in specific initial conditions;
- Empirical: observations or measurements of actual events and, in some circumstances, underlying structures or mechanisms.

*Source*: Jessop (2005: 41).

---

However, CR suggests that causal mechanisms may or may not produce events in the actual domain and, as such, not every causal mechanism manifests itself in the empirical domain. Here, the context makes the difference. Other mechanisms are not only active in the context but also in the spatio-temporal properties of the context, such as the institutional configuration and borders or the temporal organization of the context.

This ontological depth leads researchers to keep searching for the causal mechanisms that produced a certain outcome instead of focusing on the phenomena in the empirical domain (the focus of positivist research). In relation to Europeanization, this means being wary of focusing on establishing hypotheses linking variables on the empirical level. Critical realism suggests looking at the mechanisms and context in which mechanisms interact to produce events.

Critical realism ascribes causal powers to a wide range of factors, thereby broadening the traditional conception of causality. As Kurki elaborates in detail, these are the material, formal, final and efficient causes. They all hold causal powers and they bring about social and political reality when combined (Kurki, 2006: 202–208). Material causes refer to the material out of which something is made, which enables and constrains the maker. Military capabilities or certain kinds of funds, as well as institutional capacities, could be given as examples of material causes. Formal causes refer to the norms, discourses and concepts that give meaning and therefore make possible the output as a meaningful object. The conceptual basis on which we define social objects, for example the EU as a supranational entity that is based on certain responsibilities and powers vis-à-vis its member states – as much as they are contested and contingent, is an example of a formal cause. 'Final' causes are the projects for which something is done, the reasons behind actions. And finally, efficient causes are the actual makers of things (i.e., a state signing a treaty or a parliament passing legislation; Kurki, 2006: 202–208).

Some of these causal factors are structural, such as the material and the formal; others are agential, such as the final and the efficient causes, thus underlining the critical realist ontology of structure and agency. Critical realism starts from the assumption that there is an interactive relationship between structure and agency. Structures enable and constrain agents and agents pursue certain projects and strategies within those structures, thereby altering the structure through the unintended and intended consequences of their actions. What critical realists share in common is the assumption that structures pre-date agency. In Bhaskar's words,

> Society is both the ever-present *condition* (material cause) and the continually reproduced *outcome* of human agency. And praxis is both work, that is, conscious *production*, and (normally unconscious) *reproduction* of the conditions of production, that is, society.
>
> (Bhaskar, 1998b: 215)

This sketch of the critical realist ontology leaves us with the following main observations: an assumption of the pre-existence of structures to agency; the interplay of structure and agency through enablement and constraint as well as the intended and unintended consequences of action; and a broad conception of causality.

These observations are not so unfamiliar to the students of Europeanization. Radaelli's (2003: 30) oft-cited definition of Europeanization to include the creation of EU-level policies, practices and institutions in order for them to have an impact on domestic politics is an example of the pre-existence of structures. Intended and unintended consequences of action and their impact on the structure are also quite common in Europeanization literature (Börzel, 2005; Bulmer and Burch, 2005; Lavenex, 2001). Also, the 'logic of appropriateness' and the 'logic of consequences' that are usually used as proxies of sociological institutionalism and rational choice institutionalism, respectively, within Europeanization literature are bridged by such a critical realist ontology (see Box 4.5). Critical realist ontology takes agents as self-conscious, reflexive, intentional, emotional and cognitive (Carter and New, 2004: 5). Therefore, the behaviour of agents is not pre-determined by logics of consequence or appropriateness, but is strategic in the pursuit of their aims. However, it cannot be assumed that agents always seek material gain rather than social acceptance – it varies. This variation also depends on the ideas agents hold, which influence the goals they have and the ways of pursing them.

---

**Box 4.5   The logics**

– Logics of consequences and appropriateness are ideal-typical assumptions of actor behaviour. There are variations within each category.

  • Logic of consequences: individuals are rational actors, with fixed preferences pre-given to social interaction, who calculate and act in order to maximize their individual gain.
  • Logic of appropriateness: institutions shape actor preferences rather than simply shaping the interaction among individual agents, and individuals act in a legitimate and socially appropriate way.

---

Similarly, from a critical realist framework, Europeanization can be explained in terms of causal mechanisms rather than one single cause (i.e., EU policies). Ray Pawson (quoted in Carter and New, 2004: 23) formulated this critical realist conception of causality as 'mechanism + context = outcome'. Based on the causal powers ascribed to both structure and agency, causal mechanisms involve both. In the context of Europeanization it could be reinterpreted as when being part of the EU (as a member or a candidate) offers new rules and resources (both material and ideational)[5] that agency activates through strategic behaviour, in pursuit of its projects and reasons, within a certain context. This explanation is never in the form of universally generalizable statements since context matters; causal mechanisms are located in a spatio-temporal context, which is full of counteracting mechanisms that might lead to different outcomes (Sayer, 2000: 15). Therefore, the crucial aspect of Europeanization research is to establish who actualizes what mechanism and in what context.

As the previous analysis already shows, there is always a multitude of causal mechanisms simultaneously at play, which can counteract or complement each other, thereby leaving the outcome undetermined. Therefore, the task of the researcher is to move backwards from the outcome and account for the causal mechanisms that interacted in bringing about that certain outcome (Sayer, 2000: 14). Therein lays the importance of methodological safeguards that could yield realistic explanations of the political reality the researcher faces. Disentangling the causal influence of the EU is never a simple task; however, there are certain methodological options, critical realism being one.

## Critical realism and Europeanization: A methodological way forward?

At the heart of critical realist methodology lies the analysis of the interplay between structure and agency. Often the statement that structure and agency have an interactive relationship raises scepticism as to the possibility of methodologically disentangling the one from the other. To this end, a framework is proffered by Margaret Archer (1995). Archer's approach is based on structural conditioning of agency followed by the modification of the structure through intended and unintended consequences of agency. The key assumption is that these phases take place consecutively.

As Figure 4.1 shows, structural conditioning, socio-cultural interaction and structural elaboration take place in different temporal sequences: $T_1$, $T_2$ and $T_3$. Structural conditioning of agency takes place before the interaction among agents. After the interaction takes place, the intended and unintended consequences of that interaction feed back into the structure, thereby maintaining or altering the structure. Thus it is possible to trace back from an outcome to the responsible

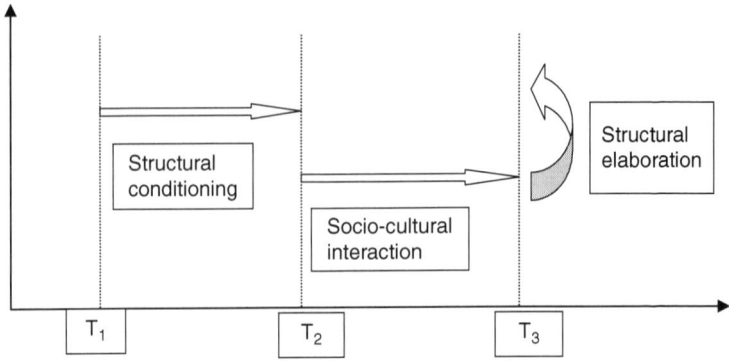

*Figure 4.1*   The relationship between structure and agency according to Archer
*Source*: Adapted from Archer (1995: 76).

mechanisms that brought it into reality. This observation highlights that historical methodology is a central issue in Europeanization research as well as in critical realism. As the past is only transformed and sustained by agents, the past is still present. As Archer puts it,

> the stratified nature of reality introduces a necessary historicity (however short the time period involved) for instead of horizontal explanations relating one experience, observable or event to another, the fact that these themselves are conditional upon antecedents, requires vertical explanations in terms of the generative relationships indispensable for their realization.
>
> (Archer, 1998: 196)

Therefore, process tracing is central in critical realism as well as in Europeanization research. Tracing back in a context-sensitive manner the events and processes and causal mechanisms that co-acted in bringing about a certain outcome is a methodological requirement for Europeanization. This process tracing (Checkel, 2006) should rely on multiple sources of data (i.e., qualitative and quantitative, interviews and document analysis, etc.), and it should utilize some thought experiments about reality in order to produce the observable outcomes. The latter is largely performed through critical realist logics of inference/thought experiments such as abduction and retroduction.

Abduction is basically redescribing and recontextualizing a phenomenon. In Danermark's words, 'to recontextualize, i.e. to observe, describe, interpret and explain something within the frame of a new context, is a central element in scientific practice' (Danermark et al., 2002: 91). Accordingly, the researcher must redefine, for example the edge of the earth dropping away as something else (i.e., the rising of the sun) (Bhaskar, 2008: 21). Through such re-descriptions, it becomes possible to refine conceptualizations about social reality and acquire an understanding of the real mechanisms at work. Within the context of Europeanization this translates into recontextualizing potential causal mechanisms that link the EU structure and domestic change from different theoretical perspectives, and when possible integrating them through empirical research (Olsen, 2004). An example could be Checkel's (2005: 806) mechanisms of social learning in Europe, which are based on Habermasian communicative action theory, bargaining from a rational choice variant and role-playing, which are all potential mechanisms linking individual action to European norms.

The second logic of inference introduced by critical realism is retroduction, whereby the researcher reasons in order to find the causal mechanisms underlying that particular event. In Danermark's words, 'by this argumentation one seeks to clarify the basic prerequisites or conditions for social relationships, people's actions, reasoning and knowledge' (Danermark et al., 2002: 96). Methods such as counterfactual reasoning and studying extreme cases are all methods of retroduction, which is the backbone of critical realist research. Retroduction answers the questions 'What must the reality be like to effect such an outcome?' and 'Would this still have happened, had this particular mechanism been absent from the picture?' The Europeanization literature is also quite familiar with suggestions that it is necessary to use methods such as counterfactual analysis, namely to ask whether a particular outcome would have happened had the EU been absent (Bache and Jordan, 2006; Haverland, 2007), with a view to identify the causal mechanisms within the EU that are capable of producing an outcome. These two thought experiments must run throughout the research, thereby keeping the researcher aware of different theoretical perspectives, as well as establishing the significance of certain mechanisms and their interplay in bringing about the outcome. Critical realist research proceeds in reverse, from the phenomenon to be explained to the causal mechanisms and their interplay in bringing it about. Therefore, in every step of this process these thought experiments should be used to give the researcher the best opportunity to identify causality.

To this end, critical realism advocates methodological pluralism, and combining qualitative and quantitative methodologies within an ontologically and epistemologically grounded framework. Quantitative methods usually aim to produce *extensive* knowledge of an aggregate of units through analysis on the basis of variables and empirical observations, whereas qualitative methods produce *intensive* knowledge of cases, an understanding of the nature, reasons and peculiarities of social action (Danermark et al., 2002: 158–163). As mentioned earlier, critical realism recognizes the causal powers of the discursive context, the material aspects of the structure, as well as actors' reasons. Therefore whenever research is undertaken, discursive context as well as the actors' beliefs, reasons and discursive strategies[6] must be analysed. This tradition of *understanding* social action from within requires qualitative methods as meaning cannot be counted or measured quantitatively (Sayer, 2000: 17).

As with Checkel's caution (above), critical realists underscore the usefulness of combining intensive and extensive research methods as long as this combination is loyal to a consistent meta-theoretical basis. Quantitative data are used to detect partial regularities in the empirical domain that are in need of causal explanation by reference to causal mechanisms producing them (Danermark et al., 2002: 166–167). Quantitative data have to be reconceptualized and explained further with qualitative research.

Intensive research methods involve the analysis of a limited number of cases through qualitative methods such as interviews, document analysis, archival research and so on. Case selection is geared towards revealing causal mechanisms behind events. Critical realist methodology offers four types of case selection:

- Normal cases, where causal mechanisms are sought in a usual case (e.g., analysis of causal mechanisms behind the everyday workings of EU Commission Directorate-Generals).
- Extreme cases (e.g., the 2004 'big bang' enlargement of the EU, which was an unusual phenomenon) give more information than average cases on the causal mechanisms.
- Extremely varied cases, which are a combination of cases that are very different from each other (e.g., the analysis of a northern EU member's responses to EU environmental policies with those of a southern EU member gives insights into how different contexts shape the operation of causal mechanisms).
- Finally, critical cases are the counter-intuitive cases, where an expected outcome never occurred or vice versa (e.g., non-EU member states adopting EU policies, or a member state not complying with the EU legislation; Saurugger, Chapter 6 in this volume), that

enable researchers to identify counteracting mechanisms that reverse the causal tendency (Danermark et al., 2002: 170–171).

Therefore, critical realism implies analysing continuity as well as change, as there is social scientific value in analysing what mechanisms maintain that political reality. This is also important for Europeanization literature since there is a lack of case selection rationale in the field (see above and also Exadaktylos and Radaelli, 2009, and Chapter 2 in this volume).

All in all, critical realism offers a methodology based on the analysis of the interplay between structure and agency, through a cautious research design that utilizes a diachronic historical methodology and logics of inference that are geared towards abstracting certain elements of the social reality at hand and establishing the interplay of causal mechanisms in bringing about that reality. This approach is implemented through methodological pluralism involving the use of both quantitative and qualitative methods and case studies within a process-tracing framework.

Some issues pertaining to a critical realist methodology must be flagged up. As Checkel (2006) demonstrated with reference to his own research, one issue is deciding where to stop the analysis. Due to the assumption of a stratified reality, critical realist methodology always aims to go beyond the level of events to mechanisms. However, there are always deeper and deeper mechanisms that could be identified, and this brings up the question of when to stop the search for deeper mechanisms. One answer to this question could be to limit the research to the boundaries of the field to which research aims to contribute. For example, when analysing the Europeanization of a policy area, the researcher could go as deep as individual psychological structures. Although this could form the basis of a new research agenda combining Europeanization literature and social psychology, the contribution of such has to be carefully framed and grounded within the Europeanization literature rather than the field of social psychology. Second, critical realism relies heavily upon thought experiments such as abduction and retroduction. The subjectivity in this method ology may alienate certain kinds of scholarship that seek generalizable knowledge through rigorous methods of falsification and verification. Critical realists do not pursue a positivist social science agenda aimed at prediction. Rather, the aim is to identify structures and mechanisms that offer explanations that are as realistic as possible for the political phenomena at hand. Thus, for critical realists all knowledge is

context-bound and fallible: more convincing explanations may later emerge.
Diligence in concept formation and triangulation become core elements of the research in the face of this subjectivity. Proxies should be selected carefully. When looking into the rationale of a national bureaucracy for a certain kind of action, what kind of data will be used to capture it? Triangulation in data is important at this point: mission statements, interviews as well as archival data could be used to triangulate causal mechanisms. It is surely difficult to 'triangulate' discursive representations and meanings of action. However, it is possible through discourse analysis of, and interviews with, the key actors from various backgrounds to get a confident level of understanding of their conceptualizations of the discursive context. Also, existing literature and half-forgotten research findings are recycled in a critical realist framework and utilized to establish structural and agential elements of causal mechanisms that bring about change, as well as non-change (i.e., non-compliance or retrenchment). Previous findings can be appropriated with certain safeguards in critical realist research and utilized. This is especially important to follow in a field such as Europeanization, which sprang out of another popular field, studies of EU integration. It is important to remember that the current generation of scholars also live in a world not of their own making, but inherited from the past generation of scholars. Therefore, past research findings should be recontextualized and used from different angles to reach a more realistic view of Europeanization.

## Conclusion

This chapter has argued that issues of research design, such as causality, should be understood within a meta-theoretical framework. It is only by having this framework in mind that methodologies acquire meaning, become explicit and can be checked for internal consistency.

Our first conclusion is that much work on Europeanization has been conducted with little reflection of this kind. And yet a number of issues, notably the relationship between structure and agency and the question of temporality, present real problems in research design for which meta-theoretical reflection can assist in the search for solutions. For instance, the frequent observation that Europeanization entails both downloading and uploading sets out a perspective on the structure–agency problem (i.e., on EU–member state relations) that is consistent with dialectical approaches to structure and agency, such as critical realism. These observations are in turn consistent with an epistemology of understanding the meanings and reasons of action and explaining the complex of causal mechanisms that bring about a certain political reality. This in turn has implications for the methodology (and thus the research design) to be used to acquire evidence about causal relations. By proceeding along these lines of research design, whether using critical realist ontology or not, there will never be a satisfactory answer to the testing question from a seminar participant concerning falsifiability. Put simply, one would have had to have commenced with a different set of assumptions about the character of Europeanization and a different epistemology. In short, meta-theory matters!

Similarly, in adopting a definition of Europeanization such as Radaelli's (2003: 30), it is important to note that it has two stages: prior EU action and impact at the domestic level. If this definition is to be fully operationalized it requires temporality to be taken seriously. Once again, the ontology of Europeanization has consequences for epistemology, methodology and, therefore, research design.

In making a plea for greater meta-theoretical awareness in Europeanization research, we have explicitly taken a critical realist perspective to shed light on some of the existing practices within the Europeanization literature. Thus in the fourth section of the chapter we outlined a meta-theoretical grounding for methodology and research design for Europeanization from a critical realist perspective. In particular we explored what critical realism distinctively offers for establishing causality as well as the highlighted issues of the structure–agency relationship and temporality.

Finally, we note the trend towards dialogue between hitherto competing ontological and methodological approaches: typically between rationalist and sociological analysis. Here again, we argue for a greater meta-theoretical appreciation of the task at hand, and suggest that insights could be brought to this dialogue from a critical realist ontology and methodology.

## Notes

1. We should note, of course, that our own understanding of meta-theory and the relationship among its components is shaped by our view of the social world rather than being in some way objectively defined.
2. Following Hall (2003), the chapter emphasizes the issue of methodology and its ontological assumptions rather than epistemological matters.
3. There are of course several other alternative philosophies of social science that could form the basis of Europeanization research, such as neo-positivism or post-structuralism.

4. We note the 'strategic-relational approach' of Bob Jessop (2008), 'morphogenetic approach' of Margaret Archer (1995), 'transformational model of social
   activity' of Roy Bhaskar (2008), the 'structurationist' social theory of Anthony
   Giddens (1986) and the 'as-if-realism' of Colin Hay (2005). The peculiarities
   of all these approaches and their positioning in the critical realist literature
   have been at the centre of an intense debate. See, for example, Archer (1995),
   Hay (2005), Jessop (2005); McAnulla (2005). It suffices here only to highlight
   that we are sticking as closely as possible with the most common assumptions
   across these variants, and when we go beyond those common assumptions
   we draw upon 'Bhaskarian' critical realists as Milja Kurki called them (Kurki,
   2006: 204).
5. It is useful here to note that being part of the EU structure offers more than
   one causal mechanism, which might be contradictory or complementary to
   each other.
6. For discourse, both as a context and an agential variable, see Lynggaard, this
   volume.

## References

Archer, M. (1995) *Realist Social Theory: The Morphogenetic Approach* (Cambridge:
   Cambridge University Press).
Archer, M. (1998) 'Introduction: Realism in the Social Sciences', in M. Archer,
   R. Bhaskar, A. Collier et al. (Eds.), *Critical Realism: Essential Readings* (London:
   Routledge), pp. 189–206.
Bache, I. (2008) *Europeanization and Multilevel Governance: Cohesion Policy in the
   European Union and Britain* (Lanham, MD: Rowman and Littlefield).
Bache, I. and Jordan, A. (2006) 'The Europeanization and Domestic Change', in
   I. Bache and A. Jordan (Eds.), *Europeanization of British Politics* (Basingstoke:
   Palgrave Macmillan).
Bhaskar, R. (1998a) 'General Introduction', in M. Archer, R. Bhaskar, A. Collier
   et al. (Eds.), *Critical Realism: Essential Readings* (London: Routledge), pp. ix–1.
Bhaskar, R. (1998b) 'Societies', in M. Archer, R. Bhaskar, A. Collier et al. (Eds.),
   *Critical Realism: Essential Readings* (London: Routledge), pp. 206–258.
Bhaskar, R. (2008) *A Realist Theory of Science* (Abingdon: Routledge).
Blaikie, N. (2003) *Approaches to Social Inquiry* (Cambridge: Polity Press).
Börzel, T. (2005) 'Europeanization: How the European Union Interacts with Its
   Member States', in S. Bulmer and C. Lequesne (Eds.), *The Member States of the
   European Union* (Oxford: Oxford University Press), pp. 45–69.
Buller, J. and Gamble, A. (2002) 'Conceptualising Europeanization', *Public Policy
   and Administration*, 17(4), 4–24.
Bulmer, S. (2007) 'Theorizing Europeanization', in P. Graziano and M. Vink (Eds.),
   *Europeanization: New Research Agendas* (Basingstoke: Palgrave Macmillan),
   pp. 46–58.
Bulmer, S. (2009) 'Politics in Time Meets the Politics of Time: Historical
   Institutionalism and the EU Timescape', *Journal of European Public Policy*, 16(2),
   307–324.
Bulmer, S. and Burch, M. (2005) 'The Europeanization of UK Government:
   From Quiet Revolution to Explicit Step-Change', *Public Administration*, 83(4),
   861–890.

Bulmer, S. and Lequesne, C. (2005) 'The EU and Its Member States: An Overview', in S. Bulmer and C. Lequesne (Eds.), *The Member States of the European Union* (Oxford: Oxford University Press), pp. 1–20.

Bulmer, S. and Radaelli, C. (2005) 'The Europeanization of National Policy', in S. Bulmer and C. Lequesne (Eds.), *The Member States of the European Union* (Oxford: Oxford University Press), pp. 338–359.

Carter, B. and New, C. (2004) 'Introduction', in B. Carter and C. New (Eds.), *Making Realism Work: Realist Social Theory and Empirical Research* (Abingdon: Routledge).

Checkel, J.T. (2005) 'International Institutions and Socialization in Europe: Introduction and Framework', *International Organization*, 59(4), 801–826.

Checkel, J.T. (2006) 'Tracing Causal Mechanisms', *International Studies Review*, 8(2), 363–370.

Checkel, J.T. (2010) 'Theoretical Synthesis in IR: Possibilities and Limits' Simons Papers in Security and Development, no. 6, Simon Fraser University, School for International Studies. Available online at «http://www.sfu.ca/internationalstudies/PDFs/WP6.pdf», retrieved 5 February 2010.

Cini, M. (2006) 'Competition Policy', in I. Bache and A. Jordan (Eds.), *The Europeanization of British Politics* (Basingstoke: Palgrave Macmillan), pp. 216–230.

Cowles, M., Caporaso, J. and Risse, T. (Eds.) (2001) *Transforming Europe: Europeanization and Domestic Change* (Ithaca and London: Cornell University Press).

Danermark, B. et al. (2002) *Explaining Society: Critical Realism in Social Sciences* (New York: Routledge).

Exadaktylos, T. and Radaelli, C.M. (2009) 'Research Design in European Studies: The Case of Europeanization', *Journal of Common Market Studies*, 47(3), 507–530.

Giddens, A. (1986) *The Constitution of Society* (Berkeley, CA: University of California Press).

Goetz, K. (2009) 'How Does the EU Tick? Five Propositions on Political Time', *Journal of European Public Policy*, 16(2), 202–220.

Hall, P. (2003) 'Aligning Ontology and Methodology in Comparative Research', in J. Mahoney and D. Rueschemeyer (Eds.), *Comparative Historical Analysis in the Social Sciences* (Cambridge: Cambridge University Press), pp. 373–404.

Haverland, M. (2005) 'Does the EU Cause Domestic Developments? The Problem of Case Selection in Europeanization Research' European Integration online Papers (EIoP), 9(2) available online at: http://www.eiop.at/eiop/pdf/2005-002.pdf

Haverland, M. (2007) 'Methodology', in P. Graziano and M. Vink (Eds.), *Europeanization: New Research Agendas* (Basingstoke: Palgrave Macmillan).

Hay, C. (2002) *Political Analysis: A Critical Introduction* (Basingstoke: Palgrave Macmillan).

Hay, C. (2005) 'Making Hay... Or Clutching Ontological Straws: Notes on Realism, "As-If-Realism" and Actualism', *Politics*, 25(1), 39–45.

Hay, C. (2007) 'Does Ontology Trump Epistemology: Notes on the Directional Dependence of Ontology and Epistemology in Political Analysis', *Politics*, 27(2), 115–118.

Hay, C. (2009) 'Your Ontology, My Ontic Speculations... On the Importance of Showing One's (Ontological) Working', *Political Studies*, 57(4), 892–898.

Hay, C. and Rosamond, B. (2002) 'Globalisation, European Integration and the Discursive Construction of Economic Imperatives', *Journal of European Public Policy*, 9(2), 147–167.

Hollis, M. and Smith, S. (1991) *Explaining and Understanding in International Relations* (Oxford: Clarendon Press).

Jessop, B. (2005) 'Critical Realism and the Strategic-Relational Approach', *New Formations*, 56, 40–53.

Jessop, B. (2008) *State Power* (Cambridge: Polity Press).

Jupille, J. (2006) 'Knowing Europe: Metatheory and Methodology in European Union Studies', in M. Cini and A. Bourne (Eds.), *Palgrave Advances in European Union Studies* (Basingstoke: Palgrave Macmillan), pp. 209–232.

Kurki, M. (2006) 'Causes of a Divided Discipline: Rethinking the Concept of Cause in International Relations Theory', *Review of International Studies*, 32(2), 189–216.

Ladrech, R. (1994) 'Europeanization of Domestic Politics and Institutions: The Case of France', *Journal of Common Market Studies*, 32(1), 69–88.

Lavenex, S. (2001) 'The Europeanization of Refugee Policies: Normative Challenges and Institutional Legacies', *Journal of Common Market Studies*, 39(5), 851–874.

McAnulla, S. (2005) 'Making Hay with Actualism: The Need for a Realist Concept of Structure', *Politics*, 25(1), 31–38.

Olsen, J. (2002) 'The Many Faces of Europeanization', *Journal of Common Market Studies*, 40(5), 921–952.

Olsen, W. (2004) 'Methodological Triangulation and Realist Research: The Indian Exemplar', in B. Carter and C. New (Eds.), *Making Realism Work* (Abingdon: Routledge).

Overton, W. (1998) *Metatheory and Methodology in Developmental Psychology* (Philadelphia, PA: Temple University).

Radaelli, C. (2003) 'The Europeanization of Public Policy', in K. Featherstone and C. Radaelli (Eds.), *The Politics of Europeanisation* (Oxford: Oxford University Press), pp. 27–56.

Radaelli, C. and Pasquier, R. (2007) 'Conceptual Issues', in P. Graziano and M. Vink (Eds.), *Europeanization: New Research Agendas* (Basingstoke: Palgrave Macmillan), pp. 35–45.

Sayer, A. (2000) *Realism and Social Science* (London: Sage).

Wight, C. (2002) 'Philosophy of Social Science and International Relations', in W. Carlsnaes, T. Risse and B.A. Simmons (Eds.), *The Handbook of International Relations* (London: Sage Publications), pp. 23–52.

Woll, C. and Jacquot, S. (2010) 'Using Europe: Strategic Action in Multi-level Politics', *Comparative European Politics*, 8(1), 110–126.

# 5
# Discursive Institutional Analytical Strategies

*Kennet Lynggaard*

## Introduction

This chapter addresses the question of how discursive approaches deal with causality claims in Europeanization. Discourse analysis as a methodological tool is not commonly associated with traditional notions of causality. At the same time discourse analysis is very much directed at the study of causal *representations* among agents. The puzzle is how we may proceed from the study of discursive causalities towards substantive causal claims.

Discourse analysis is often reluctant about making theoretical causal claims testable against an objective and stable reality (however, neo-positivist approaches to narratives and discourse have their own place in the literature, as shown by Jones and McBeth, 2010). The ambition is instead to develop research strategies that enable the study of concrete historical discursive developments. Europeanization research is a good example to explore for issues of causality in discursive accounts.

Discourse has become at least one potential explanatory variable among a number of variables in accounts of Europeanization (Chapter 2 in this volume). This is the case whether discourse is seen as an independent variable, a dependent variable or, alternatively, more broadly if discourses are seen as making up the context within which decision makers operate. Regardless if these types of variables are put forward as mutually exclusive or as potentially complementing, we are faced with the challenge of how discursive variables and their causal claims are interrelated with other types of variables and causal claims.

To achieve more comprehensive knowledge of the implications of European integration for European societies, one cannot employ one-dimensional research strategies. The study of domestic change in the face of European integration is rarely, if ever, a matter of studying a single cause-and-effect relation, just as European Union (EU) institutional and policy initiatives may be considered both in terms of implications for domestic institutional arrangements and discourses. Thus, the puzzle of moving towards claims of causality raises the question of how discourse analytical strategies may 'speak' to other theoretical and analytical frameworks.

Think, for instance, of the establishment and implications of the Economic and Monetary Union (EMU). On the one hand, the EMU is at the very least conditional for member state fiscal policies, and the introduction of the euro among other things involves national adoption of payment systems and affects cross-border trade and financial market integration. On the other hand, the EMU as a reflection of a neo-liberal policy paradigm has also been used strategically to legitimize national policy and institutional choices, and the euro may well be considered and studied in terms of its implications for 'nation building' and identity construction in Europe (Dyson, 2000; Risse et al., 1999). In other words, we must expect at least potentially multiple national impacts of any EU-level policy or institutional initiative, just as domestic change is likely to be caused by a mixture of independent and/or domestic mediating variables.

Finally, it will be argued that discourse analysis supplies a number of particularly helpful methodological tools for developing more analytical inductive research strategies and may form the basis for multi-theoretical analysis. Analytical inductive research strategies are acutely needed in Europeanization research. Not only were we well into the 2000s before some convergence appeared around a common conception of the object of Europeanization research – that is, the study of the domestic implications of European integration (see also Bache et al., Chapter 4 in this volume). The research area is also very much characterized by theory building, rather than inhabited by well-established and testable theoretical positions. For those reasons, it seems appropriate to commence the work on establishing substantive causal claims in Europeanization research with an open mind, allowing for multi-theoretical interpretations.

Along these lines, the discussion below moves beyond the traditional dichotomy between those scholars engaged in causal analysis (empiricists) and those engaged in studying the constitutive nature of norms, values and, indeed, discourse (reflectivists/constructivists) (Kurki, 2006; see also Gofas and Hay (2010) for a critical review; see Blyth (2010) for a critique of the review). Even if discourses have the reputation of being 'slippery' and in flux, discourses are a real-world phenomenon that may be captured and analysed by fairly well-known research techniques.

The chapter is organized as follows: the second section briefly introduces the concept of discourse and research techniques aimed at analysing discourse. The third section identifies types of causal claims as suggested – explicit or implicit – by discursive approaches to the study of Europeanization. This is followed by three sections that discuss how we may move towards establishing causality in Europeanization research through research strategies aimed at uncovering mechanisms, temporal comparative analysis and multi-theoretical analysis. Concluding remarks are made in the final section.

## What is discourse analysis and how can it be done?

This brief introduction by no means does justice to the range of approaches to discourse analysis in political science. It should also be noted that the focus below is discourse analysis – or the analysis of discourse – rather than on discourse theory (for a discussion of discourse theory in European politics, see David Howarth and Jacob Torfing, 2005). Even though discourse theory probably still has much more to offer also for Europeanization research, the focus on discourse analysis is justified by being associated with policy and institutional analysis and, thus, Europeanization research. Furthermore, discourse analysis is particularly helpful when dealing with issues of 'how to study' Europeanization.

### What is discourse analysis?

Sometimes a distinction is made between two general strands of research designs among scholars with an interest in the role of discourses in politics: namely the positivist (or structural) and post-positivist (or post-structural). The former takes its point of departure in hypothetical-deductive methodological set-ups and favours quantitative data. The latter is inductive and favours qualitative and often single case studies (for the difference between the two, see Jones and McBeth, 2010: 333). This distinction may be legitimized for heuristic purposes. However, it is probably also a distinction that is increasingly counterproductive for the development of comprehensive and empirically sensitive research strategies for specific investigations.

Almost certainly, we are better off considering the value of compound research designs guided by the research question at hand and the nature of the existing research on the area of interest. In that spirit, it has been proposed that the application of bottom-up, or more inductive method-ological set-ups, is timely and potentially helpful in Europeanization research (Radaelli and Pasquier, 2006). At the same time, it will also be argued below that we should move towards comparative research designs and strategies that enable the investigation of Europeanization mechanisms of relevance across comparable cases. The following emphasize the features of discourse analysis which promote these aims.

First, *the* research object of any discourse analysis is discourse. Hajer (1995: 44) defines discourse as 'a specific ensemble of ideas, concepts, and categorizations that are produced, reproduced and transformed in a particular set of practices and through which meaning is given to physical and social realities'. Different scholars may make use of slightly different definitions of discourse, but they all deal with the production of collective perceptions and meanings. Discourse analysis is the study of the development and effect of collective meaning systems.

While the focus here is narrower on discourse analysis and partic-ularly the role of discourse in Europeanization research, we make use of and reach out at the same time to the broader literature concerned with the study of meaning systems and their effect on political decision making. Approaching discourse analysis as a research methodology not only permits reaching out to a broad range of research tools, but also to speak to a variety of theoretical and analytical frameworks. In the broadest sense, we may even include the majority of current meso-level analytical frameworks concerned with governance, network analysis, institutional theory and policy analysis. Albeit more or less prominently meso-level analytical frameworks concerned with politics most often have some interest in discourse. This includes, for instance, the study of ideas, knowledge, political communication, public opinion or broader meaning systems variously conceptualized as policy frames, paradigms (Hall, 1993), belief systems (Sabatier, 1998) or narratives (Patterson and Monroe, 1998).

Second, discourse analysis points up the implications of discourse for political outcomes. Discourse may be seen as a kind of road switch through which a set of preferences are combined to produce one spe-cific policy or institutional choice (Goldstein and Keohane, 1993). Yet, discourse is more commonly studied in terms of its transformative powers. For instance, in Europeanization research European integra-tion may be seen as a set of concepts and conceptions that makes up a discursive context for domestic actors, policies and institutions. Dis-courses on European integration thus set out a 'space of possibility' for decision makers – including politicians, high-level civil servants, public administrative units, non-governmental organizations and business associations. This 'space of possibility' is both constraining and enabling for policy and institutional choices. On the one hand, domestic actors must articulate themselves through existing discourses in order to be considered relevant and legitimate. On the other hand, the decision-making elites in particular may make strategic use of discourses on European integration to carry through or, indeed, hinder domestic reform. Regardless, any discursive perspective assumes that discourses have real consequences for decision making. In that sense, causal conceptions among actors have a causal effect on political outcome. It is, however, also clear that the types of causalities emphasized vary in kind, as shown below.

Third, discourse analysis has a significant inductive concern and an essential task in any discourse analysis is the mapping of the discourse or discourses in focus. The first step is thus an empirical investigation uncovering ideas, concepts, categories and causal relations as articulated within the field of inquiry. The study of political identity, or 'senses of belonging' to a political system, and how such identities may affect political outcomes, can be used as an illustration of the more inductive concern of discourse analysis. It has convincingly been shown how national representatives may gradually assume supranational identities through treaty commitments and institutional affiliation (Laffan, 2004). To varying degrees, individuals or groups of individuals also conceive of themselves as Europeans, as belonging to a nation state and/or perhaps a sub-region. Euro-barometer surveys and elite interviews are central to this type of research (Gillespie and Laffan, 2006). We have also seen how discourse analysis has contributed to uncovering and investigating other identity categories. These include 'Europe as a moral community' and the existence of European 'communication communities', suggesting an emerging Europeanization of media treatment of European integration themes (Risse and Maier, 2003: 50ff). Almost certainly, additional identity categories with relevance for EU politics are waiting to be uncovered and investigated.

## How can discourse analysis be done?

This leads to the question of how we may capture discourses empirically. There are several research methods and techniques on offer to this endeavour, including content analysis (see Herrera and Braumoeller, 2004) and interpretative methods (e.g., Yanow, 2006). Both content analysis and interpretative methods do, however, have some drawbacks. Content analysis is traditionally the use of statistical analysis of the appearances of word categories across texts. One of the drawbacks is that discourse here tends to be detached from its context. Content analysis excludes analysis of, for instance, what the authoritative position of the actors producing discourse is? How is discourse related to the institutional and social context in which it is constructed? How is the discourse received by a broader audience? Interpretivists studies are, on the other hand, often criticized for being less than transparent and for failing to be 'clear enough to be wrong' (Jones and McBeth, 2010). This critique may be slightly misplaced for studies that by no means claim to be replicable or aim at making truth claims about an external political reality. In any case, while not excluding the usefulness of interpretative methods and particularly content analysis, they are probably both better seen as a supplement to other research techniques for the purpose of Europeanization research.

These research techniques are often used to capture discourse through the study of problem perceptions (Bacchi, 2009; Lynggaard, 2006; see also Mehta, 2011). Problem perceptions are here seen as ideational symptoms reflecting the discourse within which a set of actors operate. Take, for example, EU's employment policy; here we have seen how national decision makers come to think and talk about new employment policy problems (e.g., gender mainstreaming, raising employments rates and the inclusiveness of societal actors in labour market governance) through their involvements in the processes and activities related to the Open Method of Coordination. This in turn is seen as having real consequences for both national employments policies and governance on the area (Zeitlin, 2009).

Studying and recording articulations of perceptions of political problems over a certain time period may thus be a very manageable technique to uncover a discourse empirically. A discourse can be said to exist to the extent that it is possible to register and describe a systematic set of rules for how central problems, their sources and solutions are articulated among a set of agents. Such rules may be described in terms of whether the policy problem at hand is seen as caused by individual shortcomings or, alternatively, is considered the products of societal structures. For instance, is unemployment seen as being caused by a lack of individual motivation to find a job or perhaps rather the consequence of socio-economic structures disfavouring certain groups of individuals on the labour market? Clearly, whether the one or the other conception has the upper hand matters for policy choices (e.g., should employment policies be directed at creating incentives for individuals or rather address labour market structures?). To this we can be add perhaps that the preferred policy solutions among decision makers are more likely to frame their articulation of policy problems, rather than the other way around as suggested by Kingdon (1995). Other categories may also be useful to capture discursive rules including, for instance, conceptions of 'us/them', 'right/wrong' or more specific categories – possibly inspired by available case-specific research or analytical and theoretical frameworks. Finally, in the same manner, the study of discursive agency may, for instance, be conducted by registering 'first movers' on the use of specific policy perceptions, including the use of conceptions first articulated at the EU-level and then carried into a national context (see below).

Document analysis is probably the most used research technique to uncover continuity and change in discourse. Documents as data have the advantage of being fairly readily available through libraries, archives, databases and electronically. They are also available over long time periods (e.g., government reports, policy papers, newsletters and newspaper articles). This is helpful since both discourse analysis and Europeanization research require longitudinal studies (see Section 5). Whereas surveys repeated over a certain time period are also an option (e.g., opinion polls and Eurobarometer surveys), research interviews repeated in a comparable manner are much rarer. Finally, documents in essence produced by the actors involved in the discourse in focus are typically available. These are sometimes termed primary documents and are significant when we wish to map concepts, categories and causal relations as conceived by the involved actors.

In any case, we should seek to combine and make the most of different research techniques. Document analysis is probably the most suitable for studying the construction of discursive categories and causalities over time. Surveys may offer ways to quantify and measure the scope of such categories. Research interviews may come in handy when we wish to further qualify broader discursive constructs and supply inspiration for possible causal relations between discourse and political outcomes.

But what is the role of political discourses in Europeanization? How are discourses related to political outcomes? And, in particular, how can we proceed with the study of causality in Europeanization research? These are the issues we now turn to.

## Discursive causalities in Europeanization research

There are three types of discursive causal claims in Europeanization research. Types differ depending on (i) whether domestic discourses are seen as one among a number of explanatory variables, (ii) whether discourse is seen a strategic context or (iii) whether discourse is a strategic choice.

## Discourse as a variable

Rather than arguing 'ideas all the way down', discourses can be seen as one variable along with political-economic institutions' and actors' interests (Schmidt and Radaelli, 2004). In addition to variations in discourses among domestic elites, the scope, direction and timing of Europeanization may also vary according to different national policy legacies, preferences and vulnerability to increased global competition and domestic institutional paths (Schmidt, 2002).

Sometimes forceful discourses are considered to 'shape' actors' preferences in favour of certain policy or institutional choices. A notable example is Amandine Crespy's (2010) study of the impact of the French radical left discourse on the adoption of a critical French attitude to the EU Services (or 'Bolkestein') Directive. The critical French state preference in turn tipped the balance among EU member states and the European Parliament in favour of significant amendments to the directive, which was finally adopted in a watered-down version. Here we move towards discursive push/pull causes in the sense that discourses may be attributed with an independent and persuasive force that may affect domestic institutions and policy preferences. Hence, this perspective enables inquiries into *when* and *how* European integration discourse matters for domestic policy and institutional choices (Schmidt, 2003). It also powerfully promotes – and rightly so – a non-sectarian approach to the study of ideas and discourses by clear reference to political science and comparative politics.

Intuitively, it may seem most straightforward to take a starting point in causal claims that already ascribes certain push/pull powers to discourse in the Europeanization of domestic policies and institutions. However, we do face a number of challenges when pursuing analytical strategies encompassing both discursive and non-discursive variables. For instance, when is an empirical observation an observation of the existence of a discourse rather than a policy legacy? How do we differentiate between actors' discourses about national political-economic institutions and the material reality of countries economic vulnerability? And perhaps most fundamentally, how do we differentiate between actors' interests and discourses about actors' interest? However thoroughly and unambiguously pursued, these challenges are probably solved by neither means of conceptual definitions nor on the level of operationalization of variables (see Jupille (2006) for a very good and accessible epistemological discussion).

## Discourse as strategic context

Discourses may also be seen as making up a strategic context or a conceptual framework through which social, political and economic developments are ordered and understood at the domestic level (Hay and Smith, 2005; Smith and Hay, 2008). The study of discourse as strategic context tends to be based on causal assumptions, rather than empirical tests of causalities. It is thus assumed that there is a causal relation between discourses and political outcomes, even if it is probably not a one-dimensional and straightforward causal relation. Studies based on such causal assumptions are often empirically rich, yet the empirical eye is on uncovering discourses, rather than on the causal relation between discourse and policy outcomes. Discourses may be seen as constitutive for other types of causalities explaining domestic change, but is not attached with push/pull powers in themselves. The mapping of domestic discourses on European integration consequently becomes a research objective in itself, since the assumption is that *discourse always matters*. From this, it by no means follows that discourse on European integration is necessarily significant in bringing about domestic change. It is entirely possible that European integration issues are absent from domestic discourse at the expense of, for instance, discourse on globalization (although this may also be attached with significance and seen as a strategic choice).

## Discourse as strategic choices

Most studies relating to the Europeanization of domestic discourse, often in addition to the above, tend to see discourse as a strategic choice in itself. Focus is put on how decision makers respond to the conceived implications of European integration, as well as on how decision makers may use discourse on European integration strategically in bringing about or hindering domestic change (Hay and Rosamond, 2002; Schmidt, 2007). Decision making tends, most often implicitly, to be defined in such a way that discursive change constitutes a strategic choice. In that sense, discursive change is in itself an instance of decision making. The causality at play here seems to be one between discourse as process and discursive change as an instance. That is, developments and shifts in conceptions about the implications of European integration among a set of agents over a period of time may amount to a change in discourse at a given point in time. This line of thinking may lead to the study of the development of a policy discourse and its possible institutionalization through a gradual informal and formal sanctioning of a policy discourse (Lynggaard, 2007). Here the causal chain is:

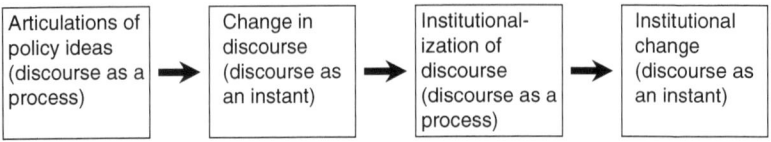

Even if this line of thinking links up ideas, discourses and institutions, the causal claims are concerned with the degree of systematic analysis and authority attached to the discourses used. In other words, causal claims are made on the ideational level(s). The challenge to this type of causal claims is whether and how we move beyond the study of discourses and tangibly engage with the study of causations between European integration and domestic policies and institutions. It may be useful to turn to the study of mechanisms focusing both on discourse as context and as strategic choice or, put slightly differently, discourse as code and as conduct.

## The study of mechanisms from a discursive institutional perspective

The point of departure of the subsequent discussion is neither *if discourse matters* in Europeanization research nor is it *when discourse matters*. Rather the question is: *how does discourse matter* in Europeanization? Essentially, how can we commence the work of specifying and giving substance to causalities in Europeanization research? For the purpose of the discussion below, we preliminarily adopt a very broad definition of causality. Causality is thus used to describe a relationship between events or situations, whether these are systematic and universal or idiosyncratic and whether causality is a theoretical claim or an empirical claim.

The identification of mechanisms aims to explain systematic relationships between observed events. In that sense, the knowledge ambition of explanatory mechanisms differs from the ambitions of establishing law-like theoretical claims, which tend to be close to universal allowing only a very few digressions. At the same time the focus on mechanisms aims at explanations of relevance across a range of comparable phenomena and thus moves beyond descriptive analysis linking a series of events in single case studies (Hedström and Swedberg, 1998).

At the heart of discursive analytical frameworks lie two mechanisms, namely (i) discursive constructs and (ii) actors' strategic use of discourse. These two basic mechanisms respectively represent more structural and more agency-based types of explanations, or discursive code and discursive conduct.

To be sure, the point of departure for any discursive analytical strategy is the existence of some sort of duality between discursive structures and agents. As summed up by Rosamond: 'Agents are bound by structures, but they are also capable through action of altering the structural environment in which they operate, albeit in way that may be structurally contained' (Rosamond, 2000: 172). This duality is commonly acknowledged. At the same time any given discursive analytical strategy may give favourable attention to the study of discursive constructs or actors' strategic use of discourse. There may very well be empirical arguments for favouring one or the other in certain fields of study. Perhaps it is fitting to uncover discursive constructs in highly institutionalized policy fields, where we must expect actors' room to manoeuvre to be particularly constrained? Perhaps it is appropriate to focus on actors' strategic use of discourse during crises, policy failures or in situations characterized by institutional contradictions? In such situations the literature generally suggests that actors have more options to change their structural context.

## Discursive code

Nonetheless, discursive constructs are most often seen as constitutive for actors' strategic actions, and there seems to be some reluctance to point to discursive constructs as causal mechanisms in their own right (Wendt, 1998). Even when discursive constructs is a central research object – including the study of policy frames, paradigms and belief systems – there is a bias towards explaining Europeanization by reference to the actions of agents. Maybe it is somehow more straightforward to point to 'who did it' and explain change in political outcome by the actions of prominent individuals or governments. There may also be more sensible reasons for the bias towards agency-based explanatory mechanisms, but here we will point up the potential of exploring more structural mechanisms. Before doing so, we will briefly consider the nature of discursive constructs.

*Table 5.1*   The study of discursive constructs

| Characteristics of discursive constructs | Research examples | Usefulness for causality research |
|---|---|---|
| Content | Implementation of tax policy reform ideas (Radaelli, 1997) National conceptions of state–European integration relations (Larsen, 1999) | Identifying conditions for Europeanization |
| Structural firmness | Conceptions at work either as background assumptions or explicated in the foreground of decision-making processes (Campbell, 2004) Beliefs which are more or less fundamental to policymakers (Dudley and Richardson, 1999; Nedergaard, 2008; Quaglia, 2010) | Identifying conditions for Europeanization |
| Interactive processes | The transformative powers of discourse (Schmidt, 2008) The translations of discourses between different social contexts (Kjær and Pedersen, 2001) | Studying causal mechanisms |

Discursive constructs have at least three characteristics, namely their content, their 'structural firmness' and the interactive process of discourses (see Table 5.1).

Both descriptive content analysis and the structural firmness of discourse are essential to studying the Europeanization of discourses. However, analysing discursive content and the structural firmness of discourses is probably more helpful in uncovering conditions for Europeanization, rather than identifying Europeanization mechanisms. The study of discursive content may reveal a 'fit' or 'misfit' between EU-level and national discourses which, in turn, may be more or less conducive to Europeanization. On the other hand, the structural firmness of discourse may tell us something about whether Europeanization is at all an option, or whether discourses among domestic actors are highly institutionalized and, thus, likely to remain in place.

It seems that it is when we engage in the study of interactive discursive processes that we move towards the study of Europeanization mechanisms. Whether interactive discursive processes give momentum to change in political outcomes appears to depend on the mixture of, on the one hand, discursive coherence and persuasion and, on the other hand, incoherence and conflict. Most authors would probably agree on this, but they vary in their emphasis.

Vivien Schmidt's *transformative power* mechanism emphasizes discursive coherence and persuasion. She suggests that interactive discursive processes are the processes through which meaning is coordinated among political elites and policy choices are communication to the public. Here the mechanism explaining variations in Europeanization is the persuasiveness of discourses, which is enhanced by discursive coherence, consistency and credibility. It is, among other things, argued that 'the credibility of a discourse is likely to benefit from consistency and coherence across policy sectors, although a modicum of vagueness or ambiguity is also to be expected' (Schmidt, 2008: 311).

Another promising mechanism for Europeanization research is *translation* (Kjær and Pedersen, 2001; Lynggaard, 2007), which puts more emphasis on discursive incoherence and conflicts. The study of processes of translation has gained some prominence in the study of how ideas travel globally (Czarniamska and Sevon, 2005), but is still largely underdeveloped for the purpose of Europeanization research. Rather than focusing on the diffusion of coherent and persuasive discourse, translation points to the more complex and selective processes through which discourses interact. Following this line of thinking, the expectation would be that EU-level discourses are probably rarely adopted in national contexts in their entirety, but rather 'bits and pieces' are selectively incorporated into existing national discourses. It may also be that EU-level discourses are 'layered' on top of exiting national discourses, possibly in a conflictual manner (see Streeck and Thelen (2005) for the comparable conception of 'institutional layering'). It is also entirely possible that ambiguous EU-level discourses may appeal to an even broader palette of decision makers and member states and, thus, contribute to Europeanization. This is still an insufficiently researched area. So for a start we should pay more attention not only to the study of discursive coherence and persuasiveness, but also to discursive incoherence and conflicts as mechanism(s) of Europeanization.

## Discursive conduct

In rational-choice accounts, the contributions of actors to Europeanization tend to be seen as happening at particular points in time. The notion of national veto players is an example of this line of thinking. The claim is that the number of veto players may explain whether Europeanization of domestic policies is likely or not: a low number of veto players increases the likeliness of domestic policies being affected by EU adaptional pressures and, by contrast, a high number of veto players favours the status quo (Börzel and Risse, 2007). We have, for instance, seen how national parliaments have decided not to ratify EU treaty amendments (e.g., The Maastricht Treaty in Denmark (1992), The Treaty establishing a Constitution for Europe in the Netherlands and France (2005) and The Treaty of Lisbon in Ireland (2008)). The actual establishment of national veto players may very well be explained by historical path-dependent developments, such as traditions of having referenda on matters that are considered to involve a transfer of state sovereignty to EU-level institutions. However, the choice of actors to veto (or not) EU-level adaptational pressure tends to be seen as an instance, rather than a process.

The social ontology of discourse analysis does not allow for one-sided explanations referring back to individual conceptions, behaviour and actions. Causal claims will be on the more structural side compared with methodological individualist starting points, regardless of whether more explanatory value is attached to discursive constructs or actors' intentional use of discourses (Jacquot and Woll, 2003). Yet, this does not mean that discourse analysis must retreat to actor-less historical accounts (Wittrock and Wagner, 1996).

Discursive actorness should rather be conceptualized as a role from where collective, but also individual, agents may exercise discursive powers and possibly contribute to Europeanization. Discursive actorness is then a role that various agents may take up simultaneously or successively. It may be useful to further explore *discursive entrepreneurship* as a Europeanization mechanism. Discursive entrepreneurship may contribute to linking up otherwise unlike discourses, involve the creation of fora for communication (e.g., public debates, hearings, conferences, etc.) as well as involve endorsements and authorizations of formerly marginalized discourse (Lynggaard, 2006). Discursive agency may also be explored further through the concepts and working of *discourse coalitions* (Hajer, 2005) and *epistemic communities* (Haas, 1992; see also Bulmer, 2007), which so far have been neglected in Europeanization research. Altogether, discursive entrepreneurship becomes an actor-in-context type of explanatory mechanism giving reason to the study of strategic actors.

## Making the most of temporal comparative analysis

The study of discursive constructs as a mechanism of Europeanization necessitates a temporal analysis of the evolvement of concepts and conceptions on the area in focus. This is also the case in the study of more agency-based mechanisms. The objective of a temporal analysis of domestic discourse is to uncover concepts and causal conceptions among a set of actors over a period of time (probably at least 10 years). The discourse(s) in focus depends first and foremost on the research question at hand. It may, for instance, involve the study of how decision makers conceive of the challenges of European integration or a more narrow focus on actors' conceptions within a policy field.

We have already seen a few large cross-country and cross-sectoral comparisons of the construction of domestic discourses and how these may affect policy and institutional choices (e.g., Schmidt and Radaelli, 2004). However, making use of discourse analysis in Europeanization research often involves single case studies (see Exadaktylos and Radaelli, Chapter 2 in this volume) among others, since cross-country and cross-sectoral studies often require larger research teams and multilinguistic resources. A comparative temporal analysis offers an opportunity to otherwise single case studies to increase the number of examples and, thus, possible comparisons. At the same time, comparative temporal analysis is certainly another option for cross-country and cross-sectoral research designs to conduct systematic comparisons of periods and events.

Having registered continuity and change through a diachronic descriptive analysis, we may thus move on to temporal comparative analysis. The increase in cases can be done essentially in two ways: (i) by characterizing periods of time and (ii) by characterizing points in time (see Figure 5.1).

A period of time may, for instance, be characterized by the institutionalization of certain conceptions of the implication of European integration among a set of domestic actors. Here Europeanization is essentially seen as a process. Yet, analytically, the point in time which marks the end of an institutionalization of a European integration discourse may also be seen as an instant of change and characterized in terms of differences before and after this point in time. Depending on

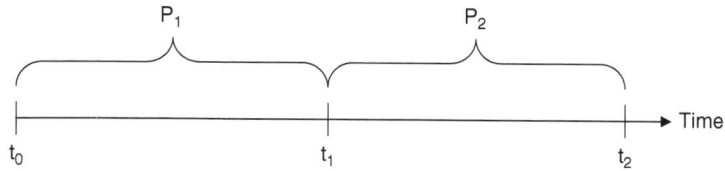

*Figure 5.1*  Temporal comparison

the number of periods (*P*) and points in time (*t*) identified, this procedure will enable us to compare a case with itself at different periods of
time and points in time. In other words, we will be able to address questions such as: What are the similarities and differences in the conditions
framing points in time characterized by change? What are the similarities and differences in periods of time characterized by change? As to the
former, our theoretical expectations include that policy failures, institutional contradictions and crises are all conducive conditions for change.
As to the latter, perhaps epistemic communities, actors' strategic use of
European integration discourses, or the diffusion or translation of ideas
may give momentum to processes of change. Regardless, a systematic
temporal analysis increases the number of cases available for comparison and does so in a way that has the advantages of the 'most-similar'
comparative research designs (see Lynggaard, 2011).

## How to conduct multi-theoretical analysis

We have already pointed to some of the challenges related to approaching discourse as one variable among other non-discursive variables.
To do that, we have to bridge different research designs. Further, after
having explored domestic discursive constructs and actors' strategic use
of discourses, we may also interpret the findings in other alternative
perspectives.

Some perspectives available for multi-theoretical analysis have already
been brought into Europeanization research. Think of the broad
institutionalist literature, the literature on state–society relations, network analysis, varieties of capitalism, party systems and so on. This
'second-order' multi-theoretical analysis raises the question of whether
and how it is possible to move from an analysis of discourses to subsequently conducting a multi-theoretical analysis including institutional
and more structural approaches.

In order to enable a multi-theoretical analysis we need to develop a
research design of relevance beyond discourse analytical frameworks.
Depending on the more specific research question at hand, this may suggest cross-country studies where countries are selected to compare, for
instance, small/large states, corporatist and pluralist political systems,
liberal market economies and coordinated market economies or dissim-
ilar electoral systems (see also Bache et al., Chapter 4 in this volume). For
instance, do domestic discourses on European integration vary between
small and large states? Are there variations in European integration discourses in corporatist and pluralist political systems? In liberal market

economies and coordinated market economies? The analytical frameworks and theoretical perspectives applied in a multi-theoretical analysis may well differ from the initial, or first-order, discourse analysis on both ontological and epistemological issues. However, for the purpose of carrying out a multi-theoretical analysis, analytical frameworks and substantive theories of relevance for the subject matter may be approached as discourses in their own right. Some might find this solution controversial. Yet, this approach allows for a comparison of discourses as articulated by actors involved in the empirical field and 'academic discourses' – all with the purpose of theoretical cross-fertilization and commencing a more comprehensive understanding of the respective implications of European integration within EU member states.

## References

Bacchi, C. (2009) *Analysing Policy: What's the Problem Represented To Be?* (Frenchs Forest, NSW: Pearson).

Blyth, M. (2010) On Setting and Upsetting Agendas: Blyth on Gofas and Hay, Tønder, and Seabrooke, in A. Gofas and C. Hay (eds) *The Role of Ideas in Political Analysis: A Portrait of Contemporary Debates* (London: Routledge), pp. 167–186.

Börzel, T. and T. Risse (2007) Europeanization: The Domestic Impact of European Union Politics, in K.E. Jørgensen, M.A. Pollack and B. Rosamond (eds) *Handbook of European Union Politics* (London: Sage Publications Ltd.), pp. 483–504.

Bulmer, S. (2007) Theorizing Europeanization, in P. Graziano and M. Vink (eds) *Europeanization: New Research Agendas* (Basingstoke: Palgrave Macmillan), pp. 46–58.

Campbell, J.L. (2004) *Institutionel forandring og globalisering* (Copenhagen: Adademisk Forlag).

Crespy, A. (2010) When 'Bolkestein' is Trapped by the French Anti-liberal Discourse: A Discursive-institutionalist Account of Preference Formation in the Realm of European Union Multi-level Politics, *Journal of European Public Policy*, Vol. 17, No. 8, pp. 1253–1270.

Czarniamska, B. and G. Sevon (eds) (2005) *Global Ideas: How Ideas, Objects and Practices Travel in the Global Economy* (Copenhagen: Copenhagen Business School).

Dudley, G. and J. Richardson (1999) Competing Advocacy Coalitions and the Process of 'Frame Reflection': A Longitudinal Analysis of EU Steel Policy, *Journal of European Public Policy*, Vol. 6, No. 2, pp. 225–248.

Dyson, K. (2000) EMU as Europeanization: Convergence, Diversity and Contingency, *Journal of Common Market Studies*, Vol. 38, No. 4, pp. 645–666.

Gillespie, P. and B. Laffan (2006) European Identity: Theory and Empirics, in M. Cini and A.K. Bourne (eds) *European Union Studies* (Basingstoke: Palgrave Macmillan), pp. 131–150.

Gofas, A. and C. Hay (2010) Varieties of Ideational Explanations, in A. Gofas and C. Hay (eds) *The Role of Ideas in Political Analysis: A Portrait of Contemporary Debates* (London: Routledge), pp. 13–55.

Goldstein, J. and R.O. Keohane (1993) *Ideas and Foreign Policy: Beliefs, Institutions, and Political Change* (Cornell: Cornell University Press).

Haas, P.M. (1992) Introduction: Epistemic Communities and International Policy Coordination, *International Organization*, Vol. 46, No. 1, pp. 1–35.

Hajer, M.A. (1995) *The Politics of Environmental Discourse: Ecological Modernisation and the Policy Process* (Oxford: Clarendon Press).

Hajer, M.A. (2005) Coalitions, Practices, and Meaning in Environmental Politics: From Acid Rain to BSE, in D. Howarth and J. Torfing (eds) *Discourse Theory in European Politics: Identity, Policy and Governance* (Basingstoke: Palgrave Macmillan), pp. 297–315.

Hall, P.A. (1993) Policy Paradigms, Social Learning, and the State: The Case of Economic Policymaking in Britain, *Comparative Politics*, Vol. 25, No. 3, pp. 275–296.

Hay, C. and Rosamond, B. (2002) Globalization, European Integration and the Discursive Construction of Economic Imperatives, *Journal of European Public Policy*, Vol. 9, No. 2, pp. 147–167.

Hay, C. and Smith, N. (2005) Horses for Courses: The Political Discourse of Globalisation and European Integration in the UK and Ireland, *West European Politics*, Vol. 28, No. 1, pp. 124–158.

Hedström, P. and R. Swedberg (1998) Social Mechanisms: An Introductory Essay, in P. Hedström and R. Swedberg (eds) *Social Mechanisms* (Cambridge: Cambridge University Press), pp. 1–31.

Herrera, Y.M. and B.F. Braumoeller (eds) (2004) Symposium: Discourse and Content Analysis, *Qualitative Methods*, Vol. 2, No. 1, pp. 15–39.

Howarth, D. and J. Torfing (eds) (2005) *Discourse Theory in European Politics. Identity, Policy and Governance* (Basingstoke: Palgrave Macmillan).

Jacquot, S. and C. Woll (2003) Usage of European Integration: Europeanisation from a Sociological Perspective, *European Integration online Papers (EIoP)*, Vol. 7, No. 12, http://eiop.or.at/eiop/texte/2003-012a.htm

Jones, M.D. and M.K. McBeth (2010) A Narrative Policy Framework: Clear Enough to Be Wrong, *Policy Studies Journal*, Vol. 38, No. 2, pp. 329–353.

Jupille, J. (2006) Knowing Europe: Metatheory and Methodology in European Union Studies, in M. Cini and A.K. Bourne (eds) *European Union Studies* (Basingstoke: Palgrave Macmillan), pp. 209–232.

Kingdon, J.W. (1995 [1984]) *Agendas, Alternatives and Public Policies* (New York: Harper Collins College Publisher).

Kjær, P. and O.K. Pedersen (2001) Translating Liberalization: Neoliberalism in the Danish Negotiated Economy, in J.L. Campbell and O.K. Pedersen (eds) *The Rise of Neoliberalism and Institutional Analysis* (Princeton, NJ: Princeton University Press), pp. 219–248.

Kurki, M. (2006) Causes of a Divided Discipline: Rethinking the Concept of Cause in International Relation Theory, *Review of International Studies*, Vol. 32, pp. 189–216.

Laffan, B. (2004) The European Union and its Institutions as 'Identity Builders', in R.K. Hermann, T. Risse and M.B. Brewer (eds) *Transnational Identities: Becoming European in the EU* (Lanham, MD: Rowman & Littlefield Publishers), pp. 75–96.

Larsen, H. (1999) British and Danish European Policies in the 1990s: A Discourse Approach, *European Journal of International Relations*, Vol. 5, No. 4, pp. 451–483.

Lynggaard, K. (2006) *The Common Agricultural Policy and Organic Farming: An Institutional Perspective on Continuity and Change* (Wallingford: CAB International).

Lynggaard, K. (2007) The Institutional Construction of a Policy Field: A Discursive Institutional Perspective on Change within the Common Agricultural Policy, *Journal of European Public Policy*, Vol. 14, No. 2, pp. 295–314.

Lynggaard, K. (2011) Domestic Change in the Face of European Integration and Globalization: Methodological Pitfalls and Pathways, *Comparative European Politics*, Vol. 9, No. 1, pp. 18–37.

Mehta, J. (2011) The Varied Roles of Ideas in Politics: From 'Whether' to 'How', in D. Béland and R.H. Cox (eds) *Ideas and Politics in Social Science Research* (Oxford: Oxford University Press), pp. 23–46.

Nedergaard, P. (2008) The Reform of the 2003 Common Agricultural Policy: An Advocacy Coalition Explanation, *Policy Studies*, Vol. 29, No. 2, pp. 179–195.

Patterson, M. and K.R. Monroe (1998) Narrative in Political Science, *Annual Review of Political Science*, Vol. 1, pp. 315–331.

Quaglia, L. (2010) Completing the Single Market in Financial Services: The Politics of Competing Advocacy Coalitions, *Journal of European Public Policy*, Vol. 17, No. 7, pp. 1007–1023.

Radaelli, C. (1997) How does Europeanization Produce Domestic Policy Change?: Corporate Tax Policy in Italy and the United Kingdom, *Comparative Political Studies*, Vol. 30, No. 5, pp. 553–575.

Radaelli, C.M. and R. Pasquier (2006) Encounters with Europe: Concepts, Definitions, and Research Design, *Tidsskriftet Politik*, Vol. 9, No. 3, pp. 6–14.

Risse, T., D. Engelmann-Martin, H. Knope and K. Roscher (1999) To Euro or Not to Euro?: The and Identity Politics in the European Union, *European Journal of International Relations*, Vol. 5, No. 2, pp. 147–187.

Risse, T. and M.L. Maier (2003) *Europeanization, Collective Identities and Public Discourses* (Florence: Robert Schuman Centre for Advanced Studies).

Rosamond, B. (2000) *Theories of European Integration* (Houndmills: MacMillan Press Ltd.).

Sabatier, P. (1998) The Advocacy Coalition Framework: Revisions and Relevance for Europe, *Journal of European Public Policy*, Vol. 5, No. 1, pp. 98–130.

Schmidt, V. (2002) Europeanization and the Mechanisms of Economic Policy Adjustment, *Journal of European Public Policy*, Vol. 9, No. 6, pp. 894–912.

Schmidt, V. (2003) How, Where, and When Does Discourse Matter in Small States' Welfare Adjustment, *New Political Economy*, Vol. 8, No. 1, pp. 127–146.

Schmidt, V. (2007) Trapped by Their Ideas: French Élites' Discourses of European Integration and Globalization, *Journal of European Public Policy*, Vol. 14, No. 7, pp. 992–1009.

Schmidt, V. (2008) Discursive Institutionalism: The Explanatory Power of Ideas and Discourse, *Annual Review of Political Science*, Vol. 11, pp. 303–326.

Schmidt, V. and C.M. Radaelli (2004) Policy Change and Discourse in Europe, *West European Politics*, Special Issue, Vol. 27, No. 2, pp. 183–210.

Smith, N. and C. Hay (2008) Mapping the Political Discourse of Globalisation and European Integration in the United Kingdom and Ireland Empirically, *European Journal of Political Research*, Vol. 47, No. 3, pp. 359–382.

Streeck, W. and K. Thelen (2005) *Beyond Continuity: Institutional Change in Advanced Political Economies* (Oxford: Oxford University Press)

Wendt, A. (1998) On Constitution and Causation in International Relations, *Review of International Studies*, Vol. 24, pp. 101–118.

Wittrock, B. and P. Wagner (1996) Social Science and the Building of the Early Welfare State, in T. Skocpol and D. Rueschemeyer (eds) *States, Social Knowledge, and the Origins of Modern Social Policies* (Princeton, NJ: Princeton University Press), pp. 90–113.

Yanow, D. (2006) Thinking Interpretatively: Philosophical Presuppositions and the Human Sciences, in D. Yanow and P. Schwartz-Shea (eds) *Interpretation and Method: Empirical Research Methods and the Interpretative Turn* (London: M.E. Sharpe), pp. 5–26.

Zeitlin, J. (2009) The Open Method of Coordination and Reform of National Social and Employment Policies: Influences, Mechanisms, Effects, in M. Heidenreich and J. Zeitlin (eds) *Changing European Employment and Welfare Regimes: The Influence of the Open Method of Coordination on National Reforms* (London/New York: Routledge), pp. 214–245.

# 6

# Beyond Non-Compliance with Legal Norms

*Sabine Saurugger*

## Introduction

As Chapter 1 has shown, research on Europeanization is about explaining change – change in actor's attitudes, public policies and institutions. But what about lack of change? What does the Europeanization framework say when no change occurs? This classical question in politics (Bachrach and Baratz, 1963) has been addressed by an increasingly important number of studies under the heading of non-compliance with European Union (EU) law. While both sides of Europeanization – change as well as non-change – present their own research design challenges, work on non-change suffers from its excessive concentration on the topic of non-compliance with EU law (see also Bache and Taylor, 2003).

In this chapter we go beyond non-compliance research focusing on EU law. The influence of European integration and the resistance to the change it triggers refer not only to legally binding norms such as directives, regulations or decisions. Programmes, 'new modes of governance' or soft law more generally equally influence the national level and often trigger resistance. Thus, we call for a wider research agenda beyond legal norms controlled by a jurisdiction. Our argument is that the influence of European integration at the domestic level is based not only on the existence of 'hard law'. Facilitated coordination (Bulmer and Radaelli, 2005), based on instruments such as new (and old) public management tools – programmes, declarations, benchmarking, peer review exercises or financial incentives, influences the national level and may equally trigger inertia and retrenchment. Actors mobilize tools and mechanisms in order to circumvent or oppose European decisions, programmes and discourses or to slow down their implementation. To explain resistance, one has to combine a structural approach with an actor-centred approach that underlines the room for manoeuvre of agents active in the domestic realm. Change as well as non-change is 'the result of inter-action among agents who dispose of room for manoeuvre and more general mechanisms which impose a more or less clear-cut cognitive framework' (Muller, 2005: 164).

Beyond this, current work on research design in Europeanization research has not much to say. True, the classic approach to compliance with EU law poses its own causality problems (Hartlapp and Falkner, 2009), and provides a starting point for going 'beyond compliance with law'. However, the scope of this chapter is wider and we need to enter uncharted territory. We will first present an overview of the main results in non-compliance research – the branch of the literature mostly inter-ested in attitudes of inertia or retrenchment. In a second step, the chapter will discuss the limitations, concerning both the concept of causality used (see Töller, Chapter 3 in this volume) as well as the lim-ited object of research. We will then turn to our proposals, drawing on the literature on policy instruments.

## Analysing inertia and retrenchment in non-compliance studies

From the outset, studies of both compliance and non-compliance have been concerned with the issue of convergence between EU laws and their implementation at the national level. European directives and reg-ulations were initially considered to be relatively apolitical, and the effectiveness of implementation was addressed in terms of the efficiency and capacity of national administrations: the quicker the legislative procedures, the more efficient the implementation of EU law.

After a first group of studies insisting, more or less implicitly, on convergence between different European national systems through European law, Europeanization turned to the explanation of *differen-tiated* implementation of EU law (for an overview of this research, see Falkner et al., 2005: 14–17; Treib, 2008). The differentiated degree of implementation became a dependent variable to be explained by both institutional configurations and intermediating or facilitating fac-tors (Börzel, 2001; Börzel and Risse, 2000; Duina, 1997; Risse et al., 2001). In this framework, studies submit that the degree of implemen-tation depends on the fit between national political structures and the European model(s). The more these structures (understood as histori-cal institutional, economic, social, ideological or cultural mechanisms providing order) are similar to those existing at the national level, the more adaptation will be facilitated at this level. However, the more important the differences between these two levels, the more the non-convergence hypothesis applies. The literature has now identified four possible outcomes: absorption, transformation, retrenchment and inertia (Börzel, 1999; Héritier and Knill, 2001; Héritier et al., 2001; Risse et al., 2001). While absorption and transformation describe degrees of policy change, retrenchment and inertia refer to non-change. Inertia thus refers to a lack of change. Here, European norms do not trigger any transformation at the national level. The forms inertia takes can be multiple, such as lags, delays in the transposition of directives (Radaelli, 2003) or explicit forms of resistance such as strikes, social movements or direct activism. The sustainability of inertia as a long-term strategy is, however, problematic (Olsen, 1996). Long-term resistance may lead to a crisis, and thus usher in radical change. Another possibility might be an ad hoc arrangement of the system, allowing for opting-out strategies with which the EU has long experiences (social charter, EMU, Schengen).

The other form of resistance – retrenchment – has been an active transformation process right from the start (Héritier, 2001; Héritier and Knill, 2001). Radaelli calls this form a paradox insofar as domestic policies become less European than they were initially (Radaelli, 2003). Here, opposition to European decisions allows for the creation at the domestic level of coalitions that impose reforms going in the opposite direction to those decided at the EU level. Research on inertia and retrenchment is now associated with the literature on compliance or non-compliance with EU law.[1] These studies base their hypothesis on one or, more often, a combination of three identified compliance approaches in international relations (for an extensive discussion of these approaches, see Börzel et al., 2007; Raustiala and Slaughter, 2002; Tallberg, 2002): constructivist, enforcement and management approaches.

The constructivist approach relies on the concept of the logic of appropriateness to explain compliance. The logic of appropriateness refers to the fact that actors not only choose their attitudes and strategies according to an abstract economic rationality of maximizing ones own interest, but mostly according to a complex cultural and value-based context in which the individual evolves. In the context of Europeanization research this means that member states comply with the European legal frame because, in complying, they value the commitments they have taken when joining the EU. Through a socialization process, EU member states have thus interiorized the rules. Börzel et al. (2007) use two specific elements of this approach: the domestic culture of law abidingness and the support for the EU as the rule-setting institution (for an illustration, see Panke, 2007).

Enforcement approaches argue instead that the strategic choice of the actors is based on a cost–benefit analysis of alternative behavioural choices when making compliance decisions. In other words, implementation of EU law at the domestic level occurs only if the costs of non-compliance are higher than those of compliance. Costs of non-compliance increase if effective control and sanction mechanisms are in place (for reviews, see Börzel et al., 2007; Tallberg, 2002).

Management approaches, finally, assume that non-compliance occurs if administrative capacity is insufficient and/or if legal norms are ambiguous. We distinguish between political capacities, where the government has the option to implement decisions even against opposition from public and private actors, and economic capacities referring to financial resources that the administration and the state has at its disposal. In order to increase the degree of compliance, capacity building, both politically and economically, is necessary.

The bulk of non-compliance studies, either explicitly or implicitly based on one or more of these assumptions, is anchored in either qualitative case study research (to quote but a few, Falkner et al., 2005, 2007; Falkner and Treib, 2008; Hartlapp and Falkner, 2009; Panke, Chapter 7 in this volume) based on either mixed methods (Kaeding, 2008; Toshkov, 2010) or quantitative research design (Börzel et al., 2007; König and Luetgert, 2009; Mastenbroek, 2005, again to quote but a few[2]).

In such studies, directives are used as a starting point since, contrary to regulations, these allow for the construction of a more or less robust causality. According to the majority of studies, concentrating on directives (either in the form of a database based on CELEX/EURLEX entries or on data based on the Commission database on infringement procedures) allows for observation of difficulties in implementing, or on the contrary the smooth transposition of, EU laws, as they must be incorporated into national law. Regulations, on the contrary, are directly applicable at the national level and therefore don't offer a basis of observation in regard to compliance processes.

However, the theoretical insights of these studies, both qualitative and quantitative, have been called 'inconclusive' or patchy' by some observers due to the different weight of some of the independent variables selected (Töller, 2010, and this volume; Toshkov, 2010; Treib, 2008). Based on the comparative analysis of quantitative research undertaken in this field, Toshkov (2010) offers a comprehensive typology of variables affecting non-compliance.[3] He distinguishes between variables (across different research projects) that positively affect compliance: administrative efficiency, parliamentary scrutiny and coordination strength; and variables that exert a negative (or non-positive) influence: centralized/decentralized decision making, corruption levels, veto players (both public and private), the number of relevant actors involved and domestic conflict.

Eight variables are considered significant by only some of the studies and not consistently by all: interest representation systems (corporatism, pluralism, statism), political constraints, type of government and number of parties in government, bargaining power, country disagreement with a directive, EU-level conflict, discretions and directive voting rules. Toshkov (2010) acknowledges the fact that not all quantitative studies analysed in his research concentrate on a representative sample of directives. Some have chosen only one public policy field or a limited number of countries, which might account for important variation (see also Töller, Chapter 3 in this volume). In general, though, the combination of management and enforcement hypothesis is consistent with the results found by Börzel and her colleagues (2007). According to their preliminary conclusion, '[t]he combination of managerial dialogue, capacity building, and penalties addresses the two major sources of non-compliance identified in our study' (Börzel et al., 2007: 24). In addition to Toshkov's findings of the most relevant variables (Table 6.1), the differentiation of actors' attitudes in active and passive inertia (Falkner et al., 2005) (Table 6.2), as I call it, is a pertinent conceptualization of non-compliance with EU law.

In insisting on agency embedded in structure, the differentiation might however allow progressing beyond non-compliance with EU law and analysing how actors react to 'facilitated coordination' and what variables account for these reactions.

*Table 6.1*  Variables influencing the degree of compliance

| Positive effect | Negative effect |
| --- | --- |
| Administrative efficiency | Centralized/decentralized decision making |
| Parliamentary scrutiny | Corruption levels |
| Coordination strength | Veto players (both public and private) |
|  | Number of relevant actors involved |
|  | Domestic conflict |

*Source*: Based on Toshkov (2010).

*Table 6.2*   Active and passive inertia

| Active inertia | Passive inertia |
| --- | --- |
| Opposition to specific contents<br>Opposition to EU decision mode<br>Opposition to national decision or<br>  transposition mode | Different interpretation<br>Administrative problems<br>Political instability |
| • parliaments, regions, interest groups or<br>  social movements<br>• inter- or intra-ministerial conflicts | |

*Source*: Adapted from Falkner et al. (2005: 13).

## Beyond compliance with legal norms

One of the most surprising results derived from non-compliance research is the consensus that the degree of politicization does not play a significant role in inertia or resistance to European integration. Both qualitative and quantitative studies agree that the degree of initial opposition to a normative proposal of the European Commission has only limited impact on the so-called downstream phase of adaptation at the national level.

This is in contradiction to the intergovernmentalist hypothesis according to which governments, supported by the relevant national societal actors, will try to resist the implementation process (downloading) if they were unsuccessful in making their voice heard during the policymaking process at the EU level (uploading). On the contrary, in cases where no national opposition during decision making at the EU level exists, implementation should not be problematic. This general hypothesis can be linked, according to Falkner et al. (2005), to Tsebelis' (1995) veto player argument, according to which the reform capacity of a political system decreases as the number of distinct actors whose argument is required to pass the reform increases. Thus non-compliance becomes deliberate opposition 'through the backdoor': those governments that either had not wanted a directive and therefore do not implement correctly, or that try to protect older national patterns without having shown opposition prior to decision making, also refuse to implement the European norm.

Although concerned only with a limited sample of social policy directives, Falkner and her colleagues argue that this hypothesis has no foundation. While this might be true in the context of social policy given the fact that social partners have, in a majority of member states except the UK, Hungary and Estonia, a long-standing partnership with the government, it is worth questioning this conclusion in other policy areas. In some fields, administration as well as interest groups may either oppose the norm before adoption at the European level or put it into jeopardy during implementation – either at the national or the local level. In other areas, a European decision or even idea (the so-called neo-liberal paradigm) may trigger the generation of interest groups or other veto players at the national level. Empirical evidence, such as the debate surrounding the Bolkestein directive, the Constitutional Treaty and the two negative national referenda, as well as the recent debate on minority rights in the EU, seems to contradict the apolitical hypothesis (Crespy and Verschueren, 2009; Grossman and Woll, 2011).

Whilst this body of work has reached a high theoretical level of sophistication, albeit with more limited cumulativeness (see Töller, 2010; Treib, 2008), it has concentrated exclusively on the implementation and transposition of EU law. However, if we consider European integration as a process that reaches beyond a simple legal integration, but also includes soft law embedded in governance instruments such as programmes, statistics, declarations or discourses (see Lynggaard, Chapter 5 this volume), it is very difficult empirically to understand how the influence of European integration can be understood solely as compliance with directives, regulations and decisions. If we take Radaelli's definition (2001, 2003) of Europeanization seriously, as a 'processes of (a) construction (b) diffusion and (c) institutionalization of formal and informal rules, procedures, policy paradigms, styles, "ways of doing things" and shared beliefs and norms which are first defined and consolidated in the making of EU public policy and politics and then incorporated in the logic of domestic discourse, identities, political structures and public policies' (Radaelli, 2001), to understand inertia and retrenchment one has to address dependent variables other than the degree of implementation of EU 'hard law'. The objects of research must include what Simon Bulmer and Claudio Radaelli (2005) call the fourth pattern of governance: facilitated coordination, so-called 'new' as well as old modes of governance and voluntary approaches to regulation (Töller, 2011). This pattern includes rules of conduct that are not legally enforceable. In this particular pattern, European institutions possess coercive powers other than the compulsory jurisdictional control by the European Court of Justice.

Emerging in the mid-1990s, recommendations, benchmarking, best practices, peer review or indeed EU mainstreaming gave rise to a body of literature on 'new forms of governance'. Numerous publications emphasized the flexible nature of these processes which are based on the desire of participants to agree, through collective deliberation, on procedural norms, forms of regulation and shared political objectives, whilst preserving a diversity of solutions and local measures (Bruno et al., 2006). The objective of these forms of governance is not to create legally binding norms with which all member states must comply, but to allow governments to maintain their national specificities whilst ensuring they remain compatible with the political and economic priorities of the EU. Thus, the emphasis is not on regulations and directives, but on the use of 'soft law'. It is not legally binding and requires only voluntary acceptance. The 'new forms of governance' are negotiated between public and private actors at different levels of the decision-making process, whilst actual political choice is left to the member states (Jordan and Schout, 2006).

Initially focused on the open method of coordination introduced by the Lisbon Strategy for employment (Borrás and Conzelmann, 2007; Borrás and Jacobsson, 2004; Dehousse, 2004; Goetschy, 2003), evaluated at mid-term (2005) and reformed in 2010, these projects highlighted voluntary agreements, standards, labels and diversified financial and fiscal incentive measures. The scope was broadened to include major economic policy guidelines, employment policy guidelines and objectives in other political domains. However, norms developed in this way are not directly applicable or transposable into domestic law. The national authorities agree to take them into account when forming their own policies. This form of governance enables coordination whilst limiting delegation of regulatory power to the Commission, and is not subject to review by the European Court of Justice. Furthermore, it seeks to avoid the conflict of preferences about economic governance. In other words, these modes of governance were aimed to reduce the regulatory burden on government and business by limiting the legislative output from Brussels. The impact assessment procedure shows that these regulatory innovations are important because they create their own windows of opportunity for agents to intervene and to set policy and organizational agendas (Radaelli and Meuwese, 2010).

Critical observers have drawn attention to the ancient nature of supposedly new forms of governance (Borrás and Greve, 2004). However, this body of research enables us to understand the reconstructions of the European political space, questioning the assumption that the main motivation of EU actors is concerned with the production and reformulation of law (Dehousse, 2004). The open method of coordination is a case in point. It is partially inspired by procedures of new public management. These refer to 'hands-on professional management', explicit performance standards, output controls, incentivization, competition and contractualization (Dunleavy, 2006; Hood, 1991; Lodge and Gill, 2011). Instruments developed via the open method are not legally binding. This is not the only case of soft law approaches. Several policy areas such as environmental policy, based on programmes as well as public and private partnerships (Halpern, 2010; Holzinger et al., 2006; Jordan et al., 2003), regional policy (Bache, 2010), or security (Balzacq, 2008) or foreign and defense policy (Menon and Sedelmeier, 2010) have equally developed soft law policy tools, often without the perimeter of the open method.

Resistance, retrenchment or inertia towards soft law instruments are however tricky research objects. Now, as Lynggaard underlines in Chapter 5 in this volume, neither discourse analysis nor new modes of governance are generally associated with the aim of producing clear-cut causal knowledge. What kind of causality can be established in the analysis of inertia or retrenchment attitudes towards rules that are not legally enforceable?

This is a complex question even within the traditional research on compliance. Hartlapp and Falkner (2009) show that it is difficult to pin down precise measures of timeliness and correctness of implementation. Timeliness means meeting the transposition of a directive. However, how do we know that government behaves in the way it should? As for correctness, a directive can be perfectly transposed into national legislation, but this does not necessarily lead to efficient implementation (Mastenbroek, 2005; Versluis, 2007). For example, the Bathing Water Directive calling for cleaner beaches was implemented very differently by EC member states. The British government declared that beaches with fewer than 500 people per mile did not fall under the purview of the directive. Thus, only 27 British beaches, as opposed to 8000 in the rest of the European Community, needed to comply with the Directive. Other member states decided either to ignore measures after rainfall or on different periodicities (Richardson, 1996). Versluis (2007) and Falkner et al. (2005) come to a similar conclusion when they state that the majority of technical questions in regard to implementation and enforcement such as safety are not on top of everyone's list of things to do and not very much attention is paid to them (Versluis, 2007: 58). But while Versluis considers this a consequence of weak issue salience, Falkner et al. interpret this as a lack of administrative resources. Another way of looking at this is to see it as an administrative strategy.

If we analyse inertia and retrenchment not only with regard to legal norms but also to programmes, declarations, benchmarks, peer reviews, assessment exercises or mainstreamed statistical tools more generally, the administration of causal proof becomes even more complex. However, if we succeed then the findings may allow us to go beyond the purely legal aspect of resistance to European integration that we find in contemporary compliance research and, beyond the literature on Euroscepticism which rarely takes public policies into account (Hooghe and Marks, 2009; Szczerbiak and Taggert, 2008; for an exception see Crespy and Verschueren, 2009). This chapter argues that the way to solve this problem is to link the ideas, values and debates present in the new modes of governance to debates focusing on instruments of governance, such as programmes and statistics. The analysis of the use of these instruments made by agents allows us to explain actors' motivation and outcomes. An analysis of non-compliance with non-legal norms thus goes beyond the study of transposition and looks inside the process of implementation. Implementation of European-level objectives involves national agencies and bureaucracies. It is here where inertia and retrenchments attitudes must be analysed.

## Analysing inertia and retrenchment beyond non-compliance with legal norms

How can attitudes of inertia, retrenchment or resistance towards soft law be efficiently analysed? One of the most promising research design moves, we submit, is to consider the instruments that allow for implementation of soft law. To analyse inertia and retrenchment towards EU modes of governance at the domestic level, it is necessary to understand the vectors of this influence as well as their direction and nature. Recent reflections on public policy instruments reopened a pertinent avenue of investigation in this area (Hood, 1986; Lascoumes and Le Galès, 2007; Kassim and Le Galès, 2010; Linder and Peters, 1989).

An instrument is a 'device that is both technical and social, that organizes specific social relations between the state and those it is addressed to, according to the representatives and meanings it carries. It is a particular type of institution, a technical device with the generic purpose of carrying a concrete concept of politics/society relationship and is sustained by a concept of regulation' (Lascoumes and Le Galès, 2007: 4). Instruments are not 'axiologically neutral and indifferently available tools. They are, on the contrary, sponsors of values, fed by an interpretation of social issues and specific conceptions of the form of regulation envisaged' (Lascoumes and Le Galès, 2007: 13). Thus instruments are not only tools to solve problems, although they are also that. The understanding of policy instruments, here, is based on the underlying power structures and struggles that allow for their emergence as well as their impact. Instruments are re-conceptualized as institutions that need to be brought into existence, and are therefore not readily available objects (Kassim and Le Galès, 2010: 4). Instruments are thus institutions that constrain and enable agents, privileging certain actors and interests over others.

In the field of 'new public policy instruments' (i.e., explicitly those that are not linked to the authority of legal norms), three types of instruments can be distinguished: (i) *agreement/incentive-based*, (ii) *information/communication-based* and (iii) *de facto and de jure standards/best practices* such as benchmarking and mainstreaming. These instruments represent less interventionist forms of public regulations and allow for governance by contract.

At the same time, instruments must not be considered as a materialization of an initial idea that is refined and ready to use, but as an often chaotic dynamic of adjustments and a result of power games among different agents. And, in this sense, instruments can be understood as institutions that structure public and political actions, just like the behaviour of actors, also based on thought frameworks or cognitive and normative matrices. This suggests that instruments are not just problem-solving tools. Their detailed analysis, in particular resistance and retrenchment attitudes vis-à-vis these instruments, allows for the explanation of power and legitimacy manoeuvres at the domestic level.

In the context of the new governance instruments in the EU, as shown above, the Commission in particular has developed new ways to circumvent the traditional obstacles of national vetoes or parliamentary rejection of their proposals (Héritier, 1999). These instruments were presented as more legitimate and democratic, as they allowed for the inclusion of representatives of the so-called 'civil society' in the debate and, subsequently, the decision-making process. The aim is in including the civil society, but also companies or domestic-level bureaucracy or the national level more generally, to keep resistance, retrenchment or inertia attitudes to a minimum. This assumption, however widespread, is still in search of systematic empirical analysis.

The conceptualization offered by the public policy instruments literature allows for studying the effects of these new modes of governance at the domestic level in taking the two central aims of this chapter into account: first, understanding Europeanization as a dynamic process, which certainly can be conceptualized as uploading and downloading processes but whose feedback loops make it difficult to think in exclusive terms (see also Mörth, 2003), and second, pushing the analysis beyond the object of legal integration.

In our understanding, instruments become the vectors of Europeanization. The study of inertia and retrenchment at the national level needs therefore to include both the analysis of the emergence of a specific instrument at the EU level (in which it is the dependent variable) and the degree of acceptance of this instrument at the domestic level (in which the instrument becomes the independent variable), which is certainly the most problematic aspect of Europeanization studies. In this context, the analysis of the implementation process allows for a detailed understanding of the mechanisms used to resist and circumvent soft law instruments developed at the EU level (see also Rose, 1988; Zahariadis, 2008). This method should lead us away from broad cross-country generalizations, making comparisons across programmes and within policy sectors a more nuanced exercise.

While we start from the assumption that there is no particular difference in modes of resistance or inertia with regard to the above-mentioned three types of instrument, three groups of variables are of particular importance:

- overall assumptions on how soft law instruments influence policies and agents at the domestic level;
- typology of the degree and forms of resistance and inertia;
- agents of resistance.

## Overall assumptions

Given that the norms analysed in this context do not foresee compulsory judicial control, three general assumptions are possible:

A1: Due to the non-binding character of instruments inertia or retrenchment, resistance attitudes occur constantly as no judicial sanctions can be expected in case of non-compliance. The non-binding character of 'new public policy instruments' allows for the development of particularly innovative ways of inertia or retrenchment because actors are free to play with non-binding instruments. However, in situations of asymmetric interdependence, which characterize non-judicial pressures, strategies of resistance to prevent change are more likely to be characterized by low-level forms of resistance than overt opposition (Bache and Taylor, 2003: 298). Outward agreement and cooperation disguises strategies of resistance, inertia and retrenchment.

A2: Governments, as well as European institutions, produce a shadow of hierarchy by threatening to introduce legally binding regulations if actors do not comply with voluntary or soft instruments. This assumption illustrates the complex relationship existing between voluntary regulations and statutory regulations, a relationship which is not exclusive, but most often combined (Töller, 2011).

A3: 'New public policy instruments' trigger more coherence between EU member states because the main mechanism of Europeanization is learning. This assumption, shared by a number of official Commission documents, sees in different forms of learning – learning by socialization, learning by monitoring, learning by arguing and persuasion (Radaelli, 2008) – a way of reorienting initial policy paradigms and positions. While learning might mean different things, such as coherence in policy aims or policy strategies, it follows that resistance or inertia, if occurring, would be extremely limited.

The question now is how to analyse these three assumptions given that our understanding of Europeanization is a dynamic one. This chapter argues that analysis of this question is possible by starting from the variables identified by legal non-compliance research:

- number of actors;
- administrative resources (efficiency, coordination strength...);
- institutional framework (centralized/decentralized decision making, veto players);
- dispositions (perception of policy goals by actors).

More specific hypotheses can be formulated on this basis.

H1: The greater the number of actors involved, the higher the probability that resistance attitudes appear. More actors add more complexity to the process of implementation, and thus open up a greater number of veto points. The greater the number of agencies, non-state actors and administrative services involved, the more complex the definition of what form the implementation process should take, and the greater the possibilities of resistance, inertia or retrenchment attitudes (Tsebelis, 1995).

H2: The greater the resources of an administration the greater their capacity to resist and circumvent non-legal instruments in an innovative manner. This is a counterfactual hypothesis to the arguments developed by legal compliance research arguing that missing resources are one of the main factors of non-compliance. It is argued here that resistance, inertia and retrenchment attitudes with regard to non-legal instruments represent an active decision made by domestic administrations who have the option to structure their goals hierarchically. Thus deciding not to implement an instrument can be seen as inertia, resistance or retrenchment.

H3: The higher the complexity of coordination structures, as well as their fragmentation, the greater the probability that resistance attitudes emerge. Clear, hierarchically organized coordination structures should decrease the options for veto players to intervene and slow down or stop the implementation process. A regulatory patchwork (Héritier, 1999), on the contrary, increases access points for veto players and therefore reinforces the probability of resistance attitudes.

H4: Dispositions refer to 'what implementers perceive is the programmatic impact on agency or personal goals' (Zahariadis, 2008: 225). The greater the perceived distance between the instruments' goal and the agency's goal, the greater the resistance to the implementation of these instruments and programmes. Thus the propensity to implement or even use the instrument that diverges substantially from those enshrined in organizational goals is rather low.

The effects that non-legally binding public policy instruments have at the domestic level, however, are influenced by an intervening variable, which is timing (Figure 6.1). Timing refers to the domestic political agenda (such as elections) as well as debates occupying the international political agenda (United Nations conferences on issues such as the environment, human rights or international political crises such as wars, environmental catastrophes, etc.).

### Degree and forms of resistance and inertia

While non-compliance research in regard to legal norms differentiates two types of resistance – active and passive – this chapter argues, on the contrary, that the active and passive forms cannot be clearly distinguished. Rather the three types – resistance, inertia and retrenchment – must be placed on a continuum. While the three notions have been

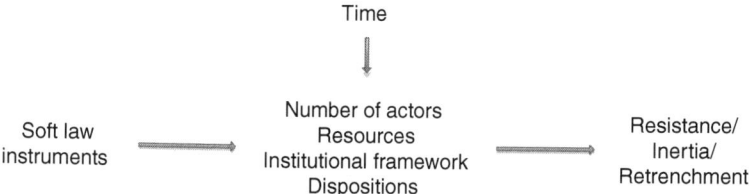

*Figure 6.1*   Resistance to European integration

used interchangeably until now, they need to be distinguished in order to clarify their meaning: inertia, resistance and retrenchment.

Thus, inertia refers to an attitude in which actors do not modify their attitudes or standard operating procedures, or as Radaelli calls it, 'their ways of doing things' (Radaelli, 2001). Thus instruments are either not used or they do not change the general workings of the administration, although they are designed to do so. Resistance, on the other hand, describes an attitude of active non-change. Here, agents are not disposed to react to implementation pressures with passive non-action but, on the contrary, actively to develop attitudes of resistance. Implementation pressures are actively challenged and rejected. Finally, retrenchment refers to an attitude in which agents develop new counter-proposals. Implementation pressures are challenged and new proposals are developed.

### Agents of resistance

Who are the agents of resistance that should be analysed in non-compliance research with soft law instruments? Contrary to political sociology approaches that concentrate on Euro-sceptic public opinion attitudes or resistance found among collective non-state actors such as non-governmental organizations, associations or interest groups, we are interested in those actors who are directly concerned with policy implementation: the bureaucracy, be they high-level offials or street-level bureaucrats. This interest is very much influenced by Hugh Heclo's assumption (Heclo, 1977) that the real power of the bureaucracy is not its capacity for disobedience or sabotage but its power to withhold services. Thus, implementation or better/poorer implementation within the bureaucracy is not characterized by rational, hierarchical modes of interaction. Principal–agent relations are not always clearly established and information is not always efficiently disseminated. This may lead to different forms of resistance or retrenchment attitudes among implementation officers, ranging from clear opposition to strategies of circumvention.

The discretion and power of national administrations is crucial to explaining Europeanization outcomes and thus, equally, inertia and resistance attitudes. National administrations play a central role in implementing European norms. Conceiving the analysis of their attitudes, as well as their relations with non-state actors such as interest groups, associations or firms as the primary objective when studying resistance to European norms at the national level, allows for linking research centred on collective action and Euro-scepticism to public policy research on implementation difficulties. By analysing national administrations in their interaction with their environment, we no longer see them as monolithic agents.

At the same time, political agendas influence the way 'new public policy instruments' are perceived by these agents at the domestic level and by the degree of salience of a particular instrument at this level. Here again, the instruments literature is useful. Salience as such does not lead to more or less inertia or retrenchment. It influences, however, the usage made of these instruments and their interpretation through agents. In insisting more on agency than on structure it is possible to understand how instruments redistribute power and thus create inertia and retrenchment attitudes (Kassim and Le Galès, 2010).

Methodologically, quantitative as well as qualitative tools must be combined in a comparative research design, based on both a significant number of member states and a comparison between the most different policy areas, in order to understand the correlation between the variables discussed above. These policies should be both 'old' policies that have both legally and non-legally binding instruments at their disposal, as well as policies that are mainly based on new modes of governance instruments. A comparison between 'old' and 'new' member states would allow to test whether the conclusions of both qualitative and quantitative non-compliance research are correct in underlining that Central and Eastern European countries are laggards in complying with EU law mainly because their administrative resources are particularly low. If results based on resistance research are similar to results in legal non-compliance research, then the main aim of these instruments – to improve the efficiency of EU public policies through debates, peer pressure and assessment exercises – would, contrary to the EU's objectives, not have been met.

# Conclusion

The analysis of inertia, resistance and retrenchment beyond non-compliance attitudes with 'hard law' generates important issues of causality in Europeanization research. However, European integration increasingly relies on coordination mechanisms, which makes the study of these new public policy instruments absolutely crucial. Resistance and inertia are effects that these new modes of governance should avoid according to those who invented them: 'In societies with growing mobility, motivated by sectors and subsectors in search of permanent normative autonomy, only participatory instruments are supposed to be able to provide adequate modes of regulation' (Lascoumes and Le Galès, 2007: 13). Contrary to this understanding, though, inertia and retrenchment are perfectly possible outcomes that equally have to be explained.

## Notes

1. In cases of member state non-compliance, the Commission can initiate an infringement procedure with a letter of formal notice that can be followed by a reasoned opinion, a transferral to the European Court of Justice and finally a ruling by the European Court of Justice (ECJ) (art. 226 ECT/art. 258 TFEU (Treaty on the Functioning of the European Union)). If the member state does not follow the ruling, a second infringement procedure can be initiated and financial sanctions can be imposed (art. 228 ECT/art. 260 TFEU).
2. For comprehensive overviews, see Töller (2010); Toshkov (2010); Treib (2008).
3. Although Toshkov's taking stock exercise is exclusively based on quantitative non-compliance studies, the variables consistently reflect those found in qualitative studies.

## References

Bache, I. (2010) 'Partnership as EU Policy Instrument: A Political History', *West European Politics*, 31(1), 58–74.

Bache, I. and Taylor, A. (2003) 'The Politics of Policy Resistance: Reconstructing Higher Education in Kosovo', *Journal of Public Policy*, 23(3), 279–300.

Bachrach, P. and Baratz, M.S. (1963) 'Decisions and Nondecisions, An Analytical Framework', *American Political Science Review*, 57(3), 632–642.

Balzacq, T. (2008) 'The Policy Tools of Securitization: Information Exchange, EU Foreign and Interior Policies', *Journal of Common Market Studies*, 46(1), 75–100.

Borrás, S. and B. Greve. (2004) 'Concluding Remarks: New Method or Just Cheap Talk?', *Journal of European Public Policy*, 11(2), 329–336.

Borrás, S. and Conzelmann, T. (2007) 'Democracy, Legitimacy and Soft Modes of Governance in the EU: The Empirical Turn', *Journal of European Integration*, 29(5), 531–548.

Borrás, S. and Jacobsson, K. (2004) 'The Open Method of Coordination and the New Governance Patterns in the EU', *Journal of European Public Policy*, 11(2), 185–208.

Börzel, T. (1999) 'Towards Convergence in Europe? Institutional Adaptation to Europeanisation in Germany and Spain', *Journal of Common Market Studies*, 37(4), 573–596.

Börzel, T. (2001) 'Non-Compliance in the European Union: Pathology or Statistical Artefact?', *Journal of European Public Policy*, 8(1), 803–825.

Börzel, T. and Risse, T. (2000) 'When Europe Hits Home. Europeanization and Domestic Change', *European Integration Online Papers* (EIoP), 4(15), http://eiop.or.at/eiop/texte/2000-015a.htm.

Börzel, T., Dudziak, M., Hofmann, T., Panke, D. and Sprungk, C. (2007) 'Recalcitrance? Inefficiency, and Support for European Integration: Why Member States do (Not) Comply with European Law', *Center for European Studies Working Paper, No. 161*, Cambridge: Harvard University.

Bruno, I., Jacquot, S. and Mandin, L. (2006) 'Europeanization Through Its Instrumentation', *Journal of European Public Policy*, 13(4), 519–536.

Bulmer, S. and Radaelli, C.M. (2005) 'The Europeanization of National Policy', in S. Bulmer and C. Lequesne (eds.), *The Member States of the European Union*, Oxford: Oxford University Press, 338–359.

Crespy, A. and Verschueren, N. (2009) 'From Europscepticism to Resistances to European integration: An Interdisciplinary Perspective', *Perspectives on European Politics and Society*, 10(3), 377–393.

Dehousse, R. (2004) 'La méthode ouverte de coordination. Quand l'instrument tient lieu de politique', in P. Lascoumes and P. Le Galès (eds.), *Gouverner par les instruments*, Paris: Presses de Sciences Po, 331–356.

Duina, F.G. (1997) 'Explaining Legal Implementation in the European Union', *International Journal of the Sociology of Law*, 25(2), 155–180.

Dunleavy, P. (2006) *Digital-Era Governance*, Oxford: Oxford University Press.

Falkner, G., Hartlapp, M. and Treib, O. (2007) 'Worlds of Compliance: Why Leading Approaches to European Union Implementation Are Only "Sometimes-true Theories" ', *European Journal of Political Research*, 3, 395–416.

Falkner, G. and Treib, O. (2008) 'Three Worlds of Compliance or Four? The EU-15 Compared to New Member States', *Journal of Common Market Studies*, 46(2), 293–313.

Falkner, G., Treib, O., Hartlapp, M. and Leiber, S. (2005) *Complying With Europe: EU Harmonisation and Soft Law in the Member States*, Cambridge: Cambridge University Press.

Goetschy, J. (2003) 'The European Employment Strategy. Multilevel Governance and Policy Coordination', in J. Zeitlin and D. Trubeck (eds.), *Governing Work and Welfare in a New Economy: European and American Experiments*, Oxford: Oxford University Press.

Grossman, E. and Woll, C. (2011) 'The French Debate on the Bolkestein Directive', *Comparative European Politics*, 9(3), 344–366.

Halpern, C. (2010) 'Governing Despite Its Instruments? Instrumentation in EU Environmental Policy', *West European Politics*, 31(1), 39–57.

Hartlapp, M. and Falkner, G. (2009) 'Problems of Operationalization and Data in EU Compliance Research', *European Union Politics*, 10(2), 281–302.

Heclo, H. (1977) *A Government of Strangers: Executive Politics in Washington*, Washington DC: Brookings Institution Press.

Héritier, A. (1999) *Policy-Making and Diversity in Europe*, New York: Cambridge University Press.

Héritier, A. (2001) 'Differential Europe: The European Union Impact on national Policymaking', in A. Héritier et al. (eds.), *Differential Europe: New Opportunities and Restrictions for Member-State Policies*, Lanham, MD: Rowman and Littlefield, 1–22.

Héritier, A. and C. Knill (2001) 'Differential Responses to European Policies: A Comparison', in A. Héritier et al. (eds.), *Differential Europe: New Opportunities and Restrictions For member-State Policies*, Lanham, MD: Rowman and Littlefield, 257–294.

Héritier, A. et al. (2001) *Differential Europe. The European Union Impact on National Policymaking*, Lanham: Rowman & Littlefield.

Holzinger K., Knill, C. and Shafer A. (2006) 'Rhetoric or Reality? "New Governance" in EU Environmental Policy', *European Law Journal*, 12(3), 403–420.

Hood, C. (1986) *The Tools of Government*, London and Basingstoke: Macmillan.

Hood, C. (1991) 'A Public Management for all Seasons?', *Public Administration*, 63(1), 3–19.

Jordan, A. and Schout, A. (2006) *Co-ordination of European Governance*, Oxford: Oxford University Press.

Jordan, A., Wurzel, R.K.W. and Zito, A.R. (2003) *New Instruments of Environmental Governance?* London: Frank Cass.

Kaeding, M. (2008) 'Lost in Translation of Full Steam Ahead? The Transposition of EU Transport Directives across Member States', *European Union Politics*, 9(1), 115–143.

Kassim, H. and Le Galès, P. (2010) 'Exploring Governance in a Multi-Level Polity: A Policy Instruments Approach', *West European Politics*, 33(1), 1–21.

König, T. and Luetgert, B. (2009) 'Troubles with Transposition? Explaining Trends in Member-State Notification and the Delayed Transposition of EU Directives', *British Journal of Political Science*, 39(1), 163–194.

Lascoumes, P. and Le Galès, P. (2007) 'Introduction: Understanding Public Policy through Its Instruments – From the Nature of Instruments to the Sociology of Public Policy Instrumentation', *Governance*, 20(1), 1–21.

Linder, S.H. and Peters, B.G. (1989) 'Instruments of Government: Perceptions and Contexts', *Journal of Public Policy*, 9(1), 35–58.

Lodge, M. and Gill, D. (2011) 'Toward a New Era of Administrative Reform? The Myth of Post-NPM in New Zealand', *Governance*, 24(1), 141–166.

Mastenbroek, E. (2005) 'EU Compliance: Still a Black Hole?', *Journal of European Public Policy*, 12(6), 1103–1120.

Menon, A. and Sedelmeier, U. (2010) 'Instruments and Intentionality: Civilian Crisis Management and Enlargement Conditionality in EU Security Policy', *West European Politics*, 31(1), 75–92.

Mörth, U. (2003) 'Europeanization as Interpretation, Translation, and Editing of Public Polices', in K. Featherstone and C.M. Radaelli (eds.), *The Politics of Europeanization*, Oxford: Oxford University Press, 159–178.

Muller, P. (2005) 'Esquisse d'une théorie de changement dans l'action publique. Structures, acteurs et cadres cognitifs', *Revue française de science politique*, 55(1), 155–187.

Olsen, J.P. (1996) 'Europeanization and Nation-State Dynamics', in S. Gustavson and L. Lewin (eds.), *The Future of the Nation State*, London: Routledge, 245–285.

Panke, D. (2007) 'The European Court of Justice as an Agent of Europeanization? Restoring Compliance with EU Law', *Journal of European Public Policy*, 14(6), 847–866.

Radaelli, C.M. (2001) 'The Domestic Impact of European Public Policy: Notes on Concepts, Methods and the Challenge of Empirical Research', *Politique européenne*, No. 5, autumn, 107–142.

Radaelli, C.M. (2003) 'The Europeanization of Public Policy', in K. Featherstone and C. Radaelli (eds.), *The Politics of Europeanization*, Oxford: Oxford University Press, 27–56.

Radaelli, C.M. (2008) 'Europeanization, Policy Learning, and New Modes of Governance', *Journal of Comparative Policy Analysis*, 10(3), 239–254.

Radaelli, C.M. and Meuwese, A. (2010) 'Hard Questions and Equally Hard Solutions. Proceduralisation through Impact Assessment in the European Union', *West European Politics*, 31(1), 136–153.

Raustiala, K. and Slaughter, A.-M. (2002) 'International Law and Compliance', in W. Carlsnaes, T. Risse and B. Simmons (eds.), *Handbook of International Relations*, London: Sage, 338–358.

Richardson, J.J. (1996) 'Eroding EU Policies: Implementation Gaps, Cheating and Re-steering', in J.J. Richardson (ed.), *European Union: Power and Policy-Making*, London: Routledge.

Risse, T., Green Cowles, M. and Caporaso, J. (eds.) (2001) *Transforming Europe: Europeanization and Domestic Change*, Ithaca, NY: Cornell University Press.

Rose, R. (1988) 'Comparative Policy Analysis: The Program Approach', in M. Dogan (ed.), *Comparing Pluralist Democracies*, Boulder, CO: Westview.

Tallberg, J. (2002) 'Paths to Compliance: Enforcement, Management and the European Union', *International Organization*, 56(3), 609–644.

Töller, A.E. (2010) 'Measuring and Comparing the Europeanization of Public Policies', *Journal of Common Market Studies*, 48(1), 413–440.

Töller, A.E. (2011) 'Voluntary Approaches to Regulation – Patterns, Causes, and Effects', in D. Levi-Faur (ed.), *Handbook of the Politics of Regulation*, Cheltenham: Edward Elgar.

Toshkov, D. (2010) 'Taking Stock: A Review of Quantitative Studies of Transposition and Implementation of EU Law', *EIF Working Paper No. 01.2010*, February.

Treib, O. (2008) 'Implementing and Complying with EU Governance Outputs', *Living Reviews in European Governance*, 3(5), http://www.livingreviews.org/lreg-2008-5 (accessed 5.2.2010).

Tsebelis, G. (1995) *Nested Games: Rational Choice in Comparative Politics*, Berkeley, CA: U.C. Press.

Versluis, E. (2007) 'Even Rules, Uneven Practices: Opening the Black Box of EU Law in Action', *West European Politics*, 30(1), 50–67.

Zahariadis, N. (2008) 'Europeanization as Programme Implementation: Effective and Democratic?', *Journal of Comparative Policy Analysis*, 10(3), 221–238.

# 7
## Process Tracing: Testing Multiple Hypotheses with a Small Number of Cases

*Diana Panke*

### Introduction

The transposition and implementation of EU directives and regulations by EU member states is one pathway of Europeanization (Chapter 1 in this volume). Member states, in which a mismatch between EU law and domestic law occurs, need to adjust their legal acts within the transposition deadline. Instances of failed Europeanization, in which domestic legal rules and practices are not in line with EU law even after the transposition deadline expired, constitute non-compliance cases. Instances of non-compliance impair the power of EU law. Hence, in order to remedy problems associated with delayed Europeanization, the EU established an infringement system which encompasses a variety of different compliance instruments (bilateral negotiations, Court judgments, sanction threats or financial penalties). Yet, we observe that there is variation in the reaction to these instruments, which differs even on a case-by-case basis. Against this background, this chapter analyses the following research question: How and under which conditions do states that initially violated EU law catch up with Europeanization?

This chapter develops competing hypotheses to explain processes of how and under which conditions states catch up with Europeanization. This leads to a common difficulty with case-study designs: the need to test multiple hypotheses with a small number of empirical cases (Bryman, 2008). King et al. tell us that a research design is overdetermined (or indeterminate) if there are fewer cases than explanatory variables to be tested, so that we cannot gain insights relating to which of the hypotheses can indeed explain an outcome (King et al., 1994). Yet, their teachings on qualitative research designs are informed by quantitative research and they overlook that in-case variation of independent as well as dependent variables is a common feature of a case study, which in effect increases the number of observations. In addition (and even more important for this chapter), process tracing allows for definition of fine-grained observable implications of causal processes as well as outcomes, which enables qualitative researchers to test multiple hypotheses even in small-*n* settings and establish causality.[1] This chapter applies process-tracing methodology and illustrates how a single case study can be utilized to test multiple hypotheses. It concludes by discussing the added value of process-tracing methods in testing hypotheses in small-*n* settings, as well as the difficulties and downsides.

## The puzzle and hypotheses

European directives are a means of Europeanization. They formulate demands for domestic changes and pose a legal obligation on states to punctually and correctly transpose and implement them. If the European Commission suspects a state of violating EU law, it initiates an infringement proceeding. In a first step, the Commission sends a reasoned opinion to the state (Art. 226 ECT). This triggers bilateral negotiations. If the case cannot be settled at this stage with non-compliance prevailing, the Commission refers the case to the European Court of Justice (ECJ). This triggers judicial discourses between state and European advocates, at the end of which the ECJ issues binding rulings. Should a state still resist catching up with Europeanization and abstaining from domestic legal change after the Court judgment, the Commission sends a second reasoned opinion (Art. 228 ECT) and threatens the state with the possibility of a second Court judgment, in which monetary sanctions can be imposed.

The vast majority of cases are settled in the early stages of the infringement proceeding, in which the state and the Commission negotiate on a bilateral basis (Mendrinou, 1996; Tallberg, 1999). Yet, all EU member states also drag cases on to the ECJ (Börzel et al., 2009). Here we observe considerable within-country variation in the reaction to the EU's compliance instruments: while a state might end non-compliance after the judicial discourse or respond to an ECJ judgment in catching up with Europeanization, the same state may need to be threatened with sanctions in a different case (Panke, 2010a). This is puzzling in so far as the EU infringement procedure and its accompanying compliance instruments (e.g., judicial discourses, judgments, sanction threats, financial penalties) as well as a country's characteristics (e.g., economic capacities, support of EU integration, political culture) are constant and cannot, thus, explain the observed variation in catching up with Europeanization.

Against this background, researchers have asked how and under which conditions a state shifts from non-compliance into compliance (e.g., Panke, 2010a). A series of different explanations are possible to explain the dynamics of delayed Europeanization.[2]

On the one hand, changes in external costs can induce compliance (e.g., the application of a compliance instrument). The application of compliance instruments (e.g., judgments or sanction threats or sanctions) can alter cost–benefit calculations of states, so that catching up with Europeanization becomes less expensive than continuing with non-compliance. A judgment creates publicity and can, thus, impose costs of reputational losses vis-à-vis EU actors. This can have negative consequences in future negotiations and, thus, motivate the government to end non-compliance (e.g., Guzman, 2002; Kim, 1996; Satori, 2002). Hence, we might expect that states shift into compliance after the ECJ issues a judgment if it clearly states that the country in question is violating EU law, because they want to avoid reputational losses. Not only a judgment, but also the subsequent compliance instrument, sanction threats, can increase non-compliance costs as these increase the likelihood of financial costs in the immediate future (Horne and Cutlip, 2002; Martin, 1992). Thus, the second hypothesis expects that states end their resistance towards Europeanization and correctly transpose and implement EU law, if the cost associated with the threatened sanctions is sufficiently high (cf. Panke, 2010b).

On the other hand, changes at the domestic level can alter the cost–benefit calculation of responsible governments or ministries and induce delayed processes of Europeanization. Again, two different mechanisms are possible. First, domestic non-compliance constituencies might be weakened by a Court judgment or a sanction threat that increases the publicity of the case and emphasizes that non-compliance is inappropriate. On the one hand, domestic actors avoiding non-compliance could lose influence, for example because certain arguments can no longer be made legitimately. On the other hand, domestic compliance proponents could be empowered through the ability publicly to shame the government for receiving a judgment and violating EU law. Thus, if domestic compliance proponents are empowered after a judgment or a sanction threat, they can shame the government into catching up with Europeanization by increasing the reputational cost

*Table 7.1*   Overview of hypotheses

| | | |
|---|---|---|
| EU-level effects | H1 | States shift into compliance to avoid reputational losses if the ECJ issues a judgment that clearly states that the country in question is violating EU law |
| | H2 | States shift into compliance if sanction threats encompass a high lump sum that credibly threatens the government |
| Domestic-level effects | H3 | States shift into compliance if judgments or sanction threats empower domestic compliance constituencies who shame them into compliance |
| | H4 | States shift into compliance if judgments or sanction threats empower lead ministries who favour compliance from the outset but are prevented from proposing or passing demanding policies by domestic veto players |

of maintaining non-compliance. Thus, the third hypothesis expects that states catch up with Europeanization after judgments or sanction threats, if domestic compliance constituencies shame their governments into compliance. ECJ judgments or sanction threats might also empower pro-compliance ministries vis-à-vis ministries that would prefer non-compliance (cf. Panke, 2010a: 51–52). Thus, the fourth and final hypothesis is: judgments or sanction threats differentially empower lead ministries and induce compliance, if the lead ministry favoured compliance from the outset but was prevented from proposing or passing demanding policies by domestic veto players (Table 7.1).

Testing these hypotheses is a challenge, for two reasons. First, a compliance instrument can have an effect on the propensity of a state to catch up with Europeanization because of EU-level or domestic cost-related changes. Also, observable effects of compliance instruments can overlap over time. European actors strictly apply the compliance instruments in a sequential order (a judgment (Art. 226 ECT) always precedes a sanction threat (Art. 228 ECT)). Nevertheless, the impact of a compliance instrument on the dependent variable (non-compliance/compliance) can take place with a time lag, because it takes time for legal change to be completed. For example, a judgment might have increased the compliance costs considerably, but a government needs a long time to complete legal changes so that the Commission issues a sanction threat although the judgment had been effective. In addition, states might anticipate the effect of a future compliance instrument and, thus, change their legal acts before the instrument actually comes into play. For example, the chance of receiving a sanction threat in the future can impact a state's behaviour in the earlier stages of the infringement procedure (e.g., immediately after judicial discourses), although it has not yet been applied. As the study below illustrates, these problems can only be tackled through process-tracing methods.

Process tracing takes seriously 'process' as the unfolding of an event over time (Bryman, 2008: 388). It zooms into the chain of events. Unlike correlation-based analysis, process tracing does more than simply examining whether change in an independent variable (explanatory variables) at a particular point of time goes hand in hand with a change in the dependent variable (phenomena to be explained). Instead, process tracing takes the accompanying causal mechanisms seriously (Checkel, 2005; Geddes, 2003: Chapter 4 in this volume). Thus, it disentangles the different mechanisms that might be at play in producing a change in the dependent variable and formulates expectations about intermediate steps in the causal chain of events (Bennett and George, 2006). On this basis, process tracing reconstructs which of the possible causal pathways has been at stake along the timeline of events and actions in a particular case (Geddes, 2003: Chapter 4 in this volume).

In our example, we will explain why we observed a change in the dependent variable from non-compliance to delayed Europeanization in the year 2002 in the UK's nitrate case.

Correlation-based analysis would record that the sanction-threat was issued in the same year. Yet, as discussed, the correlation between change in an independent variable and that in the dependent variable would not tell us which hypothesis actually accounts for the shift into compliance. Hypotheses two, three and four all feature the issuing of a sanction threat as an independent variable (but differ in the causal mechanisms that trigger a change in the dependent variable). Even hypothesis one cannot be ruled out (the correlation between the sanction threat and the change in the dependent variable in the year 2002 could be a spurious correlation) because the judgment might have triggered policy changes, but there may have been a delay in enacting corresponding legislation.

Process tracing focuses on the four different causal mechanisms and allows us to detect which of our four hypotheses can explain why the UK caught up with Europeanization in 2002. To this end, we have to specify the causal mechanism expected by each of the hypotheses and specify indicators for the mechanisms.

*Hypothesis one* is that states shift into compliance to avoid reputational losses, if the ECJ issues a judgment that clearly states that the country in question is violating EU law. The causal mechanism here is that governments seek to avoid losses in reputation vis-à-vis EU actors, thus giving up their resistance towards Europeanization. Reputational costs cannot be directly observed, but we can observe public speech acts (e.g., in parliamentary debates, Court proceedings or newspapers) of the actors before and after the ECJ judgment. What we would expect if reputational costs were at stake is governments defending the appropriateness of their legal interpretation in Court, but later shifting into highlighting the rightfulness of the ECJ ruling and the merits of its interpretation of the legal issue at stake. If the UK, on the other hand, paid lip service to the ECJ or the Commission only before but not after the ECJ ruling, we cannot conclude that they are concerned with reputational losses after the judgment. This is additionally supported if a document analysis of parliamentary documents reveals that the government or the lead ministry did not initiate policy changes.

**Hypothesis two** expects that states shift into compliance if sanction threats involve a large lump sum that credibly threatens the government. The causal mechanism is that governments make cost–benefit calculations and regard compliance as less expensive than continuing non-compliance. Again, cost–benefit calculations as such cannot be directly observed, but we can observe public responses to the sanction threat. If the head of government or the minister in charge of the policy area in question publicly highlights how severe the potential future sanctions would be and emphasizes that it is necessary to act in order to avoid them, the mechanism underlying hypothesis two would be confirmed – especially if we observe that policy changes follow quickly after such statements.

**Hypothesis three** expects that states abandon their resistance towards Europeanization if judgments or sanction threats empower domestic compliance constituencies that shame them into compliance. The causal mechanism is that pro-compliance actors publicly shame the government for pursuing a policy path that violates established and strong domestic norms of appropriateness. Pro-compliance constituencies can thereby use the publicity created by the judgment or the sanction – threat, and also the fact that judgments and sanction threats show that governmental policy is out of line with EU law. While we cannot observe whether shaming campaigns indeed create threats of reputational losses for the government, we can observe whether shaming campaigns take place. Also, we can reconstruct which norms of appropriateness were domestically institutionalized (in regard to which the government could be shamed for violating them) as well as the domestic distribution of interests and positions, which allows us to evaluate whether shaming campaigns could have been damaging for the government. In this case, we would expect public statements of governmental members to shift from defending non-compliance to paying lip service to the non-compliance constituency.

*Hypothesis four* expects that states shift into compliance if judgments or sanction threats empower lead ministries vis-à-vis domestic veto players. Through analysing public speeches (e.g., in parliament, media) prior to judgments and sanction threats, we can find out whether the lead ministry indeed favoured compliance while other ministries opted for non-compliance. If this is the case, interviews can be used to analyse whether the lead ministry was prevented from proposing or passing demanding policies by domestic veto players prior to the judgment or the sanction threat, but was enabled to push for policy reforms once pressure from the EU level increased.

The next section uses process-tracing methodology in order to test the four hypotheses as outlined above.

## Illustrative study – Delayed Europeanization in the UK's nitrates case

The Nitrates Directive (91/676) seeks to protect the environment by reducing the level of nitrates in fresh water and groundwater. It focuses in particular on nitrates from agricultural sources, which are the main water polluter. The directive prescribes the designation of Nitrate Vulnerable Zones (NVZ) and Action Programmes as instruments to protect water from the effects of nitrates. The UK legally transposed the directive with three regulations in 1996 ('The Protection of Water Against Agricultural Nitrate Pollution Regulations'). However, instead of applying the Nitrates Directive to all groundwater and fresh water, the regulations referred only to drinking water. This restriction in scope was in line with the widely held British perception of the early and mid-1990s that water quality is not an environmental but a public health issue (House of Commons, 1994a: 9, 1996: 814–815, 1997).

The Commission regarded the UK approach as an instance of non-compliance and, consequently, referred the case to the ECJ in

February 1999 (case C-69/99).[3] In December 2000, the ECJ issued a judgment clarifying that the UK had indeed violated the Nitrates Directive (European Court of Justice, 2000). In May 2002, the European Commission proposed a financial penalty for violating the Nitrates Directive. Subsequently, the UK finally complied with the EU nitrates regime.

Why did the UK choose to comply in 2002? Was it due to the reputational costs imposed by the ECJ judgment that induced domestic changes that were finalized in 2002? Was it due to the threatening financial costs of the looming sanctions that triggered swift adaptations? Did the judgment or the sanction threat empower domestic society actors who shamed the government into compliance? Did judgment or the sanction threat alter the balance between domestic veto players and empower pro-compliance ministries vis-à-vis their compliance-adverse colleagues in other departments?

Hypothesis one cannot account for the fact that the UK delayed Europeanization until 2002. On 7 December 2000, the ECJ issued a judgment according to which the UK was deemed to have incorrectly transposed the Nitrates Directive concerning all issues at stake (European Court of Justice, 2000). Nonetheless, the judgment did not increase the reputational costs vis-à-vis EU actors and other states and did not induce catching-up processes with Europeanization. UK officials paid lip service to the Commission prior to the ECJ judgment, emphasizing that 'The United Kingdom Government accepts that in the present case the submissions of the Commission are well founded ( ... ) it had initially interpreted the scope of the Directive differently ( ... ) and that the transposition of the Directive into national law was based on that interpretation' (European Court of Justice, 2000: 20). In addition, the UK promised to change its policies prior to the ECJ ruling: 'It also sets out the implementing measures which it has adopted or are in the process of being adopted in order for it to comply with its obligations under the Directive' (European Court of Justice, 2000: 20). However, once the ECJ issued its judgment, the UK did not continue rhetorically to pacify EU actors, which would have been a rational strategy, if the UK indeed wanted to avoid losing reputation vis-à-vis EU actors. Instead, the government never mentioned that action programmes were required for all areas designated as NVZs, nor did the government refine existing programmes or adopt additional action programmes in response to the judgment (House of Commons, 2002e, 2002f, 2002g). Thus, the ECJ ruling did not increase reputational costs and the government did not adjust its nitrates policy in order to avoid losses of reputation.

Consequently, the UK did not even undertake the first steps towards the legal and practical implementation after the judgment, but instead continued with non-compliance (cf. House of Commons, 2002e, 2002f, 2002g). Hypothesis three also fails to explain the Europeanization dynamics in the nitrates case. Neither the judgment nor the sanction threat enabled pro-compliance constituencies effectively to shame the government into compliance (see also Panke, 2010a). In the immediate period after the judgment, domestic non-compliance benefits were considerable.[4] Farmers as domestic non-compliance proponents were well organized and received broad public support, not least because of the bovine spongiform encephalitis (BSE) – or 'mad cow' – crisis and foot-and-mouth disease. In this context, societal actors did not shame the government publicly. As expected, the Blair government did not introduce any preparatory steps towards domestic change (House of Commons, 2000a, 2001b). Thus, Europeanization was further delayed.

Over one year later, the Royal Society for the Protection of Birds publicly criticized the Labour government for its 'half-hearted attempt to implement the directive' and its failure to comply with the ECJ ruling (*Financial Times*, 2002b; see also Panke, 2010a). During this period, which coincided with a second reasoned opinion (Art 228 ECT) of the European Commission, the government launched consultations with farmers and stakeholders on how to implement the Nitrates Directive. Was this policy adaptation due to effective shaming by the societal compliance proponents? As the consultation process came to an end in 2002, the UK designated 55 per cent rather than 80 per cent or 100 per cent of the territory as NVZs (*The Guardian*, 2002). This did not reflect a compromise that the government had constructed in response to successful shaming campaigns by environmental organizations: the domestic context was unfavourable. First, public debates were still dominated by farmers' associations and their concerns about implementation costs (*Farmers Guardian*, 2002; *Financial Times*, 2002b). Second, media coverage increased after the second reasoned opinion, but British newspapers overwhelmingly opposed a compliant approach to the Nitrates Directive (e.g., *Aberdeen Press*, 2002; *Sunday Times*, 2002). Third, due to BSE and the foot-and-mouth epidemic, public opinion was in sympathy with farmers (House of Commons, 2002a, 2002b; House of Lords, 2002).[5] Hence, while solidarity with farmers was widely considered as appropriate, there was no strongly institutionalized norm of appropriateness on the basis of which the government could have been shamed for non-compliance. In this context of high domestic implementation costs, the shaming campaign was ineffective. Consequently, the government did not emphasize the environmental merits of the Nitrates Directive and the 2002 regulation, but made it clear that they would have preferred their old nitrates approach (House of Commons, 2002b: 472, 2002c, 2002e; Select Committee on Environment, 2002: 552, 2003: 14). Rather than giving in to domestic shaming endeavours and defending policy changes as the appropriate thing to do, the government and the Department for Environment, Food and Rural Affairs (DEFRA) explained to their non-compliance constituency that their minimalist policy changes of 2002 were the fault of the ECJ and were necessary to avoid the possibility of sanctions (to the tune of to £50 million per year).[6]

Hypothesis two expects that governments adapt to rising external non-compliance costs and opt for compliance if external costs increase considerably due to a credible sanction threat. This requires that the threat of penalties be eminently strong and likely to be realized in the immediate future (i.e., the government can expect to face punishment while still in office).

The European Commission sent a letter of formal notice (Art 228 ECT) in autumn 2001. This increased the external non-compliance costs for the UK, though the threat was not immediate as a second ECJ judgment issuing financial penalties was still two procedural steps away. In line with this interpretation, the Blair government was very reluctant to shift into compliance in winter 2001 (House of Lords, 2001). At the same time, the government was no longer inactive, but prepared for the initiation of a consultation process with farmers on the designation of NVZs. This endeavour was publicly labelled as a preparatory step towards legal change (House of Commons, 2001b; House of Lords, 2001). However, this in fact delayed domestic legal changes even further. The ECJ had not only already specified the content and scope of the Nitrates Directive, so that consultations with farmers were not necessary legally to transpose the Nitrates Directive correctly and completely into UK law. The government also changed the options for consultation during the process, without starting new consultations or at least providing farmers with an update on the options, which rendered the consultation obsolete (Department of the Environment, 2002b). Since the consultations were neither required nor consequently pursued, the consultation endeavour had a window-dressing character. This might indicate that the government wanted to demonstrate its new commitment regarding nitrates in order to prevent the Commission from initiating another step towards financial penalties, while saving domestic compliance costs at least temporarily.

The Commission was not satisfied with this domestic change. In May 2002, it sent a sanction threat (second reasoned opinion, Art 228 ECT) to the UK, which proposed a daily penalty of £135,000 (House of Commons, 2002d). This increased the external non-compliance costs tremendously, since an ECJ judgment issuing the proposed penalty was not only very likely, but also very likely to happen so soon that the government would still be in office. The domestic non-compliance benefits were still high, but did not exceed the threat of external penalties. In line with hypothesis two, cost–benefit calculations changed because of the sanction threat. Delayed compliance became more beneficial than maintaining non-compliance, as the sanctions were looming. In this context, the Minister for the Environment admitted that:

> We are subject to infraction proceedings if we do not implement it in full, and non-compliance fines could run as high as £135,000 a day. (...) Those constraints are unavoidable, and we have delayed implementation as long as possible (...) we now risk fines and therefore have to act.
>
> (Mr. Meacher in House of Commons, 2002d: 906)

The 2002 nitrates regulations were issued soon after the Commission threatened the UK with financial penalties (Department of the Environment, 2002b; House of Commons, 2002d). The regulations of December 2002 had a broader applicatory scope than the 1996 nitrates regulations and included all fresh and groundwater, regardless of whether it was intended for human consumption (House of Commons, 2002e). Thus, the Blair government quickly caught up with Europeanization in order to prevent a second Court judgment and penalties.

Hypothesis four theorized that judgments or sanction threats emphasize the inappropriateness of norm violations and thereby empower lead ministries. This would be expected to induce a shift to compliance if the lead ministry favoured compliance from the outset, but was prevented from proposing or passing demanding policies by domestic veto players. The explanatory value of this theoretical claim is limited (Panke, 2010a). In the nitrates case, the Ministry of Agriculture, Forestry and Fisheries (predecessor of DEFRA) and later on DEFRA, as the lead ministries, had been opposed to a demanding and costly nitrates approach throughout the infringement procedure.[7] The same holds true for other ministries involved in nitrates issues.[8] Hence, the

UK persisted with the nitrates violation until 2002 not because domestic veto players prevented a shift into more demanding policies. Rather, non-compliance prevailed because it allowed the government to save considerable implementation costs in line with the health policy, rather than the environmental policy-oriented nitrates approach of the UK. Since the necessary condition for differential empowerment of lead ministries was absent, hypothesis four cannot account for policy shifts in the nitrates sector.

In sum, hypothesis three explains why the UK government shifted from non-compliance into compliance in 2002.

## Reflection: The added value of process tracing in small-*n* research designs

The process-tracing technique allows moving from correlation to causation within a case study design. It takes the causal mechanisms inherent in hypotheses seriously and analyses in detail whether a particular pathway, triggered by an independent variable, was indeed causing a particular event. In this sense, process tracing not only provides answers to 'why' questions,[9] but also 'how–come' questions.[10] Process tracing disentangles underlying mechanisms and empirically examines whether they take place. This strengthens the quality of hypothesis testing considerably as it avoids false conclusions about explanatory value that are based on spurious correlations in the sequencing of changes in independent and dependent variables.

Process tracing has another advantage. In small-*n* settings, it allows the testing of several hypotheses against one another, which is very important if none of the hypotheses can be controlled for by keeping the independent variable constant. In our example, the application of the sanction threat instrument was always preceded by the application of the compliance instrument, 'judgment'. Thus, in empirical cases in which a sanction threat has been issued or can be anticipated, all four causal mechanisms could potentially explain a change in the dependent variable (shift into compliance). It is, consequently, not possible to keep one, two or three of our four hypotheses constant through case selection. In our example, four hypotheses were tested simultaneously and without running the risk of arriving at indeterminate results, since the causal processes inherent in the four hypotheses were analysed in detail. This allowed us to establish cause and to conclude that hypothesis three on the top-down impact of sanction threats explained the dynamics of catching up with Europeanization in the UK nitrates case. Thus, it was possible to test which of the possible causal relationships between independent and dependent variables was present. If process tracing is applied, the internal validity of the extent to which a causal relationship has reliably been established is very high despite focusing only on a small number of cases (Bryman, 2008: 32). This is one key advantage of process-tracing methodology.

While the internal validity is very high (although we worked with only a single case study in this chapter), the external validity (i.e., potential for generalization) of such a study is limited. On the basis of just one case study (in which only one of the variables that was part of one causal mechanism was present), we cannot, for example, generalize that shaming by domestic constituencies (H2) is generally unimportant in regard to catching up with Europeanization. In order to arrive at these conclusions, we would also need to conduct a case study in which a strong domestic norm of appropriateness is present against which the government can be shamed (which is an essential intermediate variable in the causal mechanism of this hypothesis), but in which domestic societal shaming after the judgment or the sanction does nevertheless not trigger compliance. Thus, in order to remedy the problem of limited ability for generalizations faced by single case studies (i.e., limited external validity), and in order to combine the positive effects of high internal validity (due to the process-tracing methodology) with a research design with high external validity, it is essential to increase the number of cases within the research design. High external validity can be achieved through multiple case studies in which the cases are selected in line with most similar systems design in respect to the intermediate variables in the different causal mechanisms, so that there is an opportunity for each causal mechanism to be verified or falsified during the empirical analysis (cf. Panke, 2010a).

## Notes

1. The fourth section discusses the high internal validity of process-tracing methods and problems with low external validity in regard to single case studies in detail. On external and internal validity, see also Bryman (2008: 32–33, 376, 381–382).
2. For reasons of space, this chapter looks only at rationalist pathways to compliance while additional, constructivist explanations are not introduced. Also, the hypotheses are not extensively discussed at this point. For a comprehensive discussion, see Panke (2010a).
3. It was first contested whether all surface waters and groundwater are subject to the Nitrates Directive, or only water intended for human consumption. Second, there was dissent on whether the UK failed to designate sufficient

NVZs and, thereby, restricted the applicatory scope of the Nitrates Directive. Third, the UK and the Commission disagreed on whether the British action programmes required for the NVZs were sufficient (European Court of Justice, 2000).

4. For example, *The Daily Telegraph* (2000); *The Express* (2001); *Farmers Guardian* (2000); House of Commons (1999, 2000a).

5. 'The government has delayed taking action for years because it feared a backlash from the farming industry, which has been hit by a succession of crises, culminating in last year's foot-and-mouth epidemic. [...] Mr Meacher added that the government was not wishing to bash the agricultural community [...] We are trying to do it in a manner which is the least oppressive and the most co-operative' (*Financial Times*, 2002a).

6. For example, *The Daily Telegraph* (2002); Department of the Environment (2002a); *Financial Times* (2002a,b); *The Guardian* (2002); House of Commons (1994b, 1995, 1999, 2000a,b).

7. Cf. House of Commons, 1994b, 1995, 1999, 2000a, b, 2001a,c, DEFRA (2002a), *Financial Times* (2002b).

8. Cf. House of Commons (2001b, 2002b: 426, 2002 c,f); Select Committee on Environment (2002: 552, 2003: 14).

9. For example, why did the UK abandon non-compliance? *Because of the compliance instrument 'sanction threats'.*

10. For example, how come an EU compliance instrument can trigger domestic policy changes? *Because it affected the governmental cost–benefit calculations and rendered non-compliance more costly than catching up with Europeanization.*

# References

Aberdeen Press (2002) 'Farmers Fear High Cost of Clampdown on Nitrates', *Aberdeen Press* (5 January 2002).

Bennett, A. and George, A. (2006) *Case Studies and Theory Development in the Social Sciences* (Cambridge: MIT Press).

Börzel, T.A., Hofmann, T. and Panke, D. (2009) Opinions, Referrals, and Judgments. Analyzing Longitudinal Patterns of Non-Compliance, *Berlin Working Papers on European Integration*, http://www.polsoz.fu-berlin.de/polwiss/forsch ung/international/europa/arbeitspapiere/2009-13_Boerzel_Hofman_Panke.pdf

Bryman, A. (2008) *Social Research Methods* (Oxford: Oxford University Press).

Checkel, J.T. (2005) It's the Process Stupid! Process Tracing in the Study of European and International Politics, *ARENA Working Paper Series*, 26.

The Daily Telegraph (2000) 'EU Red Tape "Is Ruining Our Farmers" Task Force Blames "Over-Zealous" Britain', *The Daily Telegraph* (15 November 2000).

The Daily Telegraph (2002) 'Slurry Ban on Half of England', *The Daily Telegraph* (28 June 2002).

Department of the Environment, Food, and Rural Affairs (2002a) *News Release – Nitrate Controls to Spearhead Long-Term Strategy to Improve Water Quality*, 27 June 2002.

Department of the Environment, Food, and Rural Affairs (2002b) *Nitrates Directive Consultation. A Report Prepared by NOP Social & Political for the Department for Environment, Food and Rural Affairs (DEFRA)*, April 2002/433602.

European Court of Justice (2000) Court Judgment of December 7th, 2000: The European Commission against the United Kingdom Regarding the Incomplete Application of Directive 91/676, C-69/99, *Official Journal of the European Communities*, I–10979.

The Express (2001) 'GBP 1BN Clean-Up Cost of Water Pollution by Farm Pesticides', *The Express* (28 January 2001).

Farmers Guardian (2000) 'Revised Crop Input Recommendations', *Farmers Guardian* (22 December 2000).

Farmers Guardian (2002) ' "Union to Challenge Flawed" Scientific Basis Behind the NVZ Directive?', *Farmers Guardian* (5 July 2002).

Financial Times (2002a) 'Government to Implement EU Water Directive', *Financial Times* (28 May 2002).

Financial Times (2002b) 'Nitrate Pollution Zones "Will Cover Only 55% of UK" ', *Financial Times* (28 June 2002).

Geddes, B. (2003) *Paradigms and Sand Castles* (Ann Arbor, MI: University of Michigan Press).

The Guardian (2002) 'Meacher Caves in on Farm Pollution', *The Guardian* (28 June 2002).

Guzman, A.T. (2002) A Compliance-Based Theory of International Law, *California Law Review*, 90, 1826–1888.

Horne, C. and Cutlip, A. (2002) Sanctioning Costs and Norm Enforcement, *Rationality and Society*, 14: 3, 285–307.

House of Commons (1994a) *House of Commons Hansard Debates for 7 February 1994*, Hansard Debates, Column 89–100.

House of Commons (1994b) *House of Commons Hansard Debates for 14 June 1994 – Commons Written Answers*, Hansard Debates.

House of Commons (1995) *House of Commons Hansard Debates for 14 March 1995*, Hansard Debates, Column 807–816.

House of Commons (1996) *House of Commons Hansard Debates for 14 October 1996*, Hansard Debates, Column 814–816.

House of Commons (1997) *House of Commons Hansard Debates for 23 July 1997*, Hansard Debates, Column 924–927.

House of Commons (1999) *House of Commons Hansard Debates for 20 October 1999*, Hansard Debates, Column 444–499.

House of Commons (2000a) *House of Commons Hansard Debates for 10 February 2000*, Hansard Debates, Column 114–153.

House of Commons (2000b) *House of Commons Hansard Debates for 29 June 2000*, Hansard Debates, Column 1043–1047.

House of Commons (2001a) *House of Commons Hansard Debates for 12 November 2001*, Hansard Debates, Column 574–586.

House of Commons (2001b) *House of Commons Hansard Debates for 19 December 2001, Commons Written Answers*.

House of Commons (2001c) *House of Commons Hansard Debates for 28 February 2001*, Hansard Debates, Column 913–960.

House of Commons (2002a) *House of Commons Hansard Debates for 6 November 2002*, Hansard Debates, Column 299–302.

House of Commons (2002b) *House of Commons Hansard Debates for 12 December 2002*, Hansard Debates, Column 410 505.

House of Commons (2002c) *House of Commons Hansard Debates for 14 May 2002*, Hansard Debates, Column 198–219.

House of Commons (2002d) *House of Commons Hansard Debates for 16 May 2002*, Hansard Debates.

House of Commons (2002e) *House of Commons Hansard Debates for 30 January 2002, Commons Written Answers*.

House of Commons (2002f) *House of Commons Hansard Debates for 30 January 2002, Commons Written Answers*, Hansard Debates.

House of Commons (2002g) *House of Commons Hansard Debates for 31 January 2002, Commons Written Answers*, Hansard Debates.

House of Lords (2001) *House of Lords Debates, Lords Written Answers, 20 December 2001*, Hansard Debates.

House of Lords (2002) *House of Lords Debates, 11 December 2002*, Hansard Debates, Column 230–244.

Kim, J.-Y. (1996) Cheap Talk and Reputation in Repeated Pretrial Negotiation, *Rand Journal of Economics*, 27: 4, 787–802.

King, G., Keohane, R.O. and Verba, S. (1994) *Designing Social Inquiry. Scientific Inference in Qualitative Research* (Princeton, NJ: Princeton University Press).

Martin, L.L. (1992) *Coercive Cooperation – Explaining Multilateral Economic Sanctions* (Princeton, NJ: Princeton University Press).

Mendrinou, M. (1996) Non-Compliance and the European Commission's Role in Integration, *Journal of European Public Policy*, 3: 1, 1–22.

Panke, D. (2010a) *The Effectiveness of the European Court of Justice. Why Reluctant States Comply* (Manchester: Manchester University Press).

Panke, D. (2010b) Why Big States Cannot Do What They Want. International Courts and Compliance, *International Politics*, 47, 186–209.

Satori, A.E. (2002) The Might of the Pen: A Reputational Theory of Communication in International Disputes, *International Organization*, 56: 1, 121–149.

Select Committee on Environment, Food and Rural Affairs (2002) *Select Committee on Environment, Food and Rural Affairs. Select Committee Report. Memorandum submitted by Department for Environment, Food and Rural Affairs, Examination of Witnesses*, 11 December 2002.

Select Committee on Environment, Food and Rural Affairs (2003) *Select Committee on Environment, Food and Rural Affairs. Select Committee Report. Appendices to the Minutes of Evidence*, 12 March 2003.

Sunday Times (2002) 'Scots Farmers Face Pollution Crackdown', *Sunday Times* (13 January 2002).

Tallberg, J. (1999) *Making States Comply. The European Commission, the European Court of Justice and the Enforcement of the Internal Market* (Lund: Studentlitteratur).

# 8
# The Europeanization of Health Care: Processes and Factors

*Dorte Sindbjerg Martinsen*

## Introduction

In various aspects health care constitutes a less likely or critical case of both European integration and Europeanization (Eckstein, 1975).[1] As set out explicitly in the Treaty, the organization of health care is the responsibility of the member states (Art. 168(7) of the Lisbon Treaty, previously Art. 152(5)). As in other social policy areas, national governments have indeed been opposed to delegating too much competence to the European Community (EC) when it comes to the core of the welfare state. Health care continues to be a policy area of high political salience and legacy, and with a large set of national veto points opposing supranational intervention. Furthermore, it is a policy area of considerable economic attention and fragility, where the need for cost control hampers the introduction of new cross-border supplies. Nevertheless, both integration and Europeanization have taken place with considerable speed and substance. When a policy area may be classified as a less likely or critical case of Europeanization, this brings specific challenges to the research design, but may also bring out crucial theoretical and empirical insights regarding which causal factors mediate or limit the processes of Europeanization and its outcome. The second section will look further into case selection and how the classification of a case is an important first step, when planning one's research design for the study of Europeanization.

Integration of health care and subsequent Europeanization are effects of the EC that were never really meant to be. The case examined here may be regarded as the most important initiative taken to date in the area, gradually extending the right to cross-border health care and patient mobility. Public health-care governance in the

European Union (EU) contains a wider set of sub-policies (Lamping and Mau, 2009: 1361–1379), but this chapter examines the specific development concerning cross-border care and patient mobility. In 1998, the European Court of Justice (ECJ) initiated a remarkable process of integration where it interpreted that health care is a service within the meaning of the Treaty and therefore in principle shall circulate freely within the internal market. Understood literally, this would mean that a public good such as health care is similar to other internal market products and that a patient should be able to access any type of treatment in another member state, with the costs reimbursed by the competent national health-care institution. However, from 1998 onwards the ECJ has maintained that health care is a service within the meaning of the Treaty, but it has also recognized that, in the absence of harmonization at the supranational level, it is for each member state to determine the conditions for entitlement to benefits as long as these conditions comply with Community law. The justifiability of national conditions in the light of Community law therefore constitutes the central theme in the Court's ongoing interpretations, through which the integration process unfolds.

The chapter will first discuss research design within case studies on Europeanization, and argue that such design will benefit from including considerations on the characteristics of the cause, suggest plausible explanatory factors and specify the outcome variable. The next section examines the Europeanization of health care and, on the basis of existing studies, looks into plausible explanatory factors in the Europeanization process of Germany, France, the Netherlands, the UK and Denmark. Finally, some concluding remarks are provided.

## Research design

When examining Europeanization within or comparatively across policy areas or member states, the case study method is often applied. This also applies to the present examination of the Europeanization of health care. The qualitative case study method is useful when the scholar wants to analyse *why*, *how* and *to what extent* a policy area has become Europeanized. The method thus deals with some of the questions most central to political science research, all of which contain causality inquiries. *Why*: Which cause or explanatory factors explain whether Europeanization has taken place (or has not taken place)? *How*: Which cause characteristics and explanatory factors explain the process of Europeanization? *To what extent*: Which cause characteristics and explanatory factors explain the outcome of Europeanization?

The case study method is well equipped to uncover complex inter-institutional dynamics, as it provides 'a better opportunity to gain detailed knowledge of the phenomenon under investigation' (Collier et al., 2004: 87). Whereas the downside of the method is often found to be the small-*n*, the advantages are that the method enables the researcher to delve into the details and causal factors of a single unit (Gerring, 2004: 348). The case study constitutes a method capable of addressing the causal complexity often found when European policies are created in areas of high political salience, when such policies evolve and when they impact nationally in diverse and complex ways, such as the current case of EU health-care regulation (George and Bennett, 2005: 19–22).

In practical terms, *process tracing* is one way of mapping the incidents, organizations, actors, mechanisms and other causal factors that interplay when a specific Europeanization process unfolds. Process tracing enables the scholar to link incidents at the supranational and the national level, and through detailed analysis identify the link between a European cause, intermediate variables and national effects – as they unfold over time. Process tracing aims to identify the causal chain between an independent variable (X) and a dependent variable (Y), and hereby identify the explanatory factors assumed to link $X$ and Y (George and Bennett, 2005: 206–207). The method is therefore especially useful when one addresses causal interference in qualitative research (Beach and Pedersen, 2010). When tracing the process that links X and Y, one seeks to identify the *explanatory factors* (i.e., the *intervening variables* and *causal mechanisms* in between). Intervening variables and mechanisms are those connecting factors between an input and an output that we need to identify to analytically reconstruct the causal chain (Checkel, 2006: 363). The identification of the factors in between is analytically essential, as cause and effect are unlikely to be immediately related to one another. A long time span research period will often be needed as Europeanization tends to effectuate gradually or in delayed manner (Panke, Chapter 7 in this volume), through criss-cross links between a European cause and national intermediate variables that either hinder or mediate the effects of such cause (Martinsen, 2007a). A diachronic process-tracing study may uncover complex Europeanization, whereas a more immediate, synchronic study is likely to encounter difficulties in tracing complex dynamics and delayed effects of Europeanization.

When the scholar undertakes his/her Europeanization study and aims to uncover such causal complexity, a carefully drawn *research design* serves as a helpful analytical guide. We suggest here that when designing the research model that serves as the analytical wallpaper, it will be useful to include considerations of *the classification of the case*, the *characteristics* of the independent variable (i.e., the *cause*), the *intermediate variables* assumed to matter within and across units and finally to specify the *dependent variable* as part of the research design (i.e., does this study examine Europeanization as a process or an outcome variable? (Exadaktylos and Radaelli, Chapter 2 in this volume)). And, if it includes an outcome variable, what kind of Europeanization effect has occurred and (eventually) to what extent has it taken place? (Töller, Chapter 3 in this volume).

### The classification of a case

When undertaking within-case analysis (Bennett and Elman, 2006: 455–457) of issues such as Europeanization of health care or studies of other policy areas, a meaningful first step is to classify the case in terms of its likelihood of theory confirmation or invalidation. That is, is this a least likely (critical) or most likely case to confirm a theoretical or empirically generated hypothesis? Such classification tells us something about the generalizability of the case and how its analytical results may contribute to more general theory development.

In this way, a case can be selected for strategic-theoretical purposes. The case may then aim to test a theory or findings of other studies, to test their more general application. If the case seems *a priori* unlikely to support theory or analytical findings of other studies, it constitutes the 'least likely' case or, on the contrary, a 'most likely' case. The 'least likely' case may confirm the theory or existing studies against our expectations. The propositions of the theory thus appear stronger and more likely to hold in other (more likely) cases as well. It has gained explanatory value. As, for example, when Europeanization of a policy area is unlikely due to national characteristics, actors or the lack of direct supranational competence, but is found to have taken place. The opposite account is true for the 'most likely' case. If, contrary to expectations, it invalidates the theory, that theory has been significantly weakened. The 'least likely' case is thus foremost tailored to confirmation, and the 'most likely' case to invalidation of a theory (Eckstein, 1975: 119). By choosing one's case strategically along the continuum of 'least likely' and 'most likely', the case study becomes a highly suitable method for testing and improving theories and existing studies: 'A single crucial case may certainly score a clean knockout over a theory' (Eckstein, 1975: 127).

## Research design: Cause, explanatory factors and outcome

When designing the analytical model for one's Europeanization study, the characteristics of the independent variable, the *cause*, should also be considered, because the degree of coerciveness and thus the imperative to Europeanize may vary considerably from one EU regulatory area to the other. One needs to specify the degree of institutionalization and adjustment pressure that the European cause, driving Europeanization, exerts (Schmidt, 2002). According to Schmidt's 'Europeanization flow chart', adjustment pressure varies in relation to the degree to which rules are specified (Schmidt, 2002: 901). But other characteristics of the cause are also likely to be decisive to the process of Europeanization. First of all, Schmidt's degree of *rule specifity* and coerciveness need to be taken into account. A directive or regulation may both be binding rules, but their individual articles set out to detail member states' obligations may be very specific or very vaguely formulated, open to interpretation and mirroring political compromise. When vaguely formulated, the national executives have more discretionary space on how to implement. Non-binding rules also vary in the extent to which they specify the normative obligation to be followed by member states. Secondly, the *means of regulation* vary. Within some areas judicial policymaking plays a larger role than in others. An area that is mainly or heavily regulated by the case law of the ECJ may undergo distinct processes of Europeanization. Other areas may be supported by regulatory agencies that exert some regulatory authority within the policy areas, formulate recommendations and interpret the extent and meaning of the regulatory scope (Martens, 2008; Thatcher, 2005). Third, *time* is likely to matter with regard to the characteristics of a cause. When a policy area has been integrated for decades, it tends to be more detailed and its regulatory scope wider. Within such areas, actors and institutions have had more time to agree on objectives, instruments and confront misapplications. Time also implies that most causes are dynamic and the European imperative to change at a given $T_2$ may vary significantly from $T_0$ when the regulation was initially adopted. Some member states may be less willing or able to adapt to the ongoing dynamism of European integration, thus ignoring incremental change as it takes place.

The characteristics of the independent variable, the cause, further affect the subsequent *intervening variables and mechanisms* in play. The research design should consider which intermediate variables are likely to influence the Europeanization process and its line of causation. Hence we move beyond a simple causal logic that addresses only how X causes Y, and according to which causation means 'if X then Y' and the logic runs as 'X is a cause of Y because without X, Y would not have occurred' (Mahoney and Goertz, 2006: 232). Explaining variables extend the line of causation, since such variables link cause and effect. The proposition of causal mechanisms is that Y may not occur even though X is there, if causal mechanisms and other variables in between are not present or if their presence directly hinders causation between X and Y. Furthermore, intermediate variables may also intensify the effects of a cause and thus facilitate a process of change. An analytical focus on explaining variables highlights that there is seldom an automatic relation between X and Y.

In many ways this is what studies of Europeanization tell us. In fact, causal mechanisms and other sets of intervening variables are crucial to most Europeanization studies. The recent critique raised by Gerring (2010) on what he calls 'mechanism-centered explanations' therefore questions central parts of Europeanization research. Gerring argues that 'mechanism' has too many meanings and may mean different things to different people (ibid.), thus becoming too linked to the specific case. Without doubt this often goes for Europeanization case studies, where there is no consensus as to what constitutes a mechanism and thus what we are trying to measure (Exadaktylos and Radaelli, Chapter 2 in this volume). Here, a mechanism is understood to be related to actors and their action (i.e., the activities and behaviour of entities), relying on Hedström's definition according to which a mechanism 'refers to a constellation of entities and activities that are organized, such that they regularly bring about a particular type of outcome, and we explain an observed outcome by referring to the mechanism by which such outcomes are regularly brought about' (Hedström, 2008: 321).

One way of meeting the critique of Gerring, while maintaining that causal mechanisms may be one set of explanatory factors decisive to causality processes in Europeanization, could be to let one's research design specify the plausible causal mechanisms alongside the intervening variables for which the subsequent analysis will test.[2] That is, setting out explicitly and in relation to theory as well as existing studies what we assume are the significant variables and mechanisms that link independent variable X with dependent variable Y, and thus constitute part of the causal chain of the given Europeanization process.

As demonstrated by the findings of Exadaktylos and Radaelli's meta-analysis, Europeanization studies operate with a wide and quite different set of explanatory factors (Exadaktylos and Radaelli, Chapter 2 in this volume). Researching the impact of such different variables demands again different analytical grips. It takes a different handle to examine mechanisms, focusing on actors and actions, compared with the intervening variables of, for example, national institutions, preferences and positions of a group of actors or type of political system. These different sets of explanatory factors may be equally important for causal inference, but they require analytical distinction in the sense that the exemplified variables cannot produce outcomes themselves, but may heavily influence the way individuals act (Hedström, 2008: 322).

Instead, intervening variables can be seen as 'extraindividual entities' (Hedström, 2008) and 'static' before being paired with specific actors and action, mechanisms are relational and behavioural (Exadaktylos, 2010: 34). Together, variables and mechanisms constitute the explanatory factors between cause and effect, and the way they condition one another is essential for causal inference in Europeanization analysis. In concrete, plausible important intervening variables in our research design are likely to include national institutions, the core executive, bureaucracy, type of political system, pressure groups/non-governmental organizations (NGOs), preferences, the judiciary, political parties and media among others. Mechanisms, on the other hand, relate to what those institutions or organizations do, have done for decades, interpret or respond to European causes and count mechanisms such as institutional compatibility, the legacy of national institutions, discourse, ideas, norms, frames, socialization, identity, opportunity structures, veto positions and compliance culture among others (Exadaktylos and Radaelli, 2009; Falkner et al. 2005; Knill and Lehmkuhl, 2002).

When preparing our research design, hypotheses on intervening variables and causal mechanisms can be formulated. In addition, more crude process-tracing questions may be useful to give direction to what we are looking for and help to compare what we find (Table 8.1).

When conducting within-case studies, we may find explanatory factors that we did not consider in the first place. Furthermore, comparative case studies across policy areas or member states are likely to point out that whereas some intervening variables or mechanisms are highly important to the Europeanization of some policies or to the process in some member states, they are not in others.

Having considered plausible causal mechanisms finally brings us to the dependent or *outcome* variable of the research design, where we may hypothesize different degrees of effect ranging from retrenchment to transformation (Radaelli, 2003; Töller, Chapter 3 in this volume).

*Table 8.1*   Process-tracing questions

**Process-tracing questions in relation to intervening variables and causal mechanisms**

|  | Intervening variables | Causal mechanisms |
|---|---|---|
| Which intervening variables or causal mechanisms do we assume constitute part of the causal chain within a given case study? | Examples:<br>• bureaucracy<br>• political system<br>• pressure groups | Examples:<br>• socialization<br>• discourse<br>• identity |
|  | **Hindering variables or mechanisms** | **Mediating variables or mechanisms** |
| Do we assume that their presence hinders or mediates the process of Europeanization? | Examples:<br>• bureaucracy<br>• political system<br>• discourse<br>• identity | Examples:<br>• pressure groups<br>• socialization |
| Why are different variables or mechanisms eventually assumed to have different functions? | Explanations with reference to theories and existing studies | |

A research design encapsulating the line of causation between X and Y may take the form shown in Figure 8.1.

Which intervening variables and causal mechanisms potentially play a part will vary from case to case. Our first explorative steps in the

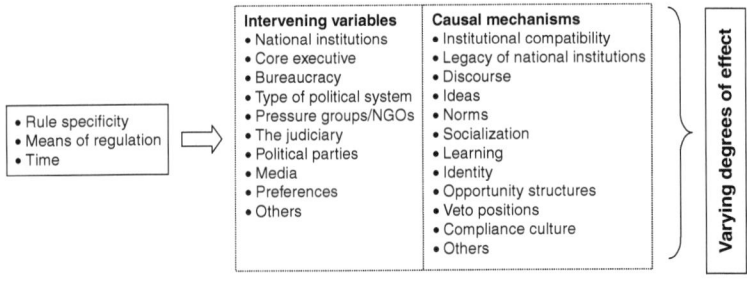

*Figure 8.1*   Research design examining the Europeanization of a policy area

research area will instruct which explanatory factors are considered important, while more in-depth analysis is likely to introduce others and refine the research design. The comparative or within-case studies will then test which ones constitute part of the causal chain – and eventually why. The different components involved in establishing a research design for the examination of causality within health-care Europeanization will be discussed in more detail in the following section.

## The Europeanization of health care

Regarding the classification of the health-care case, if placed on a continuum between 'least likely' and 'most likely' cases, it more accurately represents the 'less likely' case. Not 'least likely' in a strict sense, because internal market principles have implications for public goods, but 'less likely', because member states maintain the prerogative to organize their health-care systems and have repeatedly refused harmonization moves from the EU. The autonomy to decide on welfare policies has been zealously guarded by the member states. Integration, compromising national welfare competencies, is thus 'less likely' to happen. As a less likely case of Europeanization, we hypothesize that:

> $H_1$: Intervening variables and causal mechanisms generally oppose Europeanization.
> $H_2$: Due to the characteristics of the cause and the opposing character of explanatory factors, Europeanization is weak both as process and outcome.

When examining the *characteristics* of the independent variable, the *cause*, we find that up until March 2011 the integration process has mainly taken place by means of judicial policymaking. Nevertheless, as the ECJ has integrated quite dynamically since 1998, rule specifity has increased over time. In March 2011, the European Parliament and the Council finally managed to adopt a directive on patients' rights in cross-border health care. As the directive is still to be implemented in member states, the case law of the Court still constitutes the independent variable.[3] The cause as the input to Europeanization is therefore characterized by judicial policymaking being the regulatory means. The rule specifity has grown over time, as the ECJ has gradually extended the meaning and scope of the conditions under which one has a right to receive health care in another member state. However, the fact that the policy area is regulated by means of judicial policymaking is decisive to the subsequent Europeanization process, as member states may not accept the full wording and meaning of the rule of law but reinterpret what the Court has said more in line with their own understanding and preferences (Martinsen and Vrangbæk, 2008). The authoritative status of judicial policymaking continues to be questioned at the national level (Conant, 2002; Wasserfallen, 2010). As regulatory means, judicial policymaking may be both highly effective as it is not bound by constituencies while at the same time clearly limited, as member states reinterpret their obligation to comply. Health-care integration as the research design's independent variable is therefore characterized by judicial policymaking as regulatory means and a certain degree of rule specifity open to interpretation, and by being a dynamic process of integration indeed, where individual case law has added on and gradually but considerably extended the regulatory scope over time. The time period runs from 1998 to 2010.

Between 1998 and 2010, the ECJ laid down that health care is a service within the meaning of the Treaty, which shall in principle circulate freely. Judicial policymaking thus meant that the territorial closure of the national health-care sectors was put under severe adaptive pressure. The European imperative to change was quite fundamentally contradicting the traditional organization of the public sector: territoriality versus free movement principles (Ferrera, 2005; Martinsen, 2005). In its ongoing case law interpretations, the judiciary laid down that the free movement principles apply to all health-care services independent of how that health-care service is financed or which health-care system provides it.[4] Jurisprudence, however, also stipulates that under certain conditions national restrictions to cross-border health-care are justified. Such restrictions need to be proportional and justified (Martinsen, 2009), and the Court distinguished between non-hospital care and hospital care.[5] Judicial policymaking asserted that the EU citizen has the right to receive non-hospital care in another member state, without that right being authorized beforehand by the respective national health-care institutions. The cost of care shall then be reimbursed subsequently up to what that treatment would have cost back home by the competent health-care institution. On the other hand, member states may make the right to hospital care subject to certain conditions. According to the Court, it is justified that the right to hospital care in another member state is subject to prior authorization by the competent health-care institution, entitling the patient to receive a specific treatment in another member state and subsequently have the cost of care reimbursed up to what the same treatment would have cost in one's home member state.

In this way the Court on the one hand justifies a significant degree of national control, while on the other hand it makes such control subject to conditions. In the same area of case law, the Court also laid down that the national authority is obliged to issue the authorization if the same treatment cannot be provided without undue delay back home and the decision whether to authorize has to be based on international medical science and not purely national considerations. Furthermore, the procedure on how to apply and the condition under which such authorization is granted has to be assessable, transparent and based on objective, non-discriminatory criteria, and refusal to grant authorization must be open to challenge in judicial or quasi-judicial proceedings.[6] The Court has also clarified that there can be made no distinction as to whether health care is privately or publicly provided. Private health care may be accessed abroad even though that is not allowed in the domestic system.[7]

Health-care integration thus constitutes a dynamic cause that has its content and meaning mapped and specified over time. In many ways, it is integration by bits and pieces, two steps forward one behind and, in its fragmented manner remains open to interpretations, reinterpretations and misunderstandings.

## Explanatory factors within the Europeanization of health care

Existing studies on the implementation of the patient mobility case law have mainly examined the impact in the old member states, whereas we lack knowledge about implementation processes in southern and eastern member states. In a comparative light, they point to different *explanatory factors* in play, but a similar outcome, namely that the principle of territoriality has been weakened in the organization of national health care: a principle which for so long has bound health-care consumption to national territories (Vollaard, 2009). The degree to which the principle has been weakened, however, varies, as do the explanatory factors. This highlights the need to examine processes of Europeanization comparatively, over time and across member states. Existing studies thus give us good suggestions on plausible intervening variables and causal mechanisms, facilitating or opposing X to cause Y. Their explanatory value may then be tested in unexamined member states, as well as in other policy areas.

The *legacy of national institutions* impacts on the Europeanization of health-care. Vollaard identifies two families of health-care states: a 'command and control' health-care state and a 'corporatist' health-care state (Vollaard, 2009: 311). The distinction between two health-care categories can also be found elsewhere (Ferrera, 2005: 124; Martinsen, 2007b: 26–27). The 'command and control' type of state runs public health care as a *National Health Service* system, where health-care rights are granted on the basis of residence (Cornelissen, 1996). A person is entitled to health care because s/he is a citizen or a habitual resident, and not through individual contributions paid to a specific scheme. Health-care expenditure is generally financed by taxes. The planning is state-led and health care is provided by publicly owned health-care services. The system is governed by elected politicians and the public administration at local, regional and central level (Vollaard, 2009: 311). In practice, more and more citizens may rely on private provision of health care, and elements such as patient choice and market principles of the sector have grown over the years (Hagen and Vrangbæk, 2009). This model is found in the UK, the Scandinavian countries, Southern Europe and in some of the East European member states. The 'corporatist' health-care state organizes health-care provision differently. It is a *social insurance-based* model, where market participation generally gives access to a social security scheme, including health care, and the degree of this participation decides the level of entitlements. The provision of health care is largely regulated by hospitals and health insurance funds within a public law framework. In addition, the social partners have a say on the provision and the rights of their members. The state participates in the corporatist arrangement and may influence by means of public law, but overall the role of the state is less prominent (Vollaard, 2009: 312). We find the corporatist health-care model in France, the Netherlands, Belgium, Germany, Luxembourg, Austria and in some of the East European member states (Martinsen, 2007b: 27). The different health-care models differ as to whether they provide health care as benefit in kind, or by a principle of reimbursement, where the patient first pays for the treatment and is subsequently reimbursed by the competent health-care fund.

In his comparison of Germany and Denmark, Kostera finds that health-care institutions in Germany are comparatively better equipped to adapt to the pressures for change from the EU (Kostera, 2008: 24). On the other hand, the national institutional legacy of Danish health care has made Denmark much more hesitant in changing its legislation (Kostera, 2008). Kostera furthermore finds that the institutional setting of the Danish health-care system makes it (de facto or assumed) more economically vulnerable to cross-border provision of health care (Kostera, 2008: 29). He therefore points to the *economic variable* as an explanatory factor, which constitutes an obstacle between X and Y. The general importance of this finding could then be tested in other member states with national health service systems.

However, as processes of Europeanization are dynamic the *time* component proves to be important when examining explanatory factors, and whether they oppose or facilitate the causal link between X and Y. National institutions undergo reforms, not least in the health-care sector. Martinsen and Vrangbæk find that Danish *health-care reforms* come to mediate the impact of ECJ jurisprudence. As patient choice constitutes a vital part of domestic health-care reforms, the principles contained in the European integration process correspond closely with what happens back home. Therefore, it becomes increasingly difficult to ignore the imperatives from Europe, and Denmark needs to adapt to some extent to the ECJ jurisprudence, however not in full (Martinsen and Vrangbæk, 2008). In this sense, it is possible to speak about 'synergies of Europeanization', where domestic change patterns correspond to European ones and hereby facilitate change.

The importance of domestic reform agendas is also found in the work of Obermaier (2008, 2009). His research substantiates that one reason why the UK government decided to remove firm territorial restrictions in the National Health Service (NHS) Act was that it fitted the Labour government's agenda to make the NHS more market oriented. That also features as a causal mechanism for Germany. Political preferences played a role when Germany decided to transpose the ECJ ruling, because it was in line with the Christian Democratic Union (CDU)/Christian Social Union (CSU) preferences on greater patient choice (Obermaier, 2008: 749). We thus have political *preferences* added as an intervening variable, identified in the Europeanization of health care. Change of preferences may come to change essential parts of a blocking *institutional legacy* (i.e., a mechanism, thus facilitating change).

As a more general intervening variable, the role of the *core executive* and the *bureaucracy* is pointed out. The Danish central administration creatively reinterpreted the meaning of ECJ jurisprudence, and more specifically what constitutes a service within the meaning of the Treaty (Martinsen and Vrangbæk, 2008). Its creative reinterpretation was restrictive and thereby limited the scope of Danish health care that could be accessed in another member state. In the Netherlands, the core executive and health authorities first claimed the Dutch system largely compatible with the case law of the ECJ, thereby as a first response denying that jurisprudence obliged it to change its legislation (Vollaard, 2009: 360). The same resistance is documented by

Obermaier and found in the cases of the French, German and UK governments (Obermaier, 2008: 737). The executive and the bureaucracy are identified as key explanatory factors, decisive to the success or failure of EU-induced change. The opposition of the core executive and the bureaucracy implies that effect is indeed delayed or the full effect even hindered in the long run.

The central position of the executive and the bureaucracy suggests that the extent to which their administration of EU obligations is left unquestioned, or checked and balanced by other domestic or supranational actors or institutions, becomes crucial. To what extent is the national administration of EU obligation open to contest and trial? Obermaier's work identifies the *national judiciary* as an important variable (Obermaier, 2008, 2009). Although the role of the national judiciary tends to be disregarded in political science, Obermaier points out that it plays a decisive checks-and-balances function to how bureaucrats translate and transcend the EU imperative into national legislation and administrative practices. In France, a multiplication of court cases put more and more pressure on the French administration to end legal uncertainty and implement (Obermaier, 2008: 745). The fact that the UK had the Watts case heard before the European court, brought forward by the British judiciary, meant that no national health service system could maintain that ECJ jurisprudence did not affect their national system. Also in Germany, the national judiciary played a vital role to the Europeanization of health care, when national court cases started to address the matter and examine its impact on patients in Germany who wished to receive cross-border care (Obermaier, 2008: 749–750). In 2003, Germany finally transposed the ECJ rulings. Concerning the Netherlands, Vollaard also emphasizes the role of the Dutch judiciary. Whereas the early case law was met by uproar and deep concern among Dutch politicians (Vollaard, 2009: 337), the fact that Dutch courts sent the preliminary references of the cases of both Smits-Peerbooms *and* Müller-Faure and Van Riet directly forced the Dutch government to adapt the rulings; first in 2003, by abolishing the prior authorization procedures for pharmaceutical goods and outpatient treatment (Vollaard, 2009: 365), and second, with the health-care reform in 2006 to allow the costs of inpatient treatment provided in another member state, as well as elsewhere in the world, to be reimbursed up to what the same treatment would have cost in the Netherlands. On the other hand, the absence of social courts may partly explain the reduced extent of Europeanization in Danish health care (Kostera, 2008; Martinsen, 2005).

Another explanatory factor that may disturb the administrative autonomy of central administration in defining how to implement the case law of the Court is the existence of decentralized semi-public health authorities. *Insurance funds* in Germany have thus started to implement ECJ jurisprudence in order to put an end to legal uncertainty before the German government choose to implement it by the statutory Health Insurance Modernization Act in 2003 (Obermaier,). In contrast, Obermaier (2008, 2009) finds that the hierarchical and centralized structure encompassing the French government and insurance funds in part explains the slower and more gradual implementation process in France. French insurance funds were not in a position to put pressure on the central administration's delayed implementation, had they wished to do so. According to Obermaier, this in part explains why it took France until 2006 to comply with ECJ jurisprudence (Obermaier, 2009): there was no decentralized administrative pressure to adapt. A hypothesis generated in this regard would be that the more centralized and monopolized administration and implementation is, the lesser the effect of unwanted Europeanization. It requires dispersed power and its administration thereof to generate successful Europeanization in the less likely case. In this regard, *the media* were also found to constitute an important intervening variable in the Europeanization of health care in the UK. An aggressive press campaign focusing on the problems of the NHS put pressure on the UK government to reform the system (Obermaier, 2008: 746). This suggests that when the legacy of established national institutions is in question, dynamics of change – also when supranational – gain more momentum.

Existing studies have mainly identified different intervening variables in the five member states that they examined, whereas the importance of mechanisms has not been stressed to the same extent. In all studies, intervening variables are decisive to the Europeanization process of a less likely case and these certainly condition how actors act and are thus related to mechanisms. In general, the core executive and bureaucracy are found to hinder the process in the first place. However, all member states examined have other variables and patterns over time that pull towards Europeanization and reduce the administrative autonomy that at first constitutes obstacles to Europeanization. Thus we must assume that, over time, mechanisms such as socialization, learning, change in opportunity structure and compliance cultures play a role relevant for future investigation.

Despite the differences in explanatory factors across member states, we note a similar *outcome*, namely the weakening of the territorial principle within the organization of national health care; a weakening, however, that manifests to different degrees. France, Germany and the

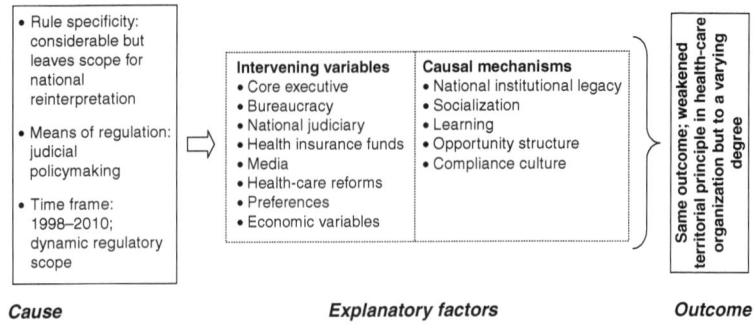

*Figure 8.2*    Research design on the Europeanization of health care

Netherlands have implemented the jurisprudence of the Court more or less in full, whereas the UK and Denmark are more reluctant compliers. The legacy of national institutions and administrative autonomy in the two systems could be hypothesized as key explanations, but that would need to be tested across a larger set of cases.

Figure 8.2 shows a representation of the Europeanization of health-care research design, drawn on the basis of existing studies.

## Concluding remarks

Existing studies demonstrate that, although judicial policy-making constitutes a rather diffuse cause open to reinterpretation, it may produce in the long run a similar outcome in different member states. The causal chain between X and Y is constituted by different explanatory factors that either facilitate, diminish or hinder the full effect of X. The five member states addressed in this chapter illustrate how the cause in itself cannot explain the process of change, but neither can a single intervening variable or causal mechanism. Instead, we have a combination of explanatory factors that drive implementation (Obermaier, 2009). This shows that case studies of Europeanization need to address both variables and mechanism (Gerring, 2010).

To date, the study of the Europeanization of health care has mainly examined processes in the old member states; Germany, France, the Netherlands, Denmark and the UK all belonged to EU-12. Here, the legacy of national institutions, the core executive and bureaucracy are central explanatory factors that have opposed the EU-induced process of change, whereas the national judiciary and other factors which challenge the administrative autonomy of bureaucracy pull towards greater Europeanization. We know little about causation in

Southern and East European member states, and future process-tracing studies will have to examine the explanatory value of the factors pointed out above in a more EU-wide setting. To date, the response of existing studies to $H_1$ and $H_2$ has been that in the less likely case of Europeanization, specific intervening variables and causal mechanisms work towards enhancing Europeanization and drive an outcome, which otherwise would have been severely hindered and delayed even more.

The causal link between X and Y thus depends on the explanatory factors in between, and no simple causal logic assuming 'if X, then Y' would capture the Europeanization process taking place. Furthermore, process tracing also documents that counterfactual logic does not apply either. If a counterfactual logic applied, then Y would occur even without X, so we have not identified the actual cause that has produced the identified outcome. The processes traced for the five different member states substantiate the fact that the strength and preferences of opposing intervening variables and causal mechanisms (i.e., the legacy of national institutions, core executive and the bureaucracy) run counter to the outcome identified. Had it not been for X (EU judicial policymaking) and facilitating explanatory factors, Y (a weakened territorial principle) would not have occurred. Therefore, the process-tracing method also stands as a useful instrument when testing counterfactual hypotheses on EU integration and Europeanization.

## Notes

1. The classification as a 'less likely case' draws on Eckstein's distinction between 'least likely' and 'most likely' cases as a selection criterion within the case study method (Eckstein, 1975). The classification as such will be further elaborated in the second section.
2. In the conclusion of his critique on mechanism-centred explanations, Gerring emphasizes that he does not make an argument against mechanisms as an instrument of causal analysis. Instead, he finds that we need 'intelligent discussion of plausible causal mechanisms, which should be subjected to testing *to the extent that it is feasible*' (Gerring, 2010: 1518).
3. Directive 2011/24/EU of the European Parliament and the Council of 9 March 2011 on the application of patients' rights in cross-border health care.
4. See, for example, cases C-157/99 Geraets-Smits and Peerbooms (2001) and C-372/04 Watts (2006).
5. See case C-372/99 Müller-Fauré and van Riet (2003). Hospital care was defined as being when one has an overnight stay in a hospital of 24 hours. Non-hospital care will then be outpatient care of less than 24 hours.
6. Para. 90 of C 157/99 Geraets-Smits and Peerbooms (repeated in the Watts case).
7. Case C-444/05 Stamatelaki (2007).

# References

Beach, D. and Pedersen, R.B. (2010) 'Process tracing: Metode, design og forskningslogik' in Andersen, L.B., Hansen, K.M. and Klemmesen, R. (eds.) *Metoder i Statskundskab* (København: Hans Reitzels Forlag), pp. 215–238.

Bennett, A. and Elman, C. (2006) 'Qualitative research: Recent developments in case study methods', *Annual Review of Political Science*, 9, 455–476.

Checkel, J.T. (2006) 'Tracing causal mechanisms', *International Studies Review*, 8 (2), 362–370.

Collier, D., Mahoney, J. and Seawright, J. (2004) 'Sources of leverage in causal inference: Towards an alternative view on methodology' in Brady, H. and Collier, D. (eds.) *Rethinking Social Inquiry: Diverse Tools, Shared Standards* (Lanham, MD: Rowman and Littlefield), pp. 85–102.

Conant, L. (2002) *Justice Contained – Law and Politics in the European Union* (Ithaca/London: Cornell University Press).

Cornelissen, R. (1996) 'The principle of territoriality and the community regulations on social security (Regulations 1408/71 and 574/72)', *Common Market Law Review*, 33, 439–471.

Eckstein, H. (1975) 'Case study and theory in political science' in Greenstein, F.L. and Polsby, N.W. (eds.) *Strategies of Inquiry* (Reading, MA: Addison-Wesley Publishing Company), pp. 79–137.

Exadaktylos, T. (2010) *The Europeanization of National Foreign Policy: The Case of Greece and Germany vis-à-vis the Eastern Enlargement of the European Union*. PhD Thesis, University of Exeter.

Exadaktylos, T. and Radaelli, C.M. (2009) 'Research design in European studies: The case of Europeanisation', *Journal of Common Market Studies*, 47 (3), 507–530.

Falkner, G., Treib, O., Hartlapp, M. and Leiber, S. (2005) *Complying with Europe. EU Harmonisation and Soft Law in the Member States* (Cambridge: Cambridge University Press).

Ferrera, M. (2005) *The Boundaries of Welfare. European Integration and the New Spatial Politics of Social Protection* (Oxford: Oxford University Press).

George, A. and Bennett, A. (2005) *Case Studies and Theory Development in the Social Sciences* (Cambridge, MA: MIT Press).

Gerring, J. (2004) 'What is a case study and what is it good for?', *American Political Science Review*, 98 (2), 341–354.

Gerring, J. (2010) 'Causal mechanisms: Yes, but …', *Comparative Political Studies*, 43 (11), 1499–1526.

Hagen, T. and Vrangbæk, K. (2009) 'The changing political governance structures of Nordic healthcare systems' in Saltman, R., Magnussen, J. and Vrangbaek, K. (eds.) *Nordic Healthcare Systems. Recent Reforms and Current Policy Challenges* (Maidenhead and New York: McGraw Hill), pp. 107–125.

Hedström, P. (2008) 'Studying mechanisms to strengthen causal inferences in quantitative research' in Box-Steffensmeier, J.M., Brady, H.E. and Collier, D. (eds.) *The Oxford Handbook of Political Methodology* (Oxford: Oxford University Press), pp. 319–335.

Knill, C. and Lehmkuhl, D. (2002) 'The national impact of European Union regulatory policy: Three Europeanisation mechanisms', *European Journal of Political Research*, 41 (2), 255–280.

Kostera, T. (2008) 'Europeanizing healthcare: Cross-border patient mobility and its consequences for the German and Danish healthcare systems', *Bruges Political Research Papers*, no. 7.

Lamping, W. and Mau, S. (2009), 'European Union and Health Policy: The "Chaordic" Dynamics of Integration'. *Social Science Quarterly*, 90(5): 1361–1379.

Mahoney, J. and Goertz, G. (2006) 'A tale of two cultures: Contrasting quantitative and qualitative research', *Political Analysis*, 14, 227–249.

Martens, M. (2008). 'Runaway Bureaucracy? Exploring the Role of Nordic Regulatory Agencies in the European Union'. *Scandinavian Political Studies*, 31(1): 27–43.

Martinsen, D.S. (2005) 'The Europeanization of welfare – The domestic impact of intra-European social security', *Journal of Common Market Studies*, 43 (5), 1027–1054.

Martinsen, D.S. (2007a) 'The Europeanisation of equality between genders. Who controls the scope of non-discrimination?', *Journal of European Public Policy*, 14 (4), 544–562.

Martinsen, D.S. (2007b) 'EU for the patients. Developments, impacts, challenges' SIEPS report, no. 6.

Martinsen, D.S. (2009) 'Conflict and conflict management in the cross-border provision of health care services', *West European Politics*, 32 (4), 792–809.

Martinsen, D.S. and Vrangbæk, K. (2008) 'The Europeanisation of health care governance – Implementing the market imperatives of Europe', *Public Administration*, 86 (1), 169–184.

Obermaier, A.J. (2008) 'The National Judiciary – Sword of European Court of Justice rulings: The example of the *Kohll Decker* jurisprudence', *European Law Journal*, 14 (6), 735–752.

Obermaier, A.J. (2009) '*The End of Territoriality? The Impact of ECJ Rulings on British, German and French Social Policy*' (Surrey: Ashgate).

Radaelli, C.M. (2003) 'The Europeanization of public policy' in Featherstone, K. and Radaelli, C. (eds.) *The Politics of Europeanization* (Oxford: Oxford University Press).

Schmidt, V. (2002) 'Europeanization and the mechanics of economic policy adjustment', *Journal of European Public Policy*, 9 (6), 894–915.

Thatcher, M. (2005) 'The third force? Independent regulatory agencies and elected politicians in Europe', *Governance*, 18 (3), 347–373.

Vollaard, H. (2009) 'Political territoriality in the European Union: The changing boundaries in the European Union: The changing boundaries of security and healthcare', Dissertation, Leiden University, the Netherlands.

Wasserfallen, F. (2010) 'The judiciary as legislator? How the European Court of Justice shapes policy-making in the European Union', *Journal of European Public Policy*, 17 (8), 1128–1146.

# 9
# How Cities Encounter Europe: Mechanisms and Modes

*Samuele Dossi*

## Introduction

Cities have gained prominence on the economic and political stage in Europe. They are centres for the accumulation and production of wealth, functioning at times as a bulwark against the effects of market forces, and at times as places of social and political inequalities (Brenner, 1999, 2004; Goldsmith, 2003; John, 2001; Le Galès, 2002). The rise of international and European institutions has favoured the transfer of regulatory authority downwards to sub-national territories, that is regions and cities, and in some circumstances, upwards in favour of supranational territorial configurations (Kazepov, 2005; Lefèvre, 1998; Le Galès, 1998).

The institutionalization of the European Union (EU) has, at times, enhanced the political importance of the category 'European City' within a context where 'European public policies, rules, procedures, conflict solving mechanisms, debates and norms, are now relevant to all cities within the EU' (Le Galès, 2002: 96). The EU provides innovative structures of opportunities for actors in urban systems of governance. These are structures that cities can exploit to promote and develop their various interests by drawing on multiple ways of interaction, both with other cities and with upper tiers of governments and regulation. Community Initiatives specifically targeted to urban and city areas have affected the ways urban-level actors 'think' about policy tasks and instruments.

The decision (of the European Commission) to terminate specific programmes addressed to cities from 2007 and to incorporate them into wider regional policies has opened up questions as to the place and role of cities and urban actors within the EU. In this connection, cities are also a key component of the attempts to create new loci of legitimacy for the EU and to learn via the open method of coordination by tapping the benefits of local knowledge (Sabel and Zeitlin, 2008; Zeitlin and Trubek, 2003).

However, when researchers try to identify the policies of the EU affecting the urban political domains, almost invariably they look for those EU programmes with 'cities' on the tin, that is, the policies formally identified as targeting cities. This is a major pitfall, since the identification of the units of policy analysis is a task of the researcher, and often formal-legalistic definitions are misleading or incomplete. In this chapter, we shed light on different causal mechanisms, instruments and arenas of Europeanization of urban politics by adopting a conceptual perspective informed by theoretical policy analysis. This is particularly relevant, because most of the literature on cities has followed a formal or legalistic approach.

Europeanization is the general framework adopted for carrying out the analysis (Exadaktylos and Radaelli,2009 and Chapter 2 in this volume). Within this framework, the focus is on the 'European domestic policy' (Jeffery, 2000), namely those domestic areas influenced by European politics and policymaking, as well as by the institutional relationships between the EU, the national and the sub-national territories. In this chapter Europeanization is defined as *an interactive process wherein domestic systems of governance are in time changed by the diffusion of ideational constructs, legal and social norms, regulations and instruments. These are first identified, negotiated, contested and agreed upon within the EU-wide arenas, and eventually used by domestic actors to shape their institutional orders.* Based on Carter and Smith, institutional orders are interactive mediations 'between sectoral regulation, usage of territory and the reproduction of the EU polity' (Carter and Smith, 2008: 266).

In cities, Europeanization leads to an intensified political and economic interaction between actors at the territorial level, providing urban areas – and so their institutions and actors – with access to, and availability of, information, legitimacy and at times financial support. Partly for these reasons, social, economic and institutional actors across urban areas are experiencing an increasing involvement within mechanisms of governance characteristic of the politics, policies and polities of the EU and of its member states (Atkinson, 2001; Chorianopoulos, 2002; John, 1996, 2000; Marshall, 2003, 2005).

The organization of the chapter is as follows. In Section 2 we peruse some of the scholarships on Europeanization of cities and outline what we contend are the main pitfalls in this field of research. Section 3 introduces the approach we endorse for the analysis and a typology for EU modes of Europeanization, while in Section 4 we advance a proposal to carry out the empirical assessment of Europeanization of cities. Section 5 concludes.

## Europeanization the urban way

The process of European integration has led to a growing bulk of legislation, rules and policy initiatives that impact European cities with different degrees of influence. Additionally, the EU official rhetoric often portrays cities as 'powerful agents of legitimization' (Le Galès, 2007) by designating urban areas as 'target populations' (Schneider and Ingram, 1993) of new dimensions of citizenship. The idea of 'Europe of cities' is also one of the components of the European polity in this legitimizing discourse.

In spite of that, within the field of European studies, academic research on the relations between cities and the EU has been confined, in practical terms, to the structural funds and cohesion policy (Marshall, 2005; Zerbinati, 2004), or to those policy programmes clearly labelled 'urban' on their tin (Cento Bull and Jones, 2006; Halpern, 2005; Tofarides, 2003), thus neglecting other dimensions where the encounter between Europe and urban systems is, theoretically at least, likely to yield transformative effects. This narrow focus creates bias in any possible proposition on the scope conditions for the Europeanization of urban areas. These studies mainly conceive of Europeanization as a twofold process of downloading new institutional models and uploading via policy networks and lobbying activities (Marshall, 2005). The process of Europeanization of cities is eventually described, rather than measured or causally explained, and the influence of the EU action is somewhat prejudged due to scarce attention being paid to the causal mechanisms that trigger change within urban systems.

The dependent variable of these analyses is often identified with the institutional arrangements of local government and eventually with the organizational structure put in place for the management and implementation of the EU programme under examination. The main flaw though is the absence of a clear research design and reference to causal conditions, eventually leading to change in the localities. This, in turn, makes it particularly difficult to disentangle the effects of the EU action – and thus to characterize or measure the process of Europeanization – from rival explanations, such as domestic processes of reform or international phenomena of policy diffusion.

An exception is provided by Zerbinati's comparative analysis of local Europeanization in Italy and England, where attention is accorded to both direct and indirect pathways for EU influence on local authorities. But also in this study the analysis is solely confined to the structural funds. Somewhat different is the approach employed by Kern and Bulkeley (2009) in their study of transnational municipal networks in the context of local policy on climate change. The character of local policy networks in the field of climate change, they argue, is influenced by the process of Europeanization, which is thus assumed to be more of an *explanans* than the phenomenon to be explained.

Turning to the field of urban studies, the EU is generally factored in as an intervening variable within a process in which Europe is reduced to a mere functional context for the action of cities (Bagnasco and Le Galès, 2000; Goldsmith, 2003; Kazepov, 2005; Le Galès, 2002). The EU is therefore somewhat equal to other international governance contexts in which, due to an enlarged opportunity structure, cities and regions are confronted with new channels for exercising 'para-diplomatic' activities beyond the control of the central government. Sometimes, the action of the EU is explicitly addressed and an attempt is made to grasp the Europeanization of cities and urban areas. Nonetheless, the analysis is limited to accounting for the transnational activity of cities within network structures (Keating, 2001; Kübler and Piliutyte, 2007). This approach, in turn, pays little attention, if any, to transformations occurring in urban systems of governance following EU policy action. It neglects elements of research design and causation concerning Europeanization at the level of cities and local authorities.

The literature suffers from an overall lack of theoretically informed approaches to EU-related urban policies grounded on specific assumptions, which in turn has reinforced the tendency to preserve the dividing between European studies and urban studies, at least within the discipline of political sciences.

Urban policies, we submit, at both the domestic level and in the context of the EU, must instead be considered as part of broader domains of public policies and their analysis should be therefore carried out accordingly. As claimed by Le Galès, 'in analytical terms, it has been a common mistake to analyse urban policy as independent from changes in public policy in general' (Le Galès, 2007: 13). This is particularly the case when the attempt is made to assess the interplay between systems and actors in the context of EU policymaking.

Therefore, to assess the nature of the process of Europeanization in the case of urban governance, we have to look at different policy areas involving cities across Europe.

However, this step has been somewhat hindered by the implicit shortcomings of the multilevel governance (MLG) approach (Marks et al., 1996). The tabloid version of MLG, which appears in studies of Europeanization of sub-national systems, reduces Europeanization to the interplay between hierarchically ordered levels of governance, where sub-national levels and central states are maintained as competing or adversarial, due to the attempt of lower levels to evade 'central control'. Thus, sub-national actors and institutions are usually treated as constituting a unique and static layer of governance.[1] Partially to overcome these drawbacks, we draw on an approach grounded in public policy analysis (Carter and Smith, 2008). In particular, we will focus on the different European policy arenas – orders – within which actors and institutions interchangeably relate in order to attain specific policy goals. Processes of interest formation, strategic decision making and regulatory competition taking place over time in the context of policy orders have the potential to influence the character of Europeanization and, eventually, the features of domestic politics within different domains. Policy arenas, as well as the institutional and individual actors therein involved, have to be conceived as constituting dynamic systems, where cities are sometimes EU-level actors, sometimes the recipients of the Commission's programmes, yet the places where EU regulatory measures and provisions are actually implemented. Either way, they are not pigeon-holed in the lower layer of governance by definition (Carter and Smith, 2008).

The analysis of Europeanization of cities offers room for applying the 'sharp public policy analysis tools' evoked by Carter and Smith by accounting for the nature and use of policy instruments, an approach that has rarely been used to date in the studies of EU cities. Focusing on policy instruments as well as on the mechanisms of transmission through which these instruments are likely to be promoted, and reacted to, allows us to move beyond functionalist approaches by integrating at the same time the understanding of the new forms of networked governance (Rhodes, 1997) with the mechanisms for the control and direction of behaviour (Hood, 1998).

## The approach: Policy modes and mechanisms of urban Europeanization

To overcome the limitations of the current literature, rather than looking at legal/formal definitions of urban policy, we have proceeded from a much wider scanning of the ways in which EU policy affects urban policy and politics. Specifically, we draw on the literature on policy types (Anderson, 1997; Gormley, 1986; Lowi, 1964, 1972; Spitzer

1987; Van Horn et al., 2001) and the literature on mechanisms of Europeanization (Eberlein and Radaelli, 2010; Knill and Lehmkuhl, 2002), as well as on the discussion on the logic of choice and the logic of appropriateness (March and Olsen, 1998).

We develop, in turn, the argument that there are four different modes of Europeanization. In consequence, to grasp the essence of a single instrument or a given EU initiative, one has to establish which mode is prevailing in the policy logic of that instrument or initiative. We will define the modes in a moment. For now we will look at the core variables that explain change, which concern the status of actors' preferences and the nature of strategic interaction.

Preferences concern the initial arrangements of preferences that can be either endogenous, and thus subject to change due to processes of learning and socialization in situations where actors' behaviours are mainly guided by a logic of appropriateness, or exogenous, therefore leaving actors with bargaining options, for the most part dictated by a logic of choice. The other dimension, nature of strategic interaction, deals with the distribution of pay-offs from Europeanization. This dimension can, in turn, be displayed on a continuum where one pole is represented by zero-sum games, where either the values at stake are mainly social values and therefore hardly negotiable or the process of interaction is likely to generate winners and losers from Europeanization (Thatcher, 2004). The other pole is positioned within the Pareto frontier.

The combination of these variables thus originates a four-dimensional space. We can therefore develop a typology for the modes of Europeanization, which chimes with current theorizations on the EU modes of governance (Borrás and Jacobsson, 2004; Eberlein and Kerwer, 2004; Héritier, 2002, 2003; Treib et al., 2005).

Cell 1 describes situations characterized by endogenous distribution of preferences and a tendency for interactions leading to zero-sum games. Therefore, within arenas of thick learning or reflexivity the main research question is about the scope conditions for reflexivity. Reflexivity has the strongest potential for transforming zero-sum games and situations of stalemate, within the decision making in regard to specific policy issues, into possible cooperative arrangements (Lenoble and Maesshalck, 2006). Dynamics of interaction characterizing reflexive domains of policy find their foundation in those ontologies and models predicting the possibility of transformative change of preferences. Change is generated by processes of socialization, discursive interaction and social learning (Adler, 1997, 2002; Checkel, 1998, 1999; Ruggie, 1998). These processes often revolve around language, norms

*Table 9.1*   The space of modes of Europeanization

|  |  | Distribution of pay-offs from Europeanization | |
| --- | --- | --- | --- |
|  |  | Zero-sum games Winners and losers from Europeanization | Pareto optimality Europeanization on the Pareto frontier |
|  |  | *Social values* | *Efficiency* |
| Logic of preferences | Exogenous Preferences can change *Appropriateness* | Thick Learning/ Reflexivity | Regulation |
|  | Endogenous Preferences are given *Choice* | Distribution/ Bargaining | Coordination |

and intersubjectivity (Checkel, 2005; Christiansen et al., 2001) and the political role of legitimizing discourses (Schmidt, 2008; Schmidt and Radaelli, 2004). Other key mechanisms through which conflicting preferences of actors involved over policy issues generate reflexivity are deliberation (Elster, 1998) and framing (Schön and Rein, 1994), defined as 'the process of selecting, emphasising and organising aspects of complex issues according to an overriding evaluative or analytical criterion' (Daviter, 2007: 654).

On the other hand, cell 2 captures situations of non-fixed preferences where the overall objective of interaction around policies is to attain procedural efficiency. Therefore, we have regulation as a mode of Europeanization. Domains, where regulation is the characteristic mode of interaction, have a rank of values that is not disputed and is eventually composed by actors. The defining logic of policy action is its tension towards preserving efficiency over equity. Thus, regulation and efficiency can be maintained as two main sets of operating procedural mechanisms (Majone, 1994). Legitimacy is sought through administrative procedures (Majone, 1996, Chapter 13). In the case of regulatory policies, the role played by the EU is one of collibration, defined as 'an intervention by government to use the social energy created by the tension between two or more social groupings [...] to achieve a policy objective by altering the conditions of engagement without destroying the tension [...]' (Dunsire, 1993: 12). The functioning of regulatory arenas is often identified with Pareto-efficiency. Regulatory regimes attempt to reach policy efficiency through differentiating the positioning of actors within the Pareto frontier, as shown by several explanations of international policy coordination (Krasner, 1991).

Cell 3, coordination, portrays arenas characterized by the fixed distribution of preferences where, nonetheless, there are gains from cooperation to be exploited. Coordination as a specific mode of interaction has been partly overlooked, and its nature remains rather under-theorized. In the case of coordination the set of preferences available to actors is exogenous and, as in the case of regulation, the rank of values at stake is not disputed and is eventually composed by actors.

Cell 4 features situations where preferences are fixed and interaction is modelled by zero-sum games. Extended processes of bargaining are the only way forward in terms of composing preferences, often via conflict management through side-payments or by using a kind of 'veil of ambiguity' to settle on long-term solutions that are amenable to short-term bargaining (Eberlein and Radaelli, 2010). The theoretical foundation of distributive arenas is the rational choice paradigm of fixed and conflicting preferences that need to be aggregated or instead transformed within different issues and over time (Eberlein and Radaelli, 2010). Interaction over policy issues thus can take the general form of bargaining and negotiation (Keohane, 1984: 12). Mechanisms of bargaining, especially over policy programmes having considerable net distributive effects, are therefore particularly relevant in the case of cities' involvement within EU-wide policymaking. An illustration is the negotiation of structural funds, where local representatives are often involved in the phase of domestic consultation and only in 'second instance' at the supranational level when the dynamics of grand bargaining can be considered complete (Pollack, 1997; Sandholtz, 1992). Another way to conceive interaction within distributive arenas is to think of a series of nested games (Tsebelis, 1990) taking place within different arenas of governance. City–EU interactions may also conform to mechanisms of 'two-level games' (Buchs, 2008; Putnam, 1988).

This characterization of modes of Europeanization has the merit of reducing theoretical fragmentation. It also sheds light on similarities between Europeanization and wider characterizations of modes of governance. Indeed, one advantage of Table 9.1 is that each typology cell can be associated with modes of interaction well known in the literature on governance and policy coordination. A second advantage consists in the fact that policy instruments can be observed dynamically. Depending on how they are implemented at the local level, they can move from one cell to another, revealing alternative modes of interaction as well as the mechanisms underpinning them.

The modes of Europeanization are theoretically justified patterns of interaction that may bring about Europeanization. We do not prejudge the degree of Europeanization that may eventually occur. We do not even make the assumption that, since there is a theoretically derived logic that produces Europeanization, that logic will operate. Indeed, empirically, one may find constraining or countervailing logics and mechanisms. Thus, we leave the question of 'How much Europeanization?' out of this conceptual exercise.

## From typological analysis to the assessment of urban Europeanization

The Europeanization of urban systems depends on the *nature of strategic interaction*, not on the legal 'tools' explicitly designated for cities. According to this hypothesis, the policy action of the EU allows for potential transformation to be triggered within the policymaking of urban systems of governance also in the context of policy areas not targeting cities in explicit ways. We can formulate expectations regarding the 'extent' of Europeanization and suggest *prima facie* evidence about the encounter between cities and the EU based on the modes of Europeanization:

Exp 1: When the prevailing mode is 'reflexive', stakes are high and Europeanization is expected to be robust (i.e., potentially durable).

Exp 2: When the prevailing mode is 'coordination', stakes are generally low and Europeanization is expected to be robust.

Exp 3: When the prevailing mode is 'bargaining', stakes are high and Europeanization is expected to be contingent.

Exp 4: When the prevailing mode is 'regulation', stakes are rather irrelevant and Europeanization is expected to be contingent on compliance patterns.

Exp. 1 is drawn from the argument that, despite the non-binding character of the policy measures promoted within ideational domains, there are latent potentials for their sedimentation into the logic of domestic action due to extended processes of confrontation and socialization between city actors in EU-wide policy arenas. This can eventually lead to the Europeanization of policy areas other than simply the one initially involved. Similarly, in the case of coordination (Exp. 2), the relatively 'soft' role of the EU and the coordination of reciprocal actions and exchange of ideas over policy alternatives – generally taking place within a group of experts – trigger the possibility of EU instruments becoming a substantial yardstick domestically for policy elaboration. Expectations on the character of Europeanization in the case of modes of bargaining (Exp. 3) are motivated by the distributive nature of EU action and by the generally limited duration of EU programmes, and therefore by the possible 'dispersion' of EU working methods after programmes have terminated. Exp. 4 arises from the reasoning that, given the rather irrelevant stakes, the eventual Europeanization of domestic arenas of policy depends upon compliance with EU provisions, which can be constraining to different degrees and, in the case of cities, 'filtered' through additional provisions elaborated within central national administrations.

These four modes can reveal differences based on the common governance characteristics that we expect to exemplify the encounter between cities and the EU. Thus, the approach to implementation can rely on rigid modalities, which define precise standards, rather than on more flexible criteria for the application of norms. Yet, the nature of conflict over resources can be material, thus involving political or societal confrontation over sensitive policy issues, or may be centred more on the specific procedures to be obeyed for carrying out policies and programmes set at the EU level. Also the character of proceduralization may vary between areas of policy where there are binding (mandatory) steps to be followed – no matter what the substance of the decision (or policy) is – and less stringent requirements that allow the actors involved to manage the issue at stake through more flexible modalities. In addition, a distinction can be made as to the level of transparency of the interaction within a specific area and the nature of deliberation over policy issues, which can be encouraged and diffused, or limited to a strict range of actors.

Furthermore, these modes are likely to feature different structures of actors. A distinction in this sense can be made as to the institutional and territorial level of their 'affiliation' – EU, national or local, the fact that those are public rather than private actors; however, in regard to the source of their legitimization, that can be technocratic or political. Apart from that, differences are likely to be detected in relation to the structure of networks eventually operating, as well as in regard to the type of access to network structures, which can be open or constrained in terms of actors' participation. Finally, other distinguishing features relate to the prevailing institutional structure of interaction that may follow market-like patterns or more hierarchical modes, and the locus of authority that can be centralized or dispersed.

Examples of cell 1 in our typology are the series of 'fora' for discussion and exchange of policy ideas, such as the URBACT II[2] support programme, the CIVITAS[3] forum in the field of transport and the CONCERTO[4] initiative for the exchange of ideas in the field of energy efficiency – yet, the Covenant of Mayors[5] aimed at promoting sustainable energy use at the local level. These instruments can be considered as preponderantly ideational, thus conforming to logics of learning and reflexivity. However, they have the potential to trigger alternative logics – bargaining and regulation – especially if they are endowed with financial provisions and/or eventually rules of implementation. Further, inherently regulative instruments typical of cell 2, such as the EU rules on public procurement and services of general interest,[6] the water framework directive,[7] the waste framework directive[8] and the directive on ambient air quality and cleaner air[9] are often evolving in their ideational elements, which may eventually substantiate into a forum for discussion and learning between actors involved in implementation (and therefore may move to cell 1 – learning and reflexivity). Another example is instruments having a distributive nature – mostly substantiated in structural programmes – which despite reflecting modes of interaction in line with cell 3 are sometimes transformed into modes of learning and reflexivity, yet still typical of cell 1. The Community Initiative URBAN II during the period 2000–2006, the LIFE+ Programme for the Environment and the various financial instruments comprising part of the Cohesion policy (ERDF and Cohesion Fund) exemplify this type of instrument. As shown by Eberlein and Radaelli (2010), the walls separating choice and appropriateness are rather porous. Having established that how should a researcher craft a possible design for empirical research? We suggest the following steps.

In a research project, policy instruments are initially associated with the four modes. Researchers then use techniques such as process tracing to verify whether instruments actually perform according to the 'mode' to which they have been initially paired, or whether they trigger contingencies that have not been theoretically/deductively foreseen. A policy instruments perspective (Hood, 1983; Salamon, 2002) looks at the instrumentation governments are endowed with – in this case the EU – rather than solely focusing on the procedures through which decisions are taken or on the whole range of activities performed. This is particularly convenient within the realm of urban policies, where the EU does not have a specific formal competence and where interactions between 'cities' and the EU are likely to take place within multiple policy areas and during different stages of the policy process. We mentioned process tracing, but this type of research can be carried out with other techniques provided that they are sensible of the time dimension.

To explore mechanisms one may not need more than one city since comparison is made between domains of policy, where variation is expected to occur. The analysis of each of the four modes proceeds along two steps.

During the first phase, the *top-down* analysis will focus on the key points that have produced change at the EU level and observe how the urban system(s) considered reacted to them. In the second phase, a *bottom-up* technique (of the type described by Radaelli and Pasquier, 2007) is employed. This step aims at establishing whether opportunities, pressures and incentives originating at the EU level (and linked to the promotion of EU policy instruments), as defined in the first step, play any actual role and conform to the expectations arising from the policy modes. Therefore, once relevant changes for the domestic urban systems of interaction have been identified, the analysis traces back to the EU (and national) level, in order to verify how the EU variables have exercised causal influence on the domestic structures of policy in the city considered. There are several examples of this combined usage of top-down and bottom-up approaches (Exadaktylos, 2010; Martinsen, 2007; Quaglia and Radaelli, 2007), although none of these look at cities. The author of this chapter is currently completing a project on the city of Turin (Italy) to fill the gap, but a whole new generation of studies on cities is needed.

## Conclusions

Although a formal EU urban policy does not yet exist, and it is very unlikely to come to light for the time being, it is nonetheless possible to produce theoretical conjectures on the influence exercised on cities and urban areas by the action (formal as well as less direct and informal) of the EU through its policy instruments.

In contrast to the classic view based on EU instruments that have 'city on the tin', we have set out to explore an alternative approach to research design. In particular, the chapter has used the initial catalogue of mechanisms and arenas to consider four ideal-typical modes.

These modes – *not* the policies legally defined as EU initiatives for the cities – are the theoretical places wherein the Europeanization effects can be traced, by examining public policies and their instruments across time.

One advantage of our approach is to extend the range of instruments that are (potentially, at least) vehicles of Europeanization way beyond the limited 'city-level initiatives' considered by the traditional approaches. Another is to enable us to theoretically reflect about governance, interaction and logics of political behaviour, thus setting the ground for theory-grounded expectations of how urban governance is affected by the action of the EU. Further, the typology contributes to the literature on modes of governance, policy instruments and Europeanization by showing how the urban dimension can be integrated into broader categories of political science. By doing so, our approach makes the urban dimension fully comparable with other territorial domains in which Europeanization effects have been studied. Further research could integrate our typological exercise with the vibrant literature on EU modes of governance and EU policy instruments (Kassim and Le Galès, 2010).

Some cautious words are in order, however. First, we have to acknowledge that our proposal is of a modest character. It is one possible way to theorize Europeanization at the city level. It brings the cost of high abstractions about logics, preferences and other concepts. Empirical work has often shown that these neat theoretical distinctions melt when researchers attend to careful empirical reconstructions of processes of changes.

The second limitation is that it is not clear at this stage whether the approach outlined in this chapter is a net sufficiently wide to catch and sort out different empirical manifestations of Europeanization, or whether it can also generate causal predictions that are testable. Third, although we have moved away from multilevel governance, it remains to be seen what applications of this alternative view may bring in terms of reassessing the theoretical status of multilevel governance.

Therefore, the research design outlined here needs to be corroborated by further analysis as to the scope conditions for Europeanization, a further specification of its observable implications and above all testable conjectures on the potential transit of the EU policy instrumentation from one domain to another, thus facilitating the collection of a sufficiently broad number of data for formulating general propositions.

## Notes

1. A more sophisticated conceptualization of MLG can be found in the recent works of Bache and Flinders (2004), Hooghe et al. (2010) and Piattoni (2010).
2. http://www.urbact.eu
3. http://www.civitas-initiative.org
4. http://www.concertoplus.eu
5. http://www.eumayors.eu
6. Directive 2004/17/EC of the European Parliament and of the Council of 31 March 2004 coordinating the procurement procedures of entities operating in the water, energy, transport and postal services sectors, OJL 134/1 of 30.4.2004.
7. European Parliament and Council Directive 2000/60/EC, OJ L 327/1 of 22.12.2000.
8. Directive 2006/12/EC of the European Parliament and of the Council of 5 April 2006 on waste.
9. Directive 2008/50/EC of the European Parliament and of the Council of 21 May 2008 on ambient air quality and cleaner air for Europe.

## References

Adler, E. (1997) 'Seizing the Middle Ground: Constructivism in World Politics', *European Journal of International Relations* 3(3): 319–363.

Adler, E. (2002) 'Constructivism and International Relations', in W. Carlsnaes et al. (eds.), *Handbook of International Relations*, London: Sage Publications, pp. 95–119.

Anderson, J. (1997) 'Response to Theodore J. Lowi's Comments', *Policy Studies Journal* 25(4): 557–560.

Atkinson, R. (2001) 'The Emerging Urban Agenda and the European Spatial Development Perspective: Towards an EU Urban Policy?', *European Planning Studies* 9(3): 385–406.

Bache, J. and Flinders, M. (eds.) (2004) *Multilevel Governance*, Oxford: Oxford University Press.

Bagnasco, A. and Le Galès, P. (eds.) (2000) *Cities in Contemporary Europe*, Oxford: Oxford University Press.

Borrás, S. and Jacobsson, K. (2004) 'The Open Method of Coordination and New Governance Patterns in the EU', *Journal of European Public Policy* 11(2): 185–208.

Brenner, N. (1999) 'Globalisation as Reterritorialisation: The Re-scaling of Urban Governance in the European Union', *Urban Studies* 36(3). 431–451.

Brenner, N. (2004) 'Urban Governance and the Production of New State Spaces in Western Europe, 1960–2000', *Review of International Political Economy* 11(3): 447–488.

Buchs, M. (2008) 'The Open Method of Coordination as a "two-level game"', *Policy and Politics* 36(1): 21–37.

Carter, C. and Smith, A. (2008) 'Revitalising Public Policy Approaches to the EU: "territorial institutionalism", Fisheries and Wine', *Journal of European Public Policy* 15(2): 263–281.

Cento Bull, A. and Jones, B. (2006) 'Governance and Social Capital in Urban Regeneration: A Comparison between Bristol and Naples', *Urban Studies* 43(4): 767–786.

Checkel, J.T. (1998) 'The Constructivist Turn in International Relations Theory', *World Politics* 50(2): 324–348.

Checkel, J.T. (1999) 'Social Construction and Integration', *Journal of European Public Policy*, Special Issue 6(4): 545–560.

Checkel, J.T. (2005) 'International Institutions and Socialization in Europe: Introduction and Framework', *International Organization* 59(4): 801–826.

Chorianopoulos, J. (2002) 'Commenting on the Effectiveness and Future Challenges of the EU Local Authority Networks', *Regional Studies* 36(8): 933–939.

Christiansen, T., Jorgensen, K.E. and Wiener, A. (eds.) (2001) *The Social Construction of Europe*, London: Routledge.

Daviter, F. (2007) 'Policy Framing in the European Union', *Journal of European Public Policy* 14(4): 654–666.

Dunsire, A. (1993) 'Manipulating Social Tensions: Collibration as an Alternative Mode of Government Intervention', *MPIFG Discussion Paper* 93(7).

Eberlein, B. and Kerwer, D. (2004) 'New Governance in the European Union: A Theoretical Perspective', *Journal of Common Market Studies* 42(1): 121–142.

Eberlein, B. and Radaelli, C.M. (2010) 'Mechanisms of Conflict Management in EU Regulatory Policy', *Public Administration* 88(3): 782–799.

Elster, J. (1998) 'A Plea for Mechanisms', in P. Hedström and R. Swedberg (eds.), *Social Mechanisms: An Analytical Approach to Social Theory*, Cambridge: Cambridge University Press, pp. 45–73.

Exadaktylos, T. (2010) *The Europeanization of National Foreign Policy: The Case of Greek and German Foreign Policies vis-à-vis the Eastern Enlargement of the European Union*, PhD Thesis, Department of Politics, University of Exeter.

Exadaktylos, T. and Radaelli, C.M. (2009) 'Research Design in European Studies: The Case of Europeanization', *Journal of Common Market Studies* 47(3): 507–530.

Goldsmith, M. (2003) 'Variable Geometry, Multilevel Governance: European Integration and Subnational Government in the New Millennium', in K. Featherstone and C.M. Radaelli (eds.), *The Politics of Europeanization*, Oxford: Oxford University Press, pp. 112–134.

Gormley, W.T.J. (1986) 'Regulatory Issue-Networks in a Federal System', *Polity* 18(4): 595–620.

Halpern, C. (2005) 'Institutional Change through Innovation: The URBAN Community Initiative in Berlin, 1994–99', *Environment and Planning C: Government and Policy* 23: 697–713.

Héritier, A. (2002) 'New Modes of Governance in Europe: Policy Making without Legislating?', in A. Héritier (ed.), *Common Goods: Reinventing European and International Governance*, Lanham, MD: Rowman and Littlefield, pp. 185–207.

Héritier, A. (2003) 'New Modes of Governance in Europe: Increasing Political Efficiency and Policy Effectiveness', in T. Borzel and R. Cichowsky (eds.), *State of the European Union*, Oxford: Oxford University Press, pp. 105–127.

Hood, C. (1983) *The Tools of Government*, London and Basingstoke: Palgrave Macmillan.

Hood, C. (1998) *The Art of the State. Culture, Rhetoric, and Public Management*, Oxford: Clarendon Press.

Hooghe, L., Marks, G. and Schakel, A.H. (2010) *The Rise of Regional Authority. A Comparative Analysis of 42 Democracies*, New York: Routledge.

Jeffery, C. (2000) 'Sub-national Mobilisation and European Integration: Does It Make Any Difference?', *Journal of Common Market Studies* 38(1): 1–23.

John, P. (1996) 'Centralisation, Decentralisation and the European Union: The Dynamics of Triadic Relationships', *Public Administration* 74(2): 293–313.

John, P. (2000) 'The Europeanization of Sub-national Governance', *Urban Studies* 37(5–6): 877–894.

John, P. (2001) *Local Governance in Western Europe*, London: Sage.

Kassim, H. and Le Galès, P. (2010) 'Exploring Governance in a Multilevel Polity: A Policy Instrument Approach', *West European Politics* 33(1): 1–21.

Kazepov, J. (ed.) (2005) *Cities of Europe. Changing Contexts, Local Arrangements, and the Challenge to Urban Cohesion*, Malden, MA: Blackwell Publishing.

Keating, M. (2001) 'Governing Cities and Regions: Territorial Restructuring in a Global Age', in A. Scott, (ed.), *Global City-Regions: Trends, Theory, Policy*, Oxford: Oxford University Press.

Keohane, R. (1984) *After Hegemony. Cooperation and Discord in the World Political Economy*, Princeton, NJ: Princeton University Press.

Kern, C. and Bulkeley, H. (2009) 'Cities, Europeanization and Multilevel Governance: Governing Climate Change through Transnational Municipal Networks', *Journal of Common Market Studies* 47(2): 309–332.

Knill, C. and Lehmkuhl, D. (2002) 'The National Impact of European Union Regulatory Policy: Three Europeanization Mechanisms', *European Journal of Political Research* 41: 255–280.

Krasner, S. (1991) 'Global Communications and National Power. Life on the Pareto Frontier', *World Politics* 43(9): 336–366.

Kübler, D. and Piliutyte, J. (2007) 'Intergovernmental Relations and International Urban Strategies: Constraints and Opportunities in Multilevel Polities', *Environment and Planning C: Government and Policy* 25: 357–373.

Le Galès, P. (1998) 'Regulations and Governance in European Cities', *International Journal of Urban and Regional Research* 22(3): 482–506.

Le Galès, P. (2002) *European Cities: Social Conflict and Governance*, New York: Oxford University Press.

Le Galès, P. (2007) *Governing Globalizing Cities, Reshaping Urban Policies. What Policies for Globalizing Cities? Rethinking the Urban Policy Agenda*, Madrid: OECD.

Lefèvre, C. (1998) 'Metropolitan Government and Governance in Western Countries: A Critical Review', *International Journal of Urban and Regional Research* 22(1): 9–25.

Lenoble, J. and Maesschalck, M. (2006) 'Beyond New-Institutionalist and Pragmatist Approaches to Governance', *Synthesis Report for the REFGOV Research Project*, REFGOV Working Paper Series: REFGOV SGI/TNU-1.

Lowi, T.J. (1964) 'American Business, Public Policy, Case Studies, and Political Theory', *World Politics* 16(4): 677–715.

Lowi, T.J. (1972) 'Four Systems of Policy, Politics, and Choice', *Public Administration Review* 32: 292–310.

Majone, G.D. (1994) 'The Rise of the Regulatory State in Europe', *West European Politics* 17(3): 77–101.

Majone, G.D. (ed.) (1996) *Regulating Europe*, London: Routledge.

March, J.G. and Olsen, J. (1998) 'The Institutional Dynamics of International Political Orders', *International Organization* 52(4): 943–969.

Marks, G., Hooghe, L. and Blank, K. (1996) 'European Integration from the 1980s: State-Centric versus Multilevel Governance', *Journal of Common Market Studies* 34(3): 341–378.

Marshall, A. (2003) 'Urban and Local Governance: The Growing European Dimension', *Journal of European Public Policy* 10(3): 478–485.

Marshall, A. (2005) 'Europeanization at the Urban Level: Local Actors, Institutions and the Dynamics of Multilevel Interaction', *Journal of European Public Policy* 12(4): 668–686.

Martinsen, D.S. (2007) 'The Europeanization of Gender Equality – Who Controls the Scope of Non-discrimination?', *Journal of European Public Policy* 14(4): 544–562.

Piattoni, S. (2010) *The Theory of Multilevel Governance. Conceptual, Empirical and Normative Challenges*, Oxford: Oxford University Press.

Pollack, M. (1997) 'The Commission as an Agent', in N. Nugent (ed.), *At the Heart of the Union: Studies of the European Commission*, New York: Palgrave Macmillan, pp. 111–131.

Putnam, R. (1988) 'Diplomacy and Domestic Politics: The Logic of Two-Level Games', *International Organization* 42(2): 427–460.

Quaglia, L. and Radaelli, C.M. (2007) 'Italian Politics and the European Union: A Tale of Two Research Designs', *West European Politics* 30(4): 924–943.

Radaelli, C. and Pasquier, R. (2007) 'Conceptual Issues', in M.P. Vink and P. Graziano (eds.) *Europeanization: New Research Agendas*, Basingstoke: Palgrave Macmillan, pp. 35–45.

Rhodes, R.A.W. (1997) *Understanding Governance. Policy Networks, Governance, Reflexivity and Accountability*, Philadelphia and Buckingham: Open University Press.

Ruggie, J.G. (1998) *Constructing the World Polity: Essays on International Institutionalization*, New York: Routledge.

Sabel, C. and Zeitlin, J. (2008) 'Learning from Difference: The New Architecture of Experimentalist Governance in the European Union', *European Law Journal* 14(3): 271–327.

Salamon, L.K. (ed.) (2002) *The Tools of Government. A Guide to the New Governance*, Oxford: Oxford University Press.

Sandholtz, W. (1992) *High-Tech Europe. The Politics of International Cooperation*, Berkeley: University of California Press.

Schmidt, V. (2008) 'Discursive Institutionalism: The Explanatory Power of Ideas and Discourse', *Annual Review of Political Science* 11: 303–326.

Schmidt, V.A. and Radaelli, C.M. (2004) 'Policy Change and Discourse in Europe: Conceptual and Methodological Issues', *West European Politics* 27(2): 183–210.

Schneider, A. and Ingram, H. (1993) 'Social Construction of Target Populations: Implications for Politics and Policy', *American Political Science Review* 87(2): 334–347.

Schön, D. and Rein, M. (1994) *Frame Reflection. Toward the Resolution of Intractable Policy Controversies*, New York: Basic Books.

Spitzer, R.J. (1987) 'Promoting Policy Theory: Revising the Arenas of Power', *Policy Studies Journal* 15(4): 675–689.

Thatcher, M. (2004) 'Winners and Losers in Europeanization: Reforming the National Regulation of Telecommunications', *West European Politics* 27(2): 284–309.

Tofarides, M. (2003) *Urban Policy in the European Union. A Multi-Gatekeeper System*, Aldershot: Ashgate.

Treib, O., Bahr, H. and Falkner, G. (2005) 'Modes of Governance: Towards Conceptual Clarification', *European Governance Papers (EUROGOV)* No. N-05-02.

Tsebelis, G. (1990) *Nested Games. Rational Choice in Comparative Politics*, Berkeley, CA: University of California Press.

Van Horn, C.E., Baumer, D.C. and Gormley, W.T.J. (2001) *Politics and Public Policy*, Washington, D.C.: Congressional Quarterly Inc.

Zeitlin, J. and Trubek, D.M. (2003) *Governing Work and Welfare in a New Economy: European and American Experiences*, Oxford: Oxford University Press.

Zerbinati, S. (2004) 'Europeanization and EU Funding in Italy and England. A Comparative Local Perspective', *Journal of European Public Policy* 11(6): 1000–1019.

# 10
# Understanding Causality and Change in Party Politics

*Robert Ladrech*

Europeanization and party change is a relatively recent area within the growing corpus of Europeanization studies. Policy and institutional change at the domestic level have constituted the main foci, helped by the fact that domestic change attributed to the European Union (EU) – or more precisely some aspect of EU activity – is relatively amenable to research methods such as process tracing (Haverland, 2007). It is also the case that explaining institutional and/or policy change had been given sustained attention early on in the development of the Europeanization research agenda, producing explanatory concepts such as 'goodness of fit' and so on. Scholarly attention to political parties and the EU is, strictly speaking, not a new area of study, as the literature on European integration *and* parties can be traced back, in general, at least to the mid- to late 1970s, coinciding with the first direct elections to the European Parliament (EP) (e.g., Henig, 1979) and formation of transnational party federations (e.g., Pridham and Pridham, 1981). The attention brought to the impact of the EU on domestic parties is also of a more recent engagement, due to the fact that parties do not come into contact, nor have regularized channels of interaction with EU decision-making bodies or are subject to EU policy outputs. At first glance, therefore, parties and the EU operate in different and non-overlapping fields of action. Research on elections to the EP focused either on intra-EP party politics (Hix et al., 2007) or on domestic factors influencing the result of elections in member states, in particular labelling their significance as 'second-order' (Reif and Schmitt, 1980). Certainly from the late 1980s onwards, attention was drawn to the position of select national parties *on* European integration, especially as the Maastricht Treaty ratification process became politicized in several EU member states (Gaffney, 1996). Linking analysis of domestic politics, broadly defined, and the

Europeanization perspective on domestic change was evident by the end of the 1990s in individual country studies such as France (Cole and Drake, 2000; Ladrech, 1994), and national institutional change early in the 2000s (for Germany and Spain, for example, see Börzel, 2002). The specific engagement of the study of national party change and the Europeanization research perspective began with Ladrech's article (2002) that promoted a framework for analysis, which has subsequently been taken up by numerous studies. Following Ladrech's proposed five areas of possible party-political change, subsequent research and literature has focused on confirming the hypothesis by searching for and identifying evidence of such change, for example, on party organization (Poguntke et al., 2007) or party programmes (Pennings, 2006). Explaining the cause(s) of party change has occupied researchers less than the search for evidence, with a general operating assumption that the EU exerts pressure on domestic political systems that in turn elicits a response from parties. Mair (2007) has confronted this under-theorized position by categorizing two types of change – direct and indirect, and providing some general suggestions as to causal triggers for each type. His challenge, to explain more rigorously the exact causes of EU-related party change (and conversely what explains a lack of response in a comparative context), is the intent of this chapter.

The next section discusses the issue of defining Europeanized party change and then leads into a discussion of possible causal triggers. Underlying the discussion is an understanding that Europeanization and party research departs from some of the key methodological components of Europeanization research, but this is made explicit in the discussion.

## Causes and types of party change

A significant methodological issue in party Europeanization research, apart from the question of causality, is identifying, if not recognizing, when a political party is reacting to EU influence (on the broader issue of causality in Europeanization studies, see Chapter 2 in this volume by Exadaktylos and Radaelli). In 'top-down' Europeanization dynamics, in particular vertical (Radaelli, 2003) or hierarchical (Bulmer and Radaelli, 2005), for example environmental policy change, legislation creating a new or altered policy responsibility or the introduction of a new policy instrument to attain the same or a new goal can be identified without too much difficulty (and therefore does not present any insurmountable problems in research design). In such cases the researcher is able to trace the origins of the new 'product' and, along the way, to identify additional or contributing causal factors. The task is made more complex, however, in horizontal or 'facilitated coordination' (Bulmer and Radaelli, 2005) in which the EU (specifically the Commission) is not in a commanding legal position, but rather practice and policy ideas are spread through a variety of non-coercive means (for an example of such a policy, see Chapter 8 in this volume by Martinsen on the Europeanization of health care). Nonetheless, there is a precise change in policy, but the researcher is faced with multiple route sources and degrees of influence.

In the case of institutional change, there are two types: direct and indirect. Evidence of direct change is represented by the creation of new offices or ministerial portfolios, as in a national executive, or resources shifted from one ministry to another in order to meet new tasks mandated by either EU legislation or by national government attempts to enhance efforts at the European level of decision making. In these examples, new characteristics are again relatively easy to identify, and subsequently to trace the origins. However, a second type of institutional change, indirect, presents a slightly more complex challenge, as it is suggested that pressure for change(s) may build within certain institutions or practices due to EU policy or decision-making practices, yet overt domestic institutional or organizational change is resisted. This phenomenon corresponds to the scope of domestic change Börzel labels 'inertia' or 'resistance', that is, when 'high misfit' (or pressure to conform to EU obligations) can 'result in inertia since domestic actors will refuse to simply replace norms, rules, and practices by new ones' (2005: 59). The pressure under which traditional activities are pursued is not easily witnessed by outside observation, nor is it apparent how to measure the degree of resistance, though the number and power of veto players can be a crucial indicator. Rather, a more intensive form of investigation that presupposes such pressure because of the hypothesized influence of the EU, or else witnessed in comparative perspective in similar member states, informs the research design and agenda. A similar phenomenon can be understood with regard to party Europeanization.

Mair (2007) categorized party Europeanization into direct and indirect types. The 'mechanism' with which the EU acted upon domestic actors was the 'penetration of EU rules, directives and norms into the domestic sphere' as well as EU 'influence and constraints'. This causal explanation becomes clearer when the differences in type of change are described. Examples of direct change are the formation of new parties, the formation of opinion on European integration and EU policy within existing parties (whether pro- or anti-) and organizational change such as the creation of new offices related to EU affairs. Indirect change in parties comes about because of changes in their operating environment, that is, the wider national political system. Mair concentrates on the effects of political system change for certain aspects of party competition. For example, the transfer of policy competences to the EU limits policy space for national government, which, in turn, removes areas of competition between parties. Additionally, the removal of certain policy instruments, such as government or national central bank manipulation of interest rates, deprives national government of specific action, again depriving parties of a means to affect domestic policy. Moreover, Mair notes that the EU limits the policy repertoire of competing parties by removing state intervention in policy areas, most significantly in those policy areas covered by Single Market legislation (i.e., the product of negative integration). Accordingly, all three 'sets of limits serve to reduce substantially the stakes of competition between political parties, and to dampen down the potential differences wrought by successive governments' (Mair, 2007: 160). Mair's argument concerning indirect effects of EU influence also extends into the issues of citizen depoliticization and disengagement from politics. Finally, a further consideration briefly highlighted by Mair is the need to integrate the analysis of the impact of the EU on parties and party systems 'into the more general theories of party change and development' (2007: 162). In this regard, certain developments which may appear at first glance to be a party adaptation to EU pressure may in fact 'be part of a consciously chosen strategy whereby vulnerable political leaders externalize their political costs and seek to evade both accountability and responsibility' (2007: 163). The task at hand is to refine these broad understandings of (i) how the EU influences parties, in both direct and indirect fashion, and (ii) to include further examples of change under the two types.

## Refining the causal link between the EU and party change

When discussing causality and party change, a concern shared with other dimensions of domestic change is proving that the EU is the responsible or a responsible factor. In other words, it may very well be the case that a newly established policy instrument was introduced as part of a range of government reforms, regardless of the precise EU relationship to the policy area in question. So too with party change: How do we discern EU-influenced change from, for example, opportunistic or strategic changes in parties? We can begin by examining in detail the classification of party change presented by Mair, direct and indirect.

## Direct party change

In this category, as Mair suggests, direct change is a result of EU policies or rules. The fact that elections to the EP mobilize partisan actors may result in the formation of a party to contest these elections, while also providing a presence in the national party system. This, in turn, can affect patterns of national party system competition. Clearly, counterfactual reasoning suggests a party formed to contest elections whose fundamental identity is EU related – either in support or against – qualifies as direct evidence of Europeanization. Two issues regarding party formation, however, spring to mind. The first, and most important for establishing causality, is explaining the exact role the EU actually plays in triggering change. After all, successful newly created EU parties are rare, suggesting that domestic factors are significant in explaining why such parties are evident in a minority of member states. If we assume that parties in competitive party systems exist to influence government policy and to win votes and office, then support for a new party must be based on perceptions by activists that such a proposed party can find some element of success. Establishing a party outside of parliament, as opposed to a group of breakaway members of parliament (MPs) forming a new party in parliament, is a formidable task in terms of resources – financial, personnel, relation to national media, and so on – as well as meeting national criteria regulating party organization, party funding and so on. Therefore, the pre-existing condition for the launch of a new (EU-related) party must be the salience of the EU in domestic politics in general, and specifically a perception by party supporters that existing parties are failing to address the issue(s) at hand. In the UK, the UK Independence Party represents just such a case in point. However, part of the problem for new EU-related party formation is the ability of existing parties to exploit an issue – even if for tactical reasons – as seen in cases of right-wing populist parties for whom Euro-scepticism is absorbed into their policy repertoire (Dechezelles and Neumayer, 2010; Lubbers and Scheepers, 2005). As this brief example demonstrates, it is less the EU causing new party formation, but more its salience or politicization as an issue in domestic politics together with national rules regulating parties that provides the conditions to launch a new party. Adapting the 'goodness of fit' proposition to party change/formation, we can assert that the politicization of the EU (i.e., the integration process and/or policies) represents a type of misfit in domestic public opinion/politics, yet as Börzel and Risse (2007: 492) suggest, 'the "goodness of fit" proposition amounts to nothing more than an enabling condition for the domestic impact of Europe, a starting point without much causal weight in and of itself'. Certainly in the case of new party formation, it takes more than the 'opportunity' of EP elections or public antipathy to certain EU policies to explain new party formation, and the domestic factors of political calculations by political operatives together with national rules may then contribute to explaining why the phenomenon is so highly variable.

It may also be the case that a party comes into existence due to a schism in an established party. As Mair has suggested, direct party Europeanization may result in the formation of new opinion on the EU or EU policy or policies within established parties. In extreme cases, internal dissent may indeed lead to a number of breakaway MPs forming a new parliamentary party. How does the EU cause changes in party internal opinion, whether it leads to a schism, altered positions or simply simmering dissent?

Similar to the example above regarding the politicized conditions conducive to new party formation, a misfit between core party positions and EU policy development must be apparent. It may be the case that latent dissent among party activists or members, or even parts of the leadership, between fundamental party positions – for example on the role of state intervention in the economy – and EU policy direction has existed for some time, only to have a combination of further EU policy development coupled with a 'trigger', such as a referendum on a EU treaty, to politicize the situation. Party leadership management of internal politics is therefore a conditioning variable that determines whether differences of opinion become destabilizing. Again, as in the example of new party formation, much depends on the perception by party activists of the domestic political calculus: the influence of such activists within the structure of the party (e.g., parliamentary party or party in central office; Katz and Mair, 1993). As most major centre-left and centre-right parties are dominated by the parliamentary party wing, for which electoral considerations are usually paramount, it is most unusual to witness internal rebellion over EU policy (or national policy with regard to the EU) beyond sentiment expressed by party members at a party congress. Interestingly, it is precisely a party dominated by its party in central office, where mid-level elites and activists have relatively more influence than the parliamentary party, namely the French Socialist Party, that experienced internal disequilibrium which was resolved through an internal party referendum on the EU Constitutional Treaty, a dynamic inextricably bound up with intra-leadership contests. In this situation, internal party policy conflict over EU position had been present for some time but additional domestic factors were required to trigger change – the EU referendum and leadership challenges; and the nature of the party organization allowed greater resources, in this case rules governing party policy, for the challengers, who based their conviction on the nature and direction of EU economic policy. In this example, the EU is present more as a contextual factor rather than a significant independent variable.

In these two examples, new party formation and opinion formation/change within parties, both types of change are based on the degree of issue salience the EU represents in individual political systems. The EU itself cannot be said to have 'caused' the changes, though of course the presence of EU policy is a necessary condition. The trigger for change is the calculations by domestic individual party actors as to the success of challenging the domestic status quo over party EU positions. Let us return to the question at the beginning of this section, namely, how to discern EU-influenced change from opportunistic or strategic changes made by parties exploiting the EU as an issue. Our discussion so far would suggest that a combination of factors led parties to 'use' the EU in party competition or generate efforts to create a new party, but these factors are primarily domestic and may involve the ideology of the party, its position within the national pattern of party competition, the political culture within which the EU is perceived and so on. It is the case, of course, that 'context matters' (Franzese, 2009), and it may be more precise to rank the *causes* of party change, in which the EU, in a multi-causal explanation, is secondary to domestic factors, at least in the case of the examples described above.

Before turning to indirect party change, there is another type of change that can also be attributed to the EU, but again its contribution to domestic change is presented in a passive manner. Organizational change related to the EU in national parties is by now widely documented (e.g., Poguntke et al., 2007). New positions have been created, particularly in the central office of party organizations (i.e., the extra-parliamentary party), though it is debatable whether these positions, such as a Europe Secretary or liaison with EP delegations, are influential in their own right. Nevertheless, most mainstream parties, as well as those on the ideological extremes that are able to expend resources on such personnel, have created positions. How can the EU be said to have influenced these organizational innovations? The revised misfit proposition used above to explain new party creation and dissent within existing parties is not especially useful to explain organizational change, as it is in explaining institutional change. In regard to the latter, the pressure to adapt institutional practices originates in the interaction between government – national and/or sub-national – and EU practices (e.g., decision making) and policies to which a misfit may have actual consequences in domestic performance. In the case of domestic political parties, it cannot be said that they have an intense interaction with EU decision-making bodies that can have clear consequences for their own performance or electoral fortunes (Ladrech, 2007). Apart from representation in transnational party federations and in the parliamentary party groups of the EP, the national political system is the arena in which domestic parties' most significant operations, resources and political fortunes are based. Performance at the European-level sites rarely has any impact on the activities of the national organization. Parties are of course intimately involved in national as well as supranational governance in the form of party government, and although the partisan complexion of government – whether single party or coalition – does have some effect in terms of intergovernmental bargaining (Aspinwall, 2002, 2007), it is rare that there are domestic political repercussions from this arena (European Council summits or Council of Ministers meetings). Consequently, the concept of a misfit generating pressure which then leads to organizational innovation within domestic parties is inappropriate, due to the absence of a specific cause (EU institutional practice or policy) that connects with the specific type of party position created. It is more realistic to suggest that the offices created in domestic parties are the result of institutional (organizational) isomorphism, in which institutions or organizations which interact on a regular basis tend to become alike, a more sociological explanation based on horizontal means of Europeanization in which 'there is no pressure to conform to EU policy models' (Radaelli, 2003: 42). Börzel points to a number of diffusion mechanisms in regard to institutional isomorphism, and the mechanism of 'imitation' seems most appropriate for national parties. When applied to national polities, imitation is understood to mean that member states 'emulate a model recommended by the EU to avoid uncertainty (*imitation*)' (2005: 57). Adapting this mechanism to political parties, it becomes clear that the primary responsibility of the EU specialist in national parties is to provide information to the leadership bodies of the party, for example on the activities and policy debates of the EP delegation, or else to represent the party in transnational European organizations, such as a Europe Secretary to the respective transnational party federation. In other words, the role of these positions is to reduce the degree of uncertainty that may emanate from the arenas in which the party is present (i.e., the EP and the affiliated transnational party federation). The diffusion mechanism is manifested through copying existing practices by 'pioneering' parties, and it is the constant interaction with colleagues from other parties in the context of meetings that 'best practice' is shared. The resource base of party organizations is also an important factor to take into account, so while the German Social Democratic Party may have a liaison officer between the national party and the EP party delegation, other lesser resourced parties may depend on the leader of the party EP delegation reporting developments and legislative initiatives directly to the national party. Ladrech (2007: 224) has labelled the role of these EU specialists an 'early warning system' for a party leadership, and the profusion of these roles (during the 1990s) coincides with the vigorous expansion of EU policy competences, which potentially raised the degree of uncertainty about the impact of the EU in domestic politics.

In the understanding of party Europeanization as direct effect, as demonstrated above, something about the EU – elections to the EP, the direction and nature of certain EU policies, and EU-level partisan bodies such as EP parliamentary groups and transnational party federations, establishes a precondition for party change. In the first two examples, a modified notion of misfit has acted as the mechanism promoting – but not necessarily determining – new party formation and new opinion formation/dissent within established parties. In the last example, organizational innovation through the creation of EU specialist positions and a modified understanding of institutional isomorphism can explain the timing and cross-national similarity of these positions. Before leaving this section, it is important to draw attention to another example of party change, perhaps obscure from most empirical observation because it is behavioural rather than institutional in the sense of a newly created party or party office. It was mentioned above that a policy misfit between the EU and core policy identity positions of parties may result in growing dissent between parts of the party and the leadership. The basis of the policy dissension may have been latent until a trigger, such as a referendum on the EU, intensifies the internal tension between dissenters and the leadership.

The case of the French Socialist Party demonstrated that a combination of a looming national referendum on the EU Constitutional Treaty and a leadership contest transformed a long-standing ambivalence about the economic direction of EU policy into an open division triggering an internal party referendum on the position for the party to advocate in the national referendum. A crucial party structural factor was the dominance of the party central office decision-making body (in which activists wield substantial influence) over the more electorally minded parliamentary wing (somewhat of a rarity among major centre-left and centre-right parties in Western Europe), illustrating the pressure on party leadership management of internal party politics. The manner in which party leaderships manage the EU as a politicized issue, for example, deciding whether to support changes in party manifestos related to the EU, or promoting or opposing a referendum relating to the EU, are all tasks that would not be incumbent unless there was a form of misfit between the party – usually on core identity issues – and the EU.

The British Conservative Party is a case in point where a leadership must walk a fine balance between voicing mild Euro-sceptic rhetoric while attempting to prevent more vociferous Euro-sceptic MPs and members of the EP from pushing the party programme to a more extreme position. The efforts expended by party leaderships, then, should be considered evidence of an impact on national parties, precisely on party leadership management.

Whereas the first three examples given above of party Europeanization evidence are amenable to outside observation, even research designs of a cross-national basis, only a more concerted in-depth case study would uncover the dynamics inside parties that are more informal. As Mair suggests, such a research strategy 'calls for quite a slow and sustained series of case-study analyses [ ... ] and the accumulation of thick descriptive accounts which can then be compared from the bottom up' (2007: 162). We shall return to the issue of research design in the final section of this chapter.

### Indirect party change

Mair's primary concern when addressing examples of the indirect effect of the EU on political parties was to concentrate on how party competition is altered. His focus was on a depoliticization, brought about because of policy transference from the national to the supranational (EU) level. By removing policy issues that had been contested, and instead redirecting the policy development to non-political EU policy experts, party competition weakens as parties have less over which to compete (another effect may be to heighten or exacerbate non-policy issues such as personality or to fuel anti-party or anti-political sentiment and mobilization). The understanding of indirect effect is therefore one that rests on changes to party government as well, for the policy choices that are removed from domestic competition also impact what parties 'in government' are able to execute and thereby employ for re-election campaign purposes. The question at hand is exactly how to frame the indirect Europeanization argument in terms of causal mechanisms? This task is made all the more challenging because one must disentangle domestic from EU causal sources, and therefore Mair's admonition to integrate party analysis with Europeanization research is a necessary step in order to avoid misattributing causal influence to the EU. The essential issue in analysing indirect effects of the EU on parties (i.e., altered patterns of party competition via the narrowing of the policy repertoire of the national executive) is determining when the EU is in fact the independent or an intervening variable. Put more succinctly, when is the EU consciously 'used' by parties as part of an electoral strategy and when is a party – reluctantly or otherwise – making changes that are a result of EU-related influence on the domestic political system?

If one brings comparative party analysis into the argument, parties may be open – under certain circumstances – to opportunities that present themselves in order to achieve a competitive edge with rivals. Articulating a Euro-sceptic rhetoric may be a strategic decision as much as a misfit between EU policy and core party principles. Apart from a few exceptions such as the British Conservative Party or the Czech Civic Democratic Party, most mainstream centre-left, centrist and centre-right political parties do not articulate a clear Euro-sceptic message. Where such a position is broadcast, it is usually by parties on both extreme sides of the political spectrum. Most right-wing populist parties have varying degrees of Euro-sceptic programmatic positions as do many parties to the left of social democrats. The reasons differ between the two ideological camps for their anti-EU position – EU economic policy for the left, national sovereignty issues, including immigration policy, for the right – but these issues are not exclusive to these parties, as social democratic and Christian democratic/conservative parties also have elements of a policy misfit to a degree with EU positions. The key difference is the competitive advantage that an anti-EU position gives in party competition in addition to the salience of the 'EU as an issue' or its politicization (Steenbergen and Scott, 2004). In the mainstream parties, suppressing or deflecting of internal issues from public scrutiny is necessary due to the need for internal stability, but also because of the mixed cues over the EU it may send to voters (Gabel and Scheve, 2007). This is less the case with far-right and far-left parties as the core party principles are in some level of discord with EU policy or polity. This explains why these types of parties are more likely to strategize or exploit the EU for electoral purposes rather than mainstream parties. However, from a Europeanization perspective, the choice or decision to actually 'use' the EU as an opportunity in party competition remains with the party itself. The structure of party opinion and the EU – a misfit – is again a precondition: what motivates a party leadership to act depends on a combination of domestic factors, both internal to the party (e.g., mobilization at a party congress) and external (the position of other parties) as well as an event (e.g., a national referendum on an EU treaty).

Mair has also suggested that the transfer of certain policy authority from the national to the supranational level is not always lamented by party leaderships, and in fact can be exploited, especially by parties in government because blame for negative policy outputs can be apportioned to the EU and away from national government (see Cole and Drake, 2000, on various ways in which the EU can be exploited in order to shift responsibility away from incumbent government and to the EU, such as a 'smokescreen for domestic political strategies' or as an 'imaginary constraint'). The fact that monetary policy or certain schemes of state aid are no longer available or permissible may certainly lead to a 'hollowing out' of the state, and thereby indirectly affect party competition in the ways that Mair has suggested. However, from a Europeanization research perspective, two issues are raised. First, along methodological lines, it is far from clear that many of the economic changes associated with the EU Single Market might not otherwise have been enacted in some form; in other words, counterfactual reasoning cannot rule out that international trends, in fact extra-European, may not also have impacted the breadth of policy choices available to national government. The example of the UK under Prime Minister Thatcher demonstrates a deregulatory and privatizing drive that may itself have influenced the development of the Single Market. Therefore, linking changes in patterns of party competition along the lines of its 'diminishment' due to policy removal and holding the EU responsible is difficult to establish. Second, if changes in patterns of party competition can be observed in one or more member states, as has been the case since the early 2000s in the Netherlands and Belgium in terms of new parties upsetting prevailing patterns and even coalition government formation, and although one can hypothesize that the EU policy has indirectly contributed to the changes, if the EU is not explicitly invoked as an issue between parties (i.e., it is absorbed into prevailing issues or ideological cleavages), how can one measure the EU impact?

New party formation, discussed above, centred on parties for whom the EU loomed large as a core principle of their identity. In new parties for whom the EU is not central to their core identity, but for whom

EU policy effects may have contributed to their popularity (e.g., Geert Wilders' Party for Freedom in the Netherlands and EU enlargement and immigration policy), the distance between the EU and national political dynamics begins to stretch the concept of 'indirect', at least in terms of operationalizing the EU as a variable in Europeanization research design. Again, the EU, or more precisely aspects of its policy output and impact on national policy agendas, is more of a contextual variable, and domestic developments act as the trigger that renders it relevant in domestic party competition.

Finally, with regard to parties and the indirect effect of the EU on the spectrum of policy choices for national government, another avenue of research is to ascertain the extent to which parties have adjusted their own policy development, that is, have EU-generated constraints led to a revised strategy for traditional goals? The Europeanization approach invoking the role of norm entrepreneurs can also be applied to parties, as policy debate – or at least the means of achieving certain goals – is ongoing in most parties, especially the more heterogeneous in terms of electorate and constituencies. The transfer of policy areas to the EU may have generated innovative alternatives, and so the indirect effects of the EU may have an impact within parties as well as at the level of the party system. It may very well be the case that there is a convergence toward the centre by centre-left parties, as the literature on social democracy has asserted (e.g., Lavelle, 2008), yet at the same time EU policy may also account for new policy areas for parties to advocate, as for example the British Labour party and environmental sustainability, and climate change in particular.

A final consideration regarding parties and Europeanization is to consider party government and its role in supranational governance. It has been suggested that the partisan complexion of a national government does have some effect on intergovernmental bargaining (Aspinwall, 2007), but the fact that most member state governments are composed of coalitions makes any process-tracing exercise in the context of a 'bottom-up' Europeanization dynamic complex, to say the least. Single party government allows a researcher an easier entry point into accounting for party influence – on the basis of its programme or campaign manifesto – on government policy proposals or other actions in the Council of Ministers, European Council or even within its delegation in the European Parliament. The point is to discover the extent to which parties may try to upload their interests (or protect them) in the process of government–EU interaction. This line of enquiry is difficult on another basis, which is that government ministers are *national* representatives, and it is in the context of coalition government that the subjective understanding of their roles as both a party politician and a national representative is blurred the most, thus mandating extra care in a research design. If indeed one can establish that in some cases a party in government does consciously attempt to introduce a partisan perspective alongside strategies to defend and promote national interests, then the researcher must establish which *part* of the party is invested with this responsibility, how it affects government strategy and so forth. There is evidence of transnational partisan cooperation – or at least an exchange of views – over national government positions prior to Council of Ministers meetings through caucuses of transnational party federations, which may suggest that even if there is not much evidence of a partisan-based argument or negotiation in Council that the individual minister is aware of a broader partisan position (Ladrech, 2000).

### Domestic factors

The basis of the argument in this chapter is that domestic factors, especially the political calculations of party actors, in particular party leaderships, are crucial for explaining ostensible domestic party change in relation to the EU. The main departure from Europeanization theory is the absence of significant points of interaction between domestic parties and powerful decision-making EU institutions or EU policy operated from a hierarchical position such that domestic parties are legally obliged to respond. This means that the 'mechanisms of change' that have been developed to explain change in domestic institutions and policy are not so amenable to party research. Nevertheless, as has been described above, there are fruitful areas in which Europeanization insights can be applied to party research, such as a modified notion of misfit between EU policy and core party identity.

The Europeanization literature has also produced an understanding of the domestic factors that contribute to change, such as veto players, facilitating institutions and cycles of reform. Applied within the context of party research, there are several such areas to incorporate in any party Europeanization research design. First, there is the nature of the party system, that is, whether it is a two- or multi-party system and in particular the presence or absence of Euro-sceptic political parties. Second, the nature of the individual party organization must be taken into account, noting the balance of internal power between the parliamentary party (the party in public office) and the central organization (in which party members may wield significant influence), for this has a decisive impact on party leadership management as well as policy development. Third, there is the relationship between government (national executive) and the party in public office, and while outwardly party discipline may suggest support from the party for government positions and decision making regarding EU developments, the 'inside story' may be different, as some parliamentary parties may influence ministerial decisions depending on the working relationship between the two, which varies from country to country (Heidar and Koole, 2000). These are essential factors to take into account in the construction of a research design which aims to isolate the EU factor in change, as well as to avoid misattributing causal influence to the EU.

## Conclusion

Europeanization and party research aims to uncover the role played by EU influence in party change. Exadaktylos and Radaelli have succinctly summarized top-down Europeanization research which 'starts from the presence of integration, controls the level of fit/misfit of the EU level policy *vis-à-vis* the Member State and then explains the presence or absence of domestic change' (2009: 510). Applying this design to parties is not so straightforward, since *where* the EU affects parties (i.e., the dependent variable of change) is not so clear; *how* the EU affects parties (i.e., mechanisms of domestic change such as misfit) cannot clearly be attributed from the outset; and precisely *what* change is (i.e., distinguishing evidence of change from domestic or non-EU sources) is difficult. None of these issues are insurmountable but it does suggest, as Mair has proposed, that there is no alternative to in-depth case study party research if the *cause* of party change is to be identified and explained. While ostensible evidence of change related to the EU may be achieved by large-*n* cross-national samples (see Chapter 3 in this volume by Töller on quantitative approaches to Europeanization), explaining causality is less amenable to such research designs.

## References

Aspinwall, M. (2002) 'Preferring Europe: Ideology and National Preferences on European Integration', *European Union Politics* 3 (1): 81–111.

Aspinwall, M. (2007) 'Government Preferences on European Integration: An Empirical Test of Five Theories', *British Journal of Political Science* 37 (1): 89–114.

Börzel, T. (2002) *States and Regions in the European Union: Institutional Adaptation in Germany and Spain* (Cambridge: Cambridge University Press).

Börzel, T. (2005) 'Europeanization: How the European Union Interacts with its member states', in S. Bulmer and C. Lequesne (eds), *The member states of the European Union* (Oxford: Oxford University Press), pp. 45–69.

Börzel, T. and Risse, T. (2007) 'Europeanization: The Domestic Impact of European Union Politics', in K. Jørgensen, M. Pollack and B. Rosamond (eds), *Handbook of European Union Politics* (London: Sage), pp. 483–504.

Bulmer, S. and Radaelli, C. (2005) 'The Europeanization of National Policy', in S. Bulmer and C. Lequesne (eds), *The member states of the European Union* (Oxford: Oxford University Press), pp. 338–359.

Cole, A. and Drake, H. (2000) 'The Europeanization of the French Polity: Continuity, Change and Adaptation', *Journal of European Public Policy* 7 (1): 26–43.

Dechezelles, S. and Neumayer, L. (2010) 'Introduction: Is Populism a Side-Effect of European Integration? Radical Parties and the Europeanization of Political Competition', *Perspectives on European Politics and Society* 11 (3): 229–336.

Exadaktylos, T. and Radaelli, C. (2009) 'Research Design in European Studies: The Case of Europeanization', *Journal of Common Market Studies* 47 (3): 507–530.

Franzese, R. (2009) 'Multicausality, Context-Conditionality, and Endogeneity', in C. Boix and S. Stokes (eds), *The Oxford Handbook of Comparative Politics* (Oxford: Oxford University Press), pp. 27–72.

Gabel, M. and Scheve, K. (2007) 'Mixed Messages: Party Dissent and Mass Opinion on European Integration', *European Union Politics* 8 (1): 37–59.

Gaffney, J. (1996) *Political Parties and the European Union* (London: Routledge).

Haverland, M. (2007) 'Methodology', in P. Graziano and M. Vink (eds), *Europeanization: New Research Agendas* (Basingstoke: Palgrave Macmillan), pp. 59–70.

Heidar, K. and Koole, R. (2000) *Parliamentary Groups in European Democracies: Political Parties Behind Closed Doors* (London: Routledge).

Henig, S. (1979) *Political Parties in the European Community* (London: Policy Studies Institute).

Hix, S., Noury, A. and Roland, G. (2007) *Democratic Politics in the European Parliament* (Cambridge: Cambridge University Press).

Katz, R. and Mair, P. (1993) 'The Evolution of Party Organizations in Europe: The Three Faces of Party Organization', *American Review of Politics* 14 (Winter): 593–617.

Ladrech, R. (1994) 'Europeanization of Domestic Politics and Institutions: The Case of France', *Journal of Common Market Studies* 32 (1): 69–88.

Ladrech, R. (2000) *Social Democracy and the Challenge of European Union* (Boulder: Lynne Rienner).

Ladrech, R. (2002) 'Europeanization and Political Parties: Towards a Framework for Analysis', *Party Politics* 8 (4): 389–403.

Ladrech, R. (2007) 'National Political Parties and European Governance: The Consequences of "Missing in Action" ', *West European Politics* 30 (5): 945–960.

Lavelle, A. (2008) *The Death of Social Democracy: Political Consequences in the 21st Century* (Aldershot: Ashgate).

Lubbers, M. and Scheepers, P. (2005) 'Political vs Instrumental Euro-scepticism: Mapping Scepticism in European Countries and Regions', *European Union Politics* 6 (2): 223–242.

Mair, P. (2007) 'Political Parties and Party Systems', in P. Graziano and M. Vink (eds), *Europeanization: New Research Agendas* (Basingstoke: Palgrave Macmillan), pp. 154–166.

Pennings, P. (2006) 'An Empirical Analysis of the Europeanization of National Party Manifestos', *European Union Politics* 7 (2): 257–270.

Poguntke, T., Aylott, N., Carter, E., Ladrech, R. and Luther, K.R. (eds) (2007) *The Europeanization of National Political Parties: Power and Organizational Adaptation* (Abingdon: Routledge).

Pridham, G. and Pridham, P. (1981) *Transnational Party Co-operation and European Integration* (London: Allen and Unwin).

Radaelli, C. (2003) 'The Europeanization of Public Policy', in K. Featherstone and C. Radaelli (eds), *The Politics of Europeanization* (Oxford: Oxford University Press), pp. 27–56.

Reif, K. and Schmitt, H. (1980) 'Nine Second-Order National Elections: A Conceptual Framework for the Analysis of European Election Results', *European Journal of Political Research* 8 (1): 3–44.

Steenbergen, M. and Scott, D. (2004) 'Contesting Europe? The Salience of European Integration as a Party Issue', in G. Marks and M. Steenbergen (eds), *European Integration and Political Conflict* (Cambridge: Cambridge University Press), pp. 165–192.

# 11
## Europeanization of Foreign Policy beyond the Common Foreign and Security Policy

*Theofanis Exadaktylos*

The purpose of this chapter is to discuss questions of causality and measurement on national foreign policy beyond the Common Foreign and Security Policy (CFSP) framework. In that respect, foreign policy is defined in a broader framework of coordination of economic, political and military tools (Jorgensen, 1997; Smith, 1999). The analysis focuses on how the conduct of national foreign policy has been influenced by the implementation of European Union (EU) enlargement policies as a soft foreign policy tool. The research puzzle then becomes whether the case of Enlargement brought about the Europeanization of the foreign policy of the old member states towards Central and Eastern European candidates. If that case can be argued, then how can we establish causality of Europeanization, isolating it from other determining domestic or global factors?

The first section examines the literature on EU foreign policy and concludes that while there may be a move towards EU policy convergence due to more coherent EU foreign policy, it is not a consistent pattern. Instead, with softer tools of foreign policy like Enlargement, we should be considering non-traditional views of what constitutes national foreign policy in the context of the EU. Within this framework, I present a modified 'goodness of fit' model of Europeanization using less ad hoc public policy tools. The second section gives an empirical overview of the impact of the recent Enlargement on the foreign policy of Germany to illustrate the method of process tracing the 'EU effect'. Finally, the third section appraises the empirical evidence from the case study, and links back to the central puzzle of this chapter. In concluding the discussion, the chapter makes the argument that complex policy areas should be broken down into different components. Further, by formulating prior expectations and following a rigorous design, we can map out the different adaptation pressures, isolating the EU effect from other determining global or domestic explanatory factors.

## EU foreign policy tools in perspective: In search of a causal framework

For the purposes of this chapter, foreign policy is defined within a broader coordination of economic, political and military tools. Within this broader definition, Enlargement as an EU policy that seeks to change the political, economic, legal and social structures of the candidate countries – a kind of structural foreign policy (Keukeleire and MacNaughtan, 2008) – can be classified as a tool of EU foreign policy. There is no doubt that foreign policy is an arena not directly influenced by the economic and political union – at least in the same way that agricultural and competition policies are – and therefore relies heavily on commonly developed historic responsibility of the member states to the world. This argument has often been cited as one of the driving forces behind the momentum to enlarge the Union to the East and leading to the establishment of the Copenhagen criteria in 1993. Despite its nonbinding nature, foreign policy at the EU level over the past 20 years has become more coherent mainly due to the consolidation of authority at the EU level, and the greater degree of national adaptation to the EU *modus operandi* on foreign policy (Smith, 2008).

These changes, along with the development of a policy for enlargement, have altered the hierarchical position of foreign ministries to other ministries involved in the EU decision-making processes; have created more open points of access to EU processes; have established clear links between economic and political processes; have intertwined domestic and foreign policy; and have led to the Europeanization of foreign policy actors (Hill, 1996; Manners and Whitman, 2000; Smith, 2000, 2004a). Assuming that we identify foreign policy as 'an attempt to design, manage and control the external activities of a state as to protect and advance agreed and reconciled objectives' (Allen, 1998: 43–44), the EU becomes a clearly defined foreign policy actor that has the potential of influencing national foreign policy strongly.

At the same time, national foreign policy actors participate in all stages of the EU foreign policymaking process, and are in essence the broad agenda setters at the European Council level (Smith, 2004b). Therefore, the close reciprocity of the national and the European policymaking processes allows us to argue that this interaction of national foreign policy elites, taking place at the EU level, leads to the establishment of the EU as a credible realm of decision making according to the socialization literature (March and Olsen, 1989; North, 1990). This may lead internally to a 'cross-fertilization of ideas and learning' (Bulmer and Radaelli, 2005), meaning that socialization at the EU level feeds back into the domestic foreign policy processes, altering the actors' positions, the deployment of policy instruments and, eventually, the beliefs in foreign policy. Enlargement became one of the softer tools of foreign policy (Grabbe, 2001; Nugent, 2004; Schimmelfennig, 1998, 2001) through which the member states themselves had to transform and adapt their national foreign policies to resonate with those of the EU towards the candidate countries (Exadaktylos, 2010), a typical case one could argue of Europeanization.

Nonetheless, this concept introduces a number of methodological and research design challenges. Starting with a common definition of Europeanization (Radaelli, 2003: 30),[1] there is a direct structural implication in terms of the policy coordination processes (Tonra, 2003: 740) that is pertinent to national foreign ministries with adaptations to bureaucratic structures and 'ways of doing things' created explicitly to link national foreign policy more effectively with EU foreign policy. In addition, the implications of the EU foreign policy beliefs do not necessarily entail adaptation (Lenschow, 2005; Mair, 2004; Radaelli and Exadaktylos, 2009).

One of the earliest definitions of Europeanization builds on the impact of EU membership on domestic politics and policies as an incremental process penetrating the organizational logic of national policies and politics (Ladrech, 1994: 69). In the case of foreign policy, Tonra suggests that common decisions trigger a Europeanization mechanism that results in the 'transformation in the way in which national foreign policies are constructed, in the way professional roles are defined and pursued and in the consequent internalization of norms and expectations arising from a complex system of collective European policymaking' (Tonra, 2000: 229). Europeanization hence is not only a process of adaptation but also one of learning (Risse et al., 2001) and requires, on the one hand, the adjustment of national instruments and procedures to external pressures – usually stemming from the EU – and on the other, changing the preferences of the actors and to a greater degree their beliefs – which in the case of foreign policy may start from simple EU-level rhetoric (Schimmelfennig, 2001). Europeanization seems to imply a process where the influence occurs fundamentally from the outside (EU level) to the inside (national foreign policy) (Torreblanca, 2001: 488) and consequently leads to the transformation of a member state's policy. With regard to foreign policy, this involves the increasing prominence of common outputs over national *domaines réservés* and internalization of the EU Enlargement policy process (Wong, 2007: 326). The process of domestic change is 'more voluntary and non-hierarchical' (Bulmer and Radaelli, 2005: 345) than in 'communitized policy areas, generated through the alteration of beliefs and expectations of actors' (Knill and Lehmkuhl, 1999: 2). Thus, the framework of Europeanization opens doors to new structured theoretical insights into European foreign policymaking.

This type of analysis, however, risks 'overestimating Europeanization as an "all explaining" factor, forgetting the importance of other endogenous or exogenous influences' (Major, 2005: 183). The methodological challenge hence is to identify and single out the 'EU effect' from other domestic or global influences – one of the ways to overcome this is to draw on process tracing, linking all elements to a time-sensitive analysis.

## Research design

In our own research design, we start from the dependent variable defined as change or shift in national foreign policy [FP]; yet, we regard it as a compound variable of four contributing components:

- actors of foreign policy [A];
- instruments of foreign policy [I];
- decision-making procedures [P];
- foreign policy beliefs [B].

Actors have been divided into *public* (state and party actors) and *civil society* actors with an emphasis on the change in their positions as a result of goals and interest competition. *Policy instruments* follow the typology of Hood (1983) and Salamon (2002) and are split into *regulatory, financial, informational* and *organizational*. The policy *procedures* following Moe and Wilson (1994) and suggestions by Radaelli and Meuwese (2010) can be classified as *design* – who is in charge of foreign policy and under what circumstances; *strategic management* – who is responsible for the implementation of foreign policy and who is held accountable; and *oversight and quality assurance* (operational management). *Beliefs* follow the typology proposed by Sabatier and

Jenkins-Smith (1999) as *deep core* (fundamental axioms), *policy core* (for strategic planning) and *secondary aspects* (for implementation). In a pseudo-mathematical connotation, [FP] = [A, I, P, B], and that holds for every episode of foreign policy; in other words, there is a different significance of role for each component, but they are all present simultaneously.[2] To measure change then, we need a finite temporal framework to detect continuity or change in any of these specific components. Change can then be measured accordingly over time as $[FP]^{X}_{t=0} \rightarrow [FP]^{X}_{t+n} = \Delta[FP]^{X}$ where $n$ signifies the end of the temporal framework, $\Delta$ denotes change and X is the country case involved. From this setting we can have four assumptions for the research question:

- *inertia*; meaning a $\Delta^{X} = 0$;
- *global geopolitics* as the determinant of variation;
- *domestic politics* in Moravcsik's (2005) intergovernmental notion;
- *Europeanization* determines change.

To assess the impact, Héritier (2001) developed a framework for measuring the direction and magnitude of change with regard to Europeanization. The process can result in 'inertia' (seen as lack of change), 'absorption' (in a sense, adaptation), 'transformation' (a deep change in policy beliefs), or even 'retrenchment' (opposition to change, or essentially less Europe than before). Here, a framework for measurement based on Héritier (2001)[3] is simplified to better measure the magnitude and direction of change:

- weak Europeanization;
- strong Europeanization;
- unclear impact (in which case rival explanations are offered).

This framework categorizes events and determines the general trend in a specific foreign policy component, also tracing its development through time, identifying at each stage the intervening variables. Using this method of process tracing, this chapter examines what goes on at the EU level on Enlargement policy, how the national foreign policy vectors respond over time and how this response feeds back dynamically (or not) into the integration process itself (Quaglia and Radaelli, 2007), reducing classic pitfalls of establishing causality in Europeanization. The connection between the two levels has been successfully demonstrated in other studies (e.g., Martinsen, 2007). Figure 11.1 exhibits a timeline

*Figure 11.1*  Model of process-tracing Europeanization in foreign policy

for process tracing, with the four components [A, I, P, B] denoted by an asterisk in terms of events in foreign policy [FP] for the case study.

As obvious from Figure 11.1, different components at different times at a different pace change or remain inert for each foreign policy episode in the case study. So the question in analysis becomes: Do the opportunities, pressures and incentives coming from Europe (identified in step one) play a causal role in determining the outcome of the four components?

## Prior expectations

In order to establish the causal path, we need to build prior expectations regarding the impact of Enlargement and juxtapose those against the empirical evidence. This chapter modifies the 'goodness of fit' causal framework suggested by Börzel and Risse (2003: 69) that builds on sociological (SI) and rationalist institutional (RI) theories, with two potential explanatory paths for change: one of more structure-based pressures and the other of more agency-based. The sociological 'logic of domestic change' emphasizes learning and socialization as the mechanisms that redefine interests and identities. The rationalist logic underlines the redistribution of resources as the starting point for change whereby the newly created differential empowerment causes change.

According to the original model, the adaptational pressures are not sufficient to cause domestic change, but are supplemented by certain intervening factors that facilitate or obstruct domestic change, giving different results for each country. If we follow the RI logic, redistribution of resources is caused by the absence of veto points or the presence of supporting formal institutions. On the other hand, the SI logic emphasizes the presence of norm entrepreneurs as agents of change and the presence of informal forums as facilitators of change. Nonetheless, since Europeanization is a process in flux, domestic change will also be in flux: the feedback into the policymaking system is continuous. Either way, the two paths are not mutually exclusive but their prominence depends on the actors' given preferences. This observation implies that they may also intersect each other. Although the two paths have the same point of origin (i.e., the *misfit* between domestic and EU policies), depending on the adaptational pressures at the EU level and the presence of facilitating factors the outcome for Europeanization is different. The claim of this chapter is that this model – as developed in its Börzel–Risse version – might unnecessarily overcomplicate matters by splitting the EU adaptation pressures into low, medium and high: although the two logics seem to be different, they are practically inseparable when it comes to the so-called medium pressures. Hence, it is necessary to redraw the boundaries of pressure between low and high. Low pressures come from low political mobilization at the EU level or from low institutionalization of the proposed policy. On the other hand, when there is high political commotion and institutional momentum at the EU level, and potentially a high-paced level of integration, then the adaptation pressures towards the member states are high. The outcomes for the degrees of domestic change are illustrated in Table 11.1.

Table 11.1 improves on Börzel and Risse's claim that the logics of change are not mutually exclusive and that they often work in a parallel fashion – or at different stages of the Europeanization process. With low adaptation pressures, both logics lead to the same outcome: strong Europeanization if the facilitating factors are present in the process and weak Europeanization if they are absent or inadequate (e.g., high number of veto points or few informal institutions). Although this appears as a self-evident realization, it is a sensible one since according to the model the two paths lead to the same outcome.

*Table 11.1* The adapted expected outcomes of Europeanization

|  | Logic of change | High pressure | Low pressure |
|---|---|---|---|
| Facilitating factors | Rational institutionalism | Strong | Strong |
|  | Sociological institutionalism | Unclear | Strong |
| No facilitating factors | Rational institutionalism | Strong | Weak |
|  | Sociological institutionalism | Unclear | Weak |

By following closely the development of various policy episodes, empirical analysis can accurately trace those small pressures emanating from the EU level and map out any facilitating factors to change. In this case, even the lowest of pressures from the EU, for example an informal socialization forum or the close contact of two high-ranking policymakers, can make a difference in the outcome of Europeanization. On high adaptation pressures the picture is even more interesting. From Table 11.1, the RI logic is expected to have the same outcome for change regardless of any facilitating factors: according to that logic, adaptation pressures originate from the presence of new opportunities for some actors due to policy download from the EU-level. Policy actors will then seek to exploit these opportunities at any cost. On the other hand, the SI logic creates unclear results at high pressures: socialization and learning due to their dependence on the development of ideas by norm entrepreneurs or the cooperation within informal institutions of policymaking are highly susceptible to incoherence of initiatives for change. Moreover, they are also vulnerable to the presence or absence of political will on behalf of the policymakers that can be translated into different outcomes depending on the domestic social, economic and political context of each member state. The following section provides a broad empirical overview of how those pressures play out for Germany vis-à-vis the Enlargement of the EU to the East.

### Empirical illustration: The case of German foreign policy vis-à-vis the Eastern enlargement

This section provides an empirical overview in applying process tracing as a method of inquiry for detecting Europeanization effects. The intention of this chapter is to present this case as an illustrative example of process tracing without providing the volume of information gained by a thorough process-tracing method (for more detailed analysis, see Exadaktylos, 2010), or entering into the details of how to conduct process tracing that have been covered by other chapters in this volume (cf. Panke (Chapter 7) on implementation, Martinsen (Chapter 8) on health care). Hence, our purpose is to present the results of such process tracing and appraise them in light of the research design methods. The timeline under examination is from 1993, marking the establishment of the Copenhagen criteria for membership, to 2004/2007 as the ending point of the 'big bang' widening to the East. The EU actions regarding Enlargement policy are *expected* to affect different components at different times and are also *expected* to produce certain Europeanization effects measured as strong, weak or unclear, depending on the expected level of contribution of other rival factors.

For example, if the trigger for change comes directly from the EU on occasions of Enlargement policy, the expected outcome is most likely to be strong: any action that emanates directly from supranational institutions, such as the Commission, is bound to have a strong effect because of the pressures it creates within the member states for policy convergence and adherence to directives and recommendations. Regular reports, twinning exercises and other tools of Enlargement policy are therefore expected to produce a strong impact. In a similar way, legally binding actions are also expected to have a strong impact on foreign policy, such as revised Treaty documents, Europe Agreements and Accession Partnerships that formally engage the member states in the process of Enlargement and exert high pressures for alignment and absorption of EU policies. Finally, we should consider high pressures arising from budgetary issues and funding of various accession programmes and actions that commit the member states in advance for a fixed period of financial planning.

In selecting the case study, namely Germany, it is necessary to provide an array of within-case foreign policy episodes, which are not necessarily limited to particular temporal points, but also cover certain time periods within the timeline (see Box 11.1). In bringing together the six episodes in the context of the overarching EU initiatives, the purpose is to address questions of process tracing to extract the net impact of the EU on foreign policy.

---

**Box 11.1   Foreign policy episode selection for Germany, in chronological order**

- The EU Summit of Copenhagen in 1993 (DE1)
- Relocation of the German capital from Bonn to Berlin (DE2)*
- The SPD/Green coalition government (DE3)
- Bilateral relations with Poland and the Czech Republic (DE4)
- The single episode of the Kosovo crisis (DE5)
- The final accession dates of the CEECs** (DE6)

* Episode DE2 is named as such for parsimony but it involved a longer-term process. The decision to relocate the German capital

was taken in 1991 upon the reunification of the country but this episode incorporates the period of transformation of the German policymaking institutions and procedures, one of them being the Foreign Office, tracing the EU effect of Enlargement in the final outcome.

\*\* CEECs: Central Eastern European Countries.

It has almost become a convention to argue that Germany represents one of the most prominent examples of Europeanization of a member state. According to Katzenstein (1997: 260), 'Germany's participation in European institutions has come to define Germany's identity and interests. Germany is the good European *par excellence*. It consistently advocates policies that support European integration, even if these policies reduce Germany's national power or run counter to its short-term interests.' The *prior expectations* for Germany derive mainly from past studies on its foreign policy. Revealing a considerable continuity despite the radical change in the international environment (Anderson, 1999; Duffield, 1998; 1999; Maull, 2000, 2006) German foreign policymakers had not abandoned a number of policy strategies due to a certain level of institutional inertia at both the domestic and international level (Marcussen et al., 1999). The end of the East–West divide indicated the development of an uncharted foreign and security setting, where Germany was liberated from any constraint to return as one of the most powerful countries in Europe. This did not happen: European integration, the development and support of the transatlantic relations and its commitment to multilateral cooperation never disappeared from its central political dialogue. Germany showed no interest in altering its post-WWII foreign policy strategies and desired to maintain the status quo in Europe (Banchoff, 1999; Hellmann, 2001).

Nonetheless, and pertinent to this chapter, what kind of evidence would prove the Europeanization argument wrong? It would be falsified if the change in any of the components reflected the outcome of a deep internal or domestic political, social or economic debate or the distillation of a longer macro-social process *discrete* from the participation of the country in the EU or from the decision of the EU to enlarge. Outcomes that favour resistance to Europeanization (cf. Saurugger, Chapter 6 in this volume) would also be important here. In addition, the argument would be falsified if the external pressures from the international community are by-products of parallel processes of globalization.

In the remainder of this section, the empirical analysis covers the most significant episodes of Box 11.1 in an illustrative manner for the purposes explained above. Hence, it is not my intention to delve into the minutiae of individual episodes.

*The Copenhagen Summit ($T_0$):* The years leading to the intergovernmental conference (IGC) Summit in Copenhagen in 1993 were marked by an inability of German policymakers to acknowledge the existence of a conflict within the German European policy of deepening versus widening. In its bilateral relations with the eligible countries, the German support appeared quite open-ended at the EU level as, by 1992, Germany was 'regarded as the CEEC's natural advocate in the [EU]' (Kohl, 1992; Tewes, 1998). The decisions of the 1993 IGC that set up the criteria for Enlargement reflected the positions of the German actors (Deubner, 1995), but the domestic reactions were also growing – for example, finance minister Theo Waigel on the financial burden (Jeffery and Paterson, 2003: 71–72) or the famous *Schäuble-Lamers Paper* on variable-speed European integration (CDU/CSU-Fraktion des Deutschen Bundestages, 1994). Nonetheless, the change was neither profound nor radical. What had changed with regard to the set of the criteria were the actors' positions and the policy instruments used to materialize them. In this case we trace a weak Europeanization effect; however, the change in positions can be attributed to the domestic debate. The second instrument to change was policy instruments, such as position papers by government members. Here, new practices seem to emerge that are not the result of domestic or other reasons, but are rather a result of socialization of the German elites in Europe, and the absorption of new ideas at the EU level into the domestic deliberations.

*From Bonn to Berlin: new procedures – new beliefs ($T_{-1}$–$T_1$–$T_4$):* The decision to relocate the German capital moved the Foreign Office only a few kilometres away from the Eastern border, facilitating the promotion of bilateral relations with CEECs and strengthening Germany's position as their natural advocate. The move to Berlin signified the beginning of a new complex institutional framework of blurred competences that went beyond the established differentiation between foreign and domestic policies (Tewes, 1998: 128). This blurring of the divide between the two, which has been noted as a sign of Europeanization in foreign policy (cf. Smith, 2004b), has brought a number of different actors each with its own policymaking procedures and beliefs. Now, when it came to implementation of Enlargement policy, the Chancellery and the Foreign Office did not always dictate the procedures. A group of ministries with genuine interests in the process, including the Defence Ministry and the Ministry of Economics, were involved, alongside others with important 'clienteles' such as the Ministry of Agriculture, the Ministries of Transport, and of Labour, who faced strong domestic pressures from the agricultural lobby, the Construction Union (*IG Bau*) and the German Trade Union Federation (*DGB*) (Hofhansel, 2005). One of the first related changes in the Foreign Office was the establishment of *Abteilung E*, or the European Directorate General, to create a safety net for the federal government's European interests and alleviate the bureaucratic burden of coordination at the Chancellery – firmly anchoring it as the constitutionally legitimate actor in the design and strategic management procedures. This shift changed the design and oversight procedures, with the Foreign Office being given new legal competences and policy coordination responsibilities. These were strongly advocated by the EU decision to enlarge: if Germany were to take maximum advantage of the new economic and geostrategic environment that Enlargement promised, it had to introduce a more centralized procedural structure and a recalibration of its policy beliefs.

*The advent of the Social Democratic Party (SPD)/Greens coalition government (T₂–T₅):* In 1998, the SPD alongside the Green Party as coalition partner was back in power. The SPD-led government was expected to introduce new policy goals, revise certain instruments and procedures and follow certain centre-left foreign policy beliefs. However, regarding the cost of Enlargement there were increasing concerns that the German contribution could rise by 10 per cent or €3.6 billion by 2006 (Quaisser, 2000). By the end of 2001, no major progress of the candidate countries had been reported in the Commission Reports and the German public began to react (Wood, 2002, 2003). The new SPD/Green coalition had to balance competing points of view not only from the political elites but also from the industrial lobbies. To alleviate the pressures, Chancellor Schröder commenced a tour of the East German states to promote the Enlargement project with the help of the Foreign Office. Despite the change of actors, there was continuity in the main line of policy towards Enlargement. Notwithstanding the change of heart of the German public and the increased contributions to the EU budget on widening, the previous political elite consensus was maintained. In other words, as expected, the European effect on the actors' positions was so strong that domestic debates and lobbies found it hard to change them. Even in cases where those interested were included in the German responses, they were not diverging from the respective points of view put forward within the EU institutions.

*Bilateral relations with Poland and the Czech Republic (T₀–T₅):* Zooming in on bilateral relations provides information on the micro-level practices of foreign policy and the informational and organization instruments, especially the use of 'best practices'. Bilateral relations between these two countries have mainly revolved around issues of free movement of labour, protection of German minorities and agricultural subsidies reform. The novelty here was the involvement of business and other interest groups in determining foreign policy positions on Poland and the Czech Republic. Support for EU-based solutions fluctuated depending on the *constellation* of domestic actor positions and German institutional instruments. On issues of non-discrimination Germany aligned its regulatory and financial instruments, tying its support to EU conditionality (Cordell and Born, 2001; Genscher, 1998; Schily, 2002). On the free movement of labour, Germany was forced to change earlier bilateral agreements that were not in accordance with EU law (Deutscher Bundestag, 1996; European Commission, 1997). With regard to agricultural subsidies on the other hand, the German Farmers Association shaped the negotiation position of the government due to its important role as the sole representative of farming interests during the consultation processes (Deutscher Bundestag, 2001: 23). While overall, German foreign policy towards these countries may have maintained continuity, when looking at particular components, actors and instruments changed to reflect more the practices of consultation, debates in parliament, new legal structures and new modes of deliberation between interest groups. Although seemingly influenced by domestic distributional conflicts, the policy outcome was a different spin on EU positions.

*The military campaign in Kosovo (T₃):* Although participation in the Kosovo campaign fell outside the scope of the Enlargement process, we can consider it as a test or control case with important consequences for the way German foreign policy towards its Eastern neighbours was conducted in the late 1990s and 2000s. With the SPD harshly opposing an increased role for Germany in crisis management and military intervention (Miskimmon, 2009), Schröder in his memoirs stresses the pressure coming from the outgoing Chancellor Kohl in 1998 to include German forces in a potential military campaign (Schröder, 2007: 110). In the first half of 1999 the German EU Presidency had to take up these issues, with a clear implication for Germany being compelled to undertake a large share of the burden in EU military crisis management. The Minister of Defence at the time, Rudolph Scharping (1999), recalls that a strong EU policy then was necessary. The German foreign policy during the crisis reflected the belief of a civilian power concerned with humanitarian tragedy and leading the diplomatic efforts post-crisis. The new policy beliefs were heavily influenced by the principles of the newly formed European Security and Defence Policy (ESDP) calling for more multilateral involvement and respect for the European institutional frameworks. This new set of beliefs came with the assumption of a higher profile in foreign affairs with international pressures for more self-confidence and awareness of the German position in the world, and a public opinion favourable to change. Hence the EU effect here is unclear.

*The final accession dates of the CEEC ($T_5$):* The incoming governments following Kohl have, overall, been less enthusiastic about the cost of integration and further enlargement beyond the 2004/2007 wave. By the end of the accession process, as the result of the *de facto* inclusion of 10 + 2 new member states, German foreign policy actors changed position. As a concluded process, Germany's new Grand Coalition government remained aligned with EU enlargement prospects. However, all member states started showing signs of reluctance towards further expansion, especially with regard to Turkey. During its 2007 EU Presidency, Germany changed course to being more cynical. The new Christian Democratic Union (CDU) leadership opposed the entry of more countries and advocated stricter criteria and further strengthening of European integration before any new member could accede. This was mainly due to a fear of further immigration and further financial cost (Janes and Szabo, 2007: 109). Here, in fact, actors in Germany have shifted due to a wider domestic fatigue by the public and the elite of being the EU's paymaster, but the EU effect from the prior momentum of the process was still keeping the previous strategy in place.

## Appraising the results of process tracing

In appraising the results of process tracing the following observation can be made. In three episodes the Europeanization effect is quite strong, mainly due to major pressures from high institutionalization of the policy at the EU level. In two cases the impact is regarded as being weak, due to either low institutionalization (Copenhagen criteria) or the less supportive informal institutions (public opinion and elite fora on further Enlargement). Table 11.2 presents a summary of the German foreign policy episodes above in comparison with the expected component change and the Europeanization pressures, based on process-tracing results. The left side presents the empirical evidence and the right side presents all the EU actions present per episode and the

Table 11.2  Comparison of empirical and expected EU impact on German foreign policy

209

| Germany | Component changed A | I | P | B | Europeanization outcome | EU action | Expected change in component A | I | P | B | Europeanization pressure | Confirmation of expectations |
|---|---|---|---|---|---|---|---|---|---|---|---|---|
| Copenhagen (DE1) | ✓ | ✓ | | | Weak | Copenhagen criteria | ✓ | ✓ | | ✓ | Low | Yes. Consistent with domestic considerations (Schäuble–Lamers paper); low institutionalization |
| Bonn–Berlin (DE2) | | | ✓ | ✓ | Strong | White Paper | ✓ | ✓ | | ✓ | High | Yes. Although an effect would be traced in Actors and Instruments, this was not the case here as actors were already aligned with the EU positions and the instruments were already in place in German foreign policy |
| | | | | | | IGC/Treaty | ✓ | ✓ | ✓ | | High | |
| | | | | | | Informal negotiations | ✓ | ✓ | ✓ | | Low | |
| | | | | | | Formal negotiations | ✓ | | | ✓ | Low | |
| | | | | | | *Aggregate* | | | | | *High* | |
| SPD–Greens (DE3) | ✓ | | | | Strong | IGC/Treaty | ✓ | ✓ | ✓ | | High | No. There is a strong impact on the Actors, however, the effect is not traced as change on the other components because they do not change, but were already in place. Prior expectations verified |
| | | | | | | Formal negotiations | ✓ | ✓ | ✓ | ✓ | Low | |
| | | | | | | Financial aid | ✓ | ✓ | ✓ | ✓ | High | |
| | | | | | | *Aggregate* | | | | | *High* | |

*Table 11.2* (Continued)

| Germany | Component changed | | | | Europeanization outcome | EU Action | Expected change in component | | | | Europeanization pressure | Confirmation of expectations |
|---|---|---|---|---|---|---|---|---|---|---|---|---|
| | A | I | P | B | | | A | I | P | B | | |
| Bilateral Relations (DE4) | ✓ | ✓ | | | strong | Regular reports | ✓ | | ✓ | ✓ | High | Yes. The impact is strong on Actors and Instruments due to the involvement of new actors in the foreign policymaking process and the introduction of new financial, organizational and informational policy instruments. There is an effect on procedures and beliefs, but this cannot be coined as change but rather as an enhancement of practices and beliefs already in place |
| | | | | | | Informal negotiations | ✓ | ✓ | ✓ | | Low | |
| | | | | | | Formal negotiations | ✓ | | | ✓ | Low | |
| | | | | | | Twinning exercises | ✓ | ✓ | ✓ | ✓ | High | |
| | | | | | | Financial aid | ✓ | ✓ | ✓ | ✓ | High | |
| | | | | | | *Aggregate* | | | | | *High* | |
| Kosovo (DE5) | | | ✓ | ✓ | Unclear | Financial Aid | ✓ | ✓ | ✓ | ✓ | High | No. Despite the fact that the expected pressure due to financial aid would be high, the pressures on Kosovo were outside the specific scope of |

| Accession (DE5) | Weak | | | | | | Enlargement policy. However, there was considerable international pressure to Germany to assume its role as an international power |
|---|---|---|---|---|---|---|---|
| | ✓ | | | | | | |
| Formal negotiations | | ✓ | | | | Low | Yes. Although the expected pressure is high, the actual pressure was in fact low: the impact was rather weak because there was simply a move along the curve of EU positions. There was no change in beliefs, for precisely this reason |
| Unanimity | | | | | ✓ | Unclear | |
| Europe Agreements | | ✓ | ✓ | | ✓ | High | |
| Financial aid | | ✓ | ✓ | ✓ | | High | |
| *Aggregate* | | ✓ | ✓ | ✓ | | *High* | |

aggregate adaptation pressures confronted by the foreign policy components. The column furthest on the right summarizes and substantiates any discrepancies found in the empirical analysis. We need to insert a caveat to warn that this is *not* a demonstration of the full process tracing; the full-length empirical analysis is available in Exadaktylos (2010).

In the case of Germany, the empirical evidence reveals a significant impact of the EU on the outlook of its foreign policy orientation and the consolidation of bilateral relations with its Eastern neighbours. The impact is more profound on the components of foreign policy where the expected Europeanization pressures were higher. However, the results defy the notion of rigidity of foreign policy, by revealing a major shift in the ways of doing things to incorporate practices and beliefs stemming from the deployment of the EU enlargement policy.

If we illustrate the results on a diagram, as in Figure 11.1, it is possible to depict the relative position of the [FP] components against each other (Figure 11.2). We can observe that national interpretation and compliance with EU beliefs and policies takes some time and this feeds back into the integration process, as the next steps often depend on agreement and implementation by the member states. Hence, the impact of the EU does not follow a consistent schedule. From Figure 11.2, various political and civil society actors [A] have an impact at the EU level taking implementation of a strategy forward. Finally, the rigidity of actors can be facilitated when the necessary instruments [I] and new beliefs [B] are already in place at the EU level. A dividing line between 1993 and 1998 is visible here, when certain instruments matured and certain procedural hurdles [P] were overcome, which increases the activity in the middle and accelerates and deepens the Europeanization process. In this

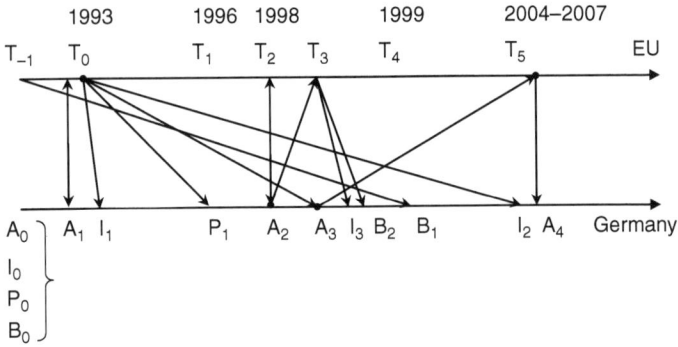

*Figure 11.2*   Process tracing the EU impact on German foreign policy

case, the entrenchment of the EU ways of doing things is so strong that even extremely controversial domestic debates cannot reverse the EU effect.

This analysis is still not sufficient to explain causality in the six foreign policy episodes examined above. These have to be placed under the prism of the two logics of domestic change, which lead us back to the broader research question on the impact of the EU on national foreign policy. Based on the research design tools of the second section and on the adapted outcomes of Table 11.1, Table 11.3 compares the model of the logics of domestic change with the actual outcomes from the case study episodes.

The findings of the process-tracing exercise from the six episodes provide interesting answers to the questions put forward by Börzel and Risse. In the overall assessment based on the modified model, both logics lead to the same Europeanization outcome in three episodes. In other words, no matter which path is followed, the outcome remains of the same magnitude and orientation. The effect of Europeanization is similar no matter which component of foreign policy it tends to influence. When the pressures are low, then both logics apply but the determining factor for the actual outcome is still the presence or absence of those facilitating factors for change to occur.

Finally, and going back to the original Börzel–Risse template, our evidence shows that neither path is dominant. Depending on the intrinsic characteristics and circumstances for each policy episode, one explanatory path may be favoured. Even so, the paths take misfit as a necessary condition and agree to the fact that lower pressures lead to weaker outcomes. Nevertheless, those pressures alone are not sufficient, but require facilitating factors to operate. These factors depend upon the capability and willingness of domestic political actors to grasp the opportunities developed at the EU level (rational path) or take advantage of the forum of ideas that exists in the EU for learning new practices and adapting old ways of doing things (sociological path). The analysis of foreign policy concludes that these logics are in no way mutually exclusive, but as the case studies have demonstrated they can operate in tandem with each other or be associated with different stages of foreign policy changes. The clearer the logic for each particular episode, the more dominant it is over the others. As a concluding remark, it suffices to mention that deeply embedded procedures and collective beliefs are less prone to change and can be mostly affected through socialization and learning. On the other hand, it may be easier to change actor positions and policy instruments as these are often influenced by the presence of new

Table 11.3 Comparing the expected with the actual outcomes from the case study

| Episodes* | Facilitating factors | Adaptation pressure | Predicted outcomes | | Actual outcome | Match |
|---|---|---|---|---|---|---|
| | | | SI | RI | | |
| DE1 | N | Low | Weak | Weak | Weak | Yes. Matches both |
| DE2 | Y | High | Unclear | Strong | Strong | RI. Supporting formal institutions and low number of veto points – agreed beforehand |
| DE3 | Y | Low | Strong | Strong | Strong | Yes. Matches both |
| DE4 | Y | High | Unclear | Strong | Strong | RI. Supporting formal institutions and low number of veto points – most players aligned |
| DE5 | N | High | Unclear | Strong | Unclear | SI. Cooperative informal institutions and high number of veto points – domestic and international |
| DE6 | N | Low | Weak | Weak | Weak | Yes. Matches both |

* DE1–6 correspond to the episodes pertinent to Germany, ordered according to their appearance in Box 11.1 above.

opportunities and constraints that are more volatile due to the moving targets of the policy.

## Concluding remarks

The purpose of the chapter was to introduce a research design for a policy area that falls outside the direct competences of the EU. What can be said upon examining foreign policy as one of those areas is that when authority is consolidated and highly institutionalized at the EU level, the member states become bearers of those policies and maintain their commitment to the foreign policy goals set. The general view that foreign policy is a restricted domain for sovereign governments and, as such, deserves special treatment in its analysis is perhaps obsolete. In line with M.E. Smith (2008), this chapter argued that it is not a different type of policy. It is just like any other public policy, especially in relation to how the internalization of EU membership and the EU integration process gain more prominence in the national agenda. The chapter also drew on already established theoretical policy analysis tools and found that they travel reasonably well for the examination of foreign policy. In this way, tracing the change in foreign policy becomes a much easier task as scholars can be less overwhelmed with ad hoc theorization for foreign policy.

The chapter clarified the methodological preconditions for applying Europeanization to a less traditional policy field, and analysed the net impact without making the EU effect 'a cause in search of an effect' (Goetz, 2000). The answer was to create the *ex ante conditions* and compare the actual outcomes for the specified period of time. Europeanization as such is not a theory: it is a process that is explained under the broader spectrum of new institutionalist theories. The chapter endorsed the Börzel–Risse argument that the two paths are not mutually exclusive, but that they can both be present depending on the given circumstances. In addition, they are not in competition with each other, as one path may intersect the other in time. This is not a novel finding, but it is important since the two logics are often juxtaposed in empirical studies informed by neo-institutionalism.

The model in this chapter proposed pressures based on low or high political commotion or institutionalization, hence confirming the need to build into the explanatory models the relationship between agency, institutions and historical development. Concluding this chapter, the main purpose was not to present one logic of change as parasitic on or a special case of the other, or try to reinvent the wheel in a greater unified theory. Rather, the purpose was to provide a mid-range framework that allows for capturing 'causal complexity – usually invoking several independent variables – over a spatially or temporally delimited frame' (Checkel, 2010), and without getting entangled in what Olsen in response to his critics would term 'unproductive tribal warfare' (Olsen, 2001: 197) contributing to the climate of dialogue between different approaches to domestic change.

## Notes

1. Radaelli, drawing on Ladrech (1994), defines Europeanization as 'processes of a) construction, b) diffusion and c) institutionalization of norms, beliefs, formal and informal rules, procedures, policy paradigms, styles, "ways of doing things" that are first defined and consolidated in the EU policy processes and then incorporated in the logic of domestic (national and sub-national) discourse, political structures and public policies'.
2. In a similar fashion, this way of reasoning could also be applied in large-*n* studies by transforming the typology into quantifiable variables. Yet, since in foreign policy the episodes are less frequent, it is difficult to construct large-*n* samples; hence, application of qualitative methods of analysis is more appropriate.
3. While Héritier's framework is quite insightful, it may not always be able to differentiate between outcomes, as will become apparent later in the chapter. Inertia or retrenchment simply denotes an 'unclear' impact; in other words, an EU pressure is present but there are other determining or explanatory factors for the direction (or lack thereof) of domestic change. Absorption as an outcome denotes low domestic change as a result of Europeanization; hence it is classified as 'weak' outcome. Finally, accommodation or transformation indicates a modest or high degree of domestic change, either by adapting or replacing the overarching policy framework, hence classified as a 'strong' effect.

## References

Allen, D. (1998) 'Who Speaks for Europe? The Search for an Effective and Coherent External Policy'. In Peterson, J. and Sjursen, H. (eds.) *A Common Foreign Policy for Europe?* (London: Routledge).

Anderson, J.J. (1999) *German Unification and the Union of Europe* (Cambridge: Cambridge University Press).

Banchoff, T. (1999) 'German Identity and European Integration'. *European Journal of International Relations*, 5(3): 259–289.

Börzel, T.A. and Risse, T. (2003) 'Conceptualizing the Domestic Impact'. In Featherstone, K. and Radaelli, C. (eds.) *The Politics of Europeanization* (Oxford: Oxford University Press).

Bulmer, S. and Radaelli, C. (2005) 'The Europeanization of National Policy'. In Bulmer, S. and Lequesne, C. (eds.) *The Member States of the European Union* (Oxford: Oxford University Press).

CDU/CSU-Fraktion des Deutschen Bundestages (1994) 'Überlegungen zur Europapolitik'. Bonn, 1 September 1994.

Checkel, J.T. (2010) 'Theoretical Synthesis in IR: Possibilities and Limits'. In Carlsnaes, W., Risse, T. and Simmons, B. (eds.) *Sage Handbook of International Relations*, 2nd edition (London: Sage Publications).

Cordell, K. and Born, K.M. (2001) 'The German Minority in Upper Silesia: Electoral Success and Organizational Patterns'. *Nationalism and Ethnic Politics*, 7(1): 41–62.

Deubner, C. (1995) *Deutsche Europapolitik: Von Maastricht nach Kerneuropa?* (Baden-Baden: Nomos).

Deutscher Bundestag (1996) 'Drucksache 13/3155. Beschlußempfehlung und Bericht des Ausschusses für Arbeit und Sozialordnung (11. Ausschuß) zu dem Gesetzentwurf der Bundesregierung Drucksachen 13/2414, 13/2839 - Entwurf eines Gesetzes über zwingende Arbeitsbedingungen bei grenzüberschreitenden Dienstleistungen (Arbeitnehmer-Entsendegesetz – AEntG)'.

Deutscher Bundestag (2001) 'Auswirkungen der EU-Osterweiterung auf die Gemeinsame Agrarpolitik und die Regionen: Öffentliche Anhörung des Ausschusses für die Angelegenheiten der Europäischen Union und des Ausschusses für Ernährung, Landwirtschaft und Forsten am 17. Januar 2001' (Ausschuss für die Angelegenheiten der Europäischen Union).

Duffield, J.S. (1998) *World Power Forsaken: Political Culture, International Institutions, and Germany Security Policy after Unification* (Stanford, CA: Stanford University Press).

Duffield, J.S. (1999) 'Political Culture and State Behavior: Why Germany Confounds Neorealism'. *International Organization*, 53(4): 765–803.

European Commission (1997) 'Official Journal No. L18, January 21, 1997'.

Exadaktylos, T. (2010) 'The Europeanization of National Foreign Policy: the case of Greece and Germany vis-à-vis the Eastern Enlargement of the European Union'. PhD Thesis, Department of Politics, University of Exeter.

Genscher, H.-D. (1998) *Rebuilding a House Divided* (New York: Broadway Books).

Goetz, K.H. (2000) 'European Integration and National Executives: A Cause in Search of an Effect?' *West European Politics*, 23(4): 211–231.

Grabbe, H. (2001) 'How does Europeanization affect CEE Governance? Conditionality, Diffusion and Diversity'. *Journal of European Public Policy*, 8(6): 1013–1031.

Hellmann, G. (2001) 'Precarious Power: Germany at the Dawn of the Twenty-first Century'. In Eberwein, W.-D. and Kaiser, K. (eds.) *Germany's New Foreign Policy: Decision-making in an Interdependent World* (Basingstoke: Palgrave Macmillan).

Héritier, A. (2001) *Differential Europe: The European Union Impact on National Policymaking* (Oxford: Rowman and Littlefield).

Hill, C. (1996) *The Actors in Europe's Foreign Policy* (London: Routledge).

Hofhansel, C. (2005) *Multilateralism, German Foreign Policy and Central Europe* (Abingdon: Routledge).

Hood, C. (1983) *The Tools of Government* (London: Macmillan).

Janes, J. and Szabo, S. (2007) 'Angela Merkel's Germany'. *Current History*, 106(698): 106–111.

Jeffery, C. and Paterson, W.E. (2003) 'Germany and European Integration: A Shifting of Tectonic Plates'. *West European Politics*, 26(4): 59–75.

Jorgensen, K.E. (ed.) (1997) *European Approaches to Crisis Management* (The Hague: Kluwer International).

Katzenstein, P.J. (1997) 'The Smaller European States, Germany and Europe'. In Katzenstein, P.J. (ed.) *Tamed Power. Germany in Europe* (Ithaca, NY: Cornell University Press).

Keukeleire, S. and J. MacNaughtan (2008). *The Foreign Policy of the European Union* (Basingstoke: Palgrave Macmillan).

Knill, C. and Lehmkuhl, D. (1999) 'How Europe Matters. Different Mechanisms of Europeanisation'. *European Integration Online Papers (EIoP)*, 3(7): http://eiop.or.at/texte/1998-1007a.htm.

Kohl, H. (1992) *Protokoll 3* (Düsseldorf: Parteitag der CDU Deutschlands), 26–28 October.

Ladrech, R. (1994) 'Europeanisation of Domestic Politics and Institutions: The Case of France'. *Journal of Common Market Studies*, 32(1): 69–88.

Lenschow, A. (2005) 'Europeanisation of Public Policy'. In Richardson, J.J. (ed.) *European Union: Power and Policy-Making* (Abingdon: Routledge).

Mair, P. (2004) 'The Europeanization Dimension'. *Journal of European Public Policy*, 11(2): 337–348.

Major, C. (2005) 'Europeanisation and Foreign and Security Policy: Undermining or Rescuing the Nation State?' *Politics*, 25(3): 175–190.

Manners, I. and Whitman, R. (eds.) (2000) *The Foreign Policies of European Union Member States* (Manchester: Manchester University Press).

March, J.G. and Olsen, J.P. (1989) *Rediscovering Institutions: The Organizational Basis of Politics* (New York: Free Press).

Marcussen, M., Risse, T., Engelmann-Martin, D., Knopf, H.J. and Roscher, K. (1999) 'Constructing Europe? The Evolution of French, British and German Nation State Identities'. *Journal of European Public Policy*, 6(4): 614–633.

Martinsen, D.S. (2007) 'The Europeanization of Gender Equality – Who Controls the Scope of Non-discrimination?' *Journal of European Public Policy*, 14(4): 544–562.

Maull, H.W. (2000) 'Germany and the Use of Force: Still a "Civilian Power"?' *Survival*, 42(2): 56–80.

Maull, H.W. (ed.) (2006) *Germany's uncertain power: foreign policy of the Berlin Republic* (Basingstoke: Palgrave Macmillan).

Miskimmon, A. (2009) 'Falling into Line? Kosovo and the Course of German Foreign Policy'. *International Affairs*, 85(3): 561–573.

Moe, T. and Wilson, S.A. (1994) 'Presidents and the Politics of Structure'. *Law and Contemporary Problems*, 57 (Spring): 1–44.

Moravcsik, A. (2005) 'Liberal Intergovernmentalism'. In Wiener, A. and Diez, T. (eds.) *European Integration Theory* (Oxford: Oxford University Press).

North, D.C. (1990) *Institutions, Institutional Change, and Economic Performance* (New York: Cambridge University Press).

Nugent, N. (ed.) (2004) *European Union Enlargement* (New York: Palgrave Macmillan).

Olsen, J.P. (2001) 'Garbage Cans, New Institutionalism, and the Study of Politics'. *American Political Science Review*, 95(1): 191–198.

Quaglia, L. and Radaelli, C.M. (2007) 'Italian Politics and the European Union: A Tale of Two Research Designs'. *West European Politics*, 30(4): 924–943.

Quaisser, W. (2000) 'Die Osterweiterung: Ein europäisches Großprojekt mit vielen Unbekannten'. Munich: *ifo Schnelldienst*, 31: 7–10.

Radaelli, C.M. (2003) 'The Europeanization of Public Policy'. In Featherstone, K. and Radaelli, C.M. (eds.) *The Politics of Europeanization* (Oxford: Oxford University Press).

Radaelli, C.M. and Exadaktylos, T. (2009) 'New Directions in Europeanization Research'. In Egan, M., Nugent, N. and Paterson, W.E. (eds.) *Research Agendas in EU Studies: Stalking the Elephant* (Basingstoke: Palgrave Macmillan).

Radaelli, C.M. and Meuwese, A.C.M. (2010) 'Hard Questions, Hard Solutions: Proceduralisation through Impact Assessment in the EU'. *West European Politics*, 33(1): 136–153.

Risse, T., Caporaso, J.A. and Cowles, M.G. (2001) 'Europeanization and Domestic Change: Introduction'. In Cowles, M.G., Caporaso, J.A. and Risse, T. (eds.) *Transforming Europe: Europeanization and Domestic Change* (Ithaca, NY: Cornell University Press).

Sabatier, P.A. and Jenkins-Smith, H.C. (1999) 'The Advocacy Coalition Framework: An Assessment'. In Sabatier, P.A. (ed.) *Theories of the Policy Process* (Boulder, CO: Westview Press).

Salamon, L.M. (ed.) (2002) *The Tools of Government: A Guide to the New Governance* (Oxford: Oxford University Press).

Scharping, R. (1999) *Wir dürfen nicht wegsehen. Der Kosovo-Krieg und Europa* (Berlin: Ullstein).

Schily, O. (2002) 'Speech: Rede von Bundesinnenminister Otto Schily beim Treffen der Sudetendeutschen Landsmannschaft am 18. Mai 2002 in Nürnberg (gekürzt)'.

Schimmelfennig, F. (1998) 'Liberal Norms and the Eastern Enlargement of the European Union: A Case for Sociological Institutionalism'. *Österreichische Zeitschrift Für Politikwissenschaft*, 27(4): 459–472.

Schimmelfennig, F. (2001) 'The Community Trap: Liberal Norms, Rhetorical Action, and the Eastern Enlargement of the European Union'. *International Organization*, 55(1): 47–80.

Schröder, G. (2007) *Entscheidungen. Mein Leben in der Politik* (Berlin: Ullstein).

Smith, K.E. (1999) *The Making of EU Foreign Policy: The Case of Eastern Europe* (London: Palgrave Macmillan).

Smith, M.E. (2000) 'Conforming to Europe: The Domestic Impact of EU Foreign Policy Co-operation'. *Journal of European Public Policy*, 7(4): 613–631.

Smith, M.E. (2004a) 'Institutionalization, Policy Adaptation and European Foreign Policy Cooperation'. *European Journal of International Relations*, 10(1): 95–136.

Smith, M.E. (2004b) 'Toward a Theory of EU Foreign Policy-Making: Multi-Level Governance, Domestic Politics, and National Adaptation to Europe's Common Foreign and Security Policy'. *Journal of European Public Policy*, 11(4): 740–758.

Smith, M.E. (2008) 'Researching European Foreign Policy: Some Fundamentals'. *Politics*, 28(3): 177–187.

Tewes, H. (1998) 'Between Deepening and Widening: Role Conflict in Germany's Enlargement Policy'. *West European Politics*, 21(2): 117–133.

Tonra, B. (2000) 'Denmark and Ireland'. In Manners, I. and Whitman, R. (eds.) *The Foreign Policies of the European Union Member States* (Manchester: Manchester University Press).

Tonra, B. (2003) 'Constructing the Common Foreign and Security Policy: The Utility of a Cognitive Approach'. *Journal of Common Market Studies*, 41(4): 731–756.

Torreblanca, J.I. (2001) 'La europeización de la política Española'. In Closa, C. (ed.) *La Europeización del Sistema Político Español* (Madrid: Istmo).

Wong, R. (2007) 'Foreign Policy'. In Graziano, P. and Vink, M.P. (eds.) *Europeanization: New Research Agendas* (Basingstoke: Palgrave Macmillan).

Wood, S. (2002) 'Germany and the Eastern Enlargement of the EU: Political Elites, Public Opinion and Democratic Processes'. *Journal of European Integration*, 24(1): 23–38.

Wood, S. (2003) 'Is Eastern Enlargement of the European Union a Beneficial Investment for Germany?' *Political Science Quarterly*, 118(2): 281–306.

# 12
# Rival Hypotheses: Comparing the Roles of the European Union and Black Sea Economic Cooperation Organization in Good Governance Reforms

*Stella Ladi*

The study of Europeanization concerns the domestic reaction to the strengthening and widening of European Union (EU) activities that directly affect domestic polities, politics and policies.[1] The literature on Europeanization has slowly moved from the study of member states to the study of candidate countries, and special attention has recently been paid to non-member states with no immediate accession prospects. This chapter focuses on the Europeanization of non-member states (i.e., the Black Sea countries) and explores rival hypotheses in order to establish causality. The novelty of this chapter is that rather than focusing the design on the relations between non-member states and the EU, it explores what else exists alongside the EU that pushes for similar reforms (i.e., other international and regional organizations). The adoption of such a research design reduces bias and shows that causality in European studies is complex and conjunctional.

The promotion of so-called good governance is an illustrative case because it is included in the lists of all international organizations (e.g., EU, Black Sea Economic Cooperation (BSEC)) active in the Black Sea area as a goal for the countries of the region. This chapter explores the exogenous pressures and the 'soft' and 'hard' mechanisms of governance transfer in the Black Sea region. The purpose is to establish causality between governance reforms and one or more specific organizations. Three rival hypotheses exist. The first hypothesis is that international and regional organizations other than the EU are responsible for the transfer of governance practices and principles in the region. The second hypothesis proposes that it is the EU that actually pushes forward good governance in the region, while the third hypothesis sees international and regional organizations and the EU as being complementary in regard to their work.

The Black Sea region is more of a political construction than a geographical space. The states bordering the Black Sea are Bulgaria, Romania, Georgia, Russia, Ukraine and Turkey, but most of the attempts at regional cooperation include neighbouring states such as Greece, Moldova, Belarus, Serbia, Montenegro, Armenia and Azerbaijan – states that are affected by and effect developments in the area (Aydin, 2004). In this chapter, the Black Sea region is understood in its broad sense and includes the members of the BSEC. It is an interesting case study because it involves countries with different levels of development, countries that are members of the EU (Romania and Bulgaria), countries that are candidate member states (Turkey) and the ex-Soviet Union republics (Georgia, Ukraine, Armenia, etc.), all of which are still going through a painful transition period.

The chapter is organized into three sections. The first section discusses the literature on the Europeanization of non-member states, the alternative research designs and the mechanisms that are in place, in order to introduce our own research design. The second section discusses good governance and the way it has been used by the international community in the Black Sea region. It focuses on a comparison between BSEC and EU initiatives in order to make a more specific assessment of the rival hypotheses. The final section compares the empirical findings on the BSEC and the EU and links them to the methodological and theoretical discussion of the first section. The purpose is to draw conclusions about the type of causality that exists between the promotion of good governance in the Black Sea area and domestic change.

## Europeanization of Non-Member States

Europeanization applies not only to EU member states but also to accession, candidate and neighbouring countries (Olsen, 2002: 923–294). The study of the impact of Europeanization in countries that are not members of the EU is interesting because it reveals a much more top-down direction than is the case for the old EU member states (Papadimitriou and Phinnemore, 2003). Even more interestingly, the study of Europeanization process in Black Sea countries can shed light on the EU's external governance strategy.

Most of the literature on Europeanization analyses the impact of the EU on new and old member states (e.g., Featherstone and Papadimitriou, 2008; Knill, 2001), but less work has been done on the impact of the EU outside of its borders – which is the focus of this chapter. As is the case with most of the literature, the research designs and methods used in studies of non-member states are often not explicit (see Töller, Chapter 3 in this volume). Grabbe and Sedelmeier (2010) rightly point out that the study of external governance or of Europeanization beyond the member states was developed in the context of the literature on enlargement, and by and large it uses similar research tools. Indeed, if we turn to a couple of key studies that were published before the accession of the Central and Eastern European (CEE) countries, many similarities with the most recent external governance literature can be found. Grabbe (2001), in her paper on the effects of Europeanization on CEE governance, focuses on the mechanisms that the EU uses to influence CEE governance and devotes only a short section to the interaction of the EU with other external and internal political dynamics. Goetz (2001) identifies Europeanization with modernization and explores the effects of the EU at the domestic level by paying special attention to the transfer of the *acquis communautaire*. No attention is paid to other external sources of change.

Turning to studies of the Europeanization of non-member states, similar research designs can be revealed. Lavenex (2004), in an attempt to explore EU external governance, looks at the spread of the *acquis communautaire* of justice and home affairs, and environmental and energy policy in the immediate EU neighbourhood. No analytical discussion of the research design is offered. Switzerland is a case of a non-member state that has attracted the attention of Europeanization researchers. For example, Sciarini, Fischer and Nicolet (2004) examine the impact of Europeanization on Switzerland by focusing on direct and indirect mechanisms and by selecting three decision-making processes where different levels of Europeanization are expected. Another interesting study by Freyburg et al. (2009) discusses the EU promotion of democratic governance in the neighbourhood using a research design that searches for EU impact at the domestic level in three countries and three policy sectors. What is remarkable is that when the explanatory variables are operationalized, no distinction is made between the EU and other international actors and, as a result, in the findings of the study it is not easy to establish whether the EU was responsible for the promotion of democratic governance. This is indicative of the main weakness of the existing literature – that it does not pay enough attention to rival hypotheses such as the impact of other international and regional organizations in non-EU member states, and as a result limits the possibility of questioning causality between Europeanization processes and domestic change.

The research design followed in this chapter has two distinct dimensions: the application of rival hypotheses and the study of mechanisms. First, in order to have a parallel study of the EU and of other exogenous sources of change and avoid a simplified Europeanization causality argument, rival hypotheses are discussed. Three rival hypotheses are put forward. The first one emphasizes the impact of international and regional organizations other than the EU; the second promotes the active role of the EU; while the third hypothesis perceives the two dimensions as complementary. Second, the mechanisms of Europeanization are explored, as in the rest of the literature, but the study is complemented by a comparison of the mechanisms used by the BSEC. This research strategy allows for the exploration of the three rival hypotheses. The domestic mediating factors, which would be another alternative, shed light on domestic factors of change or resistance but do not tell us much about the impact of other international and regional processes. The study of outcomes, which would be the third possibility, provides us with the final picture of change or inertia but only gives us limited information on the initiation of change. Empirically, it is more realistic to focus on mechanisms, because it is still too early to show results from the implementation of either the BSEC or the EU initiatives on good governance.

Turning to mechanisms, the literature on Europeanization proposes a number of mechanisms that range from 'hard' to 'soft' (Ladi, 2005, see also Exadaktylos and Radaelli, Chapter 2 in this volume). Knill (2001: 214–225) offers one of the most useful classifications and suggests that three mechanisms of Europeanization exist: institutional compliance, changing domestic opportunity structures and framing domestic beliefs and expectations. Institutional compliance refers to explicit European policies that prescribe a specific institutional model that has to be introduced at the domestic environment. It is the 'hardest' mechanism identified by Knill, given that the member states have only limited discretion about how to implement the institutional change. This mechanism is also relevant for accession and candidate member states that need to comply with the *acquis communautaire* in order to promote their membership, but it is not relevant per se for neighbouring countries such as the majority of the Black Sea countries that do not have an obligation of compliance. Nevertheless, a set of instruments that shape institutional reform can be detected. Grabbe (2001: 1019–1024) refers to these instruments that were first put in place for the accession of the CEE countries as mechanisms. The main instrument is gatekeeping, which refers to conditionality that can lead to access to negotiations for accession or when membership is not relevant to other benefits such as economic aid or trade. Other instruments include benchmarking and monitoring of progress, provision of legislative and institutional templates, aid and technical assistance and advice and twinning.

The second mechanism is changing domestic opportunity structures, which would be placed somewhere in the middle of a scale that descends from 'hard' to 'soft' mechanisms. It describes instances where European policies alter the distribution of power and resources between domestic actors and, as a result, institutional change occurs. It can also be applied to non-EU members in situations where EU funding and/or the process of negotiations with the EU empowers specific institutions and actors and alters the domestic opportunity structures.

The final and 'softest' mechanism proposed is framing domestic beliefs and expectations. The EU goal here is to prepare the ground for institutional change by changing the 'cognitive input' of domestic actors. This is the mechanism which is the most relevant for both EU and non-EU member states.

If we apply these three mechanisms to other international organizations that are pushing for domestic change, some important differences can be observed but the logic is similar. Institutional compliance resembles conditionality used by international organizations. Although most international organizations do not provide complete policies to be followed in the way the EU does, they outline the desired outcome and attach it to lending (this is typical of the World Bank and the International Monetary Fund (IMF)). Furthermore, the expectations are purely economic and not that of full membership and political unity, as expected from the EU. More specifically, after the end of the Cold War, international organizations such as the World Bank, the IMF and other donors started linking loans to political and administrative performance of the developing countries. Political conditionality has been characterized as 'the first international attempt to change states' domestic behaviours in peacetime' (Uvin and Biagiotti, 1996). So-called good governance has been on the top of its list. International expectations were high about what political conditionality and the application of good governance principles could accomplish, but its implementation soon provoked criticism. The ability of donors either to suggest successful reforms or to evaluate their results, as well as their objectivity, was soon questioned (Doornbos, 2001).

Both 'softer' mechanisms – changing domestic opportunity structures and framing domestic beliefs and expectations – are broadly used by international and regional organizations. BSEC, for example, has tried to frame domestic beliefs and expectations through the activities of its Working Group on Institutional Renewal and Good Governance, as analysed in a later section. This brings us to a first key finding when applying a Europeanization framework to domestic policy changes of non-members: similar mechanisms are used by a number of international and regional organizations other than the EU. In the next section we move to a more detailed discussion of the empirical case study in order to explore the three rival hypotheses and to further illustrate the arguments made up to now.

## Spread of good governance in the Black Sea area

The primary purpose of this section is to shed light on the different international and regional organizations that are active in the area, in order to compare them with the EU and thus identify the source of good governance transfer in the Black Sea area. Good governance, which is the main object of the transfer, is a very general term. It has normative aspirations, and suggests that governance should be 'good' and not 'bad'. The former United Nations (UN) Secretary General Kofi Annan describes good governance as a force ensuring respect for human rights and the rule of law; strengthening democracy; and promoting transparency and capacity in public administration. Recently, the use of the term good governance has been stretched even more. The areas of interest are numerous: 'universal protection of human rights, non-discriminatory laws; efficient, impartial and rapid judicial processes; transparent public agencies; accountability for decisions by public officials; devolution of resources and decision making to local levels from the capital; and meaningful participation by citizens in debating public policies and choices' (Weiss, 2000: 801). Good governance has thus become an elastic term rather than a concept in its own terms. It is used more like a flexible carrier that conveys a varying combination of messages which remain, however, in the same general logic (Doornbos, 2001). Moreover, good governance can be understood as a mechanism of capacity building for states that – although independent – are not capable of making and implementing their own decisions (Interview 1, 1 August 2008).

The use of good governance principles from international organizations in order to push for domestic reform has been novel. Traditionally, domestic politics and interference in the internal affairs of a state were formally outside the province of the international community. Article 2(7) of the UN Charter guarantees sovereignty and non-interference in the internal affairs of a state, but the pressures for development and the necessity of efficient management have led to the undermining of its absolute character (Weiss, 2000). The turning point, though, for the prominence of the good governance concept in the international fora has been the fall of the Berlin Wall. The advancement of theses such as Huntington's (1991) 'third wave' of democratization made good governance principles appear universal. Western investment in Third World and former Soviet bloc countries brought domestic politics to the forefront of the discussion.

A number of international and regional organizations as well as national international development organizations (e.g., the United States Agency for International Development (USAID)) are active in the Black Sea region in the field of good governance, working mainly on a bilateral rather than a regional basis. For example, the World Bank focuses on anti-corruption and administrative and civil reform by offering country reports, data and statistics (http://www.worldbank.org). The IMF intervenes more indirectly in the field of good governance, again mainly via research on an individual country basis (http://www.imf.org). The United Nations Development Programme (UNDP) has a broader spectrum of interest, working on governance topics such as public administration reform, ombudsmen institutions, anti-corruption, human resource management in the civil service, ex ante policy impact assessment, human rights and access to justice, local government and decentralization. Its instruments are training, publications and professional networks. The Black Sea is not seen as a region, and the projects again concern mainly individual countries. For example, there has been a project supporting implementation of local administration reform in Turkey that is funded by the EU and run by the UNDP (http://www.undp.org). USAID also prefers working with individual countries on projects for the support of media, civil society empowerment and women's rights (http://www.usaid.gov). The Organisation for Economic Co-operation and Development (OECD) has developed more of a regional approach by publishing the Black Sea and Central Asia Economic Outlook in 2000 and by establishing the South Caucasus and Ukraine Initiative, which covers part of the Black Sea and refers to investment and competitiveness issues rather than good governance topics (http://www.oecd.org). The protection of the environment was the first and main area where international organizations considered the Black Sea as a region. For example, in June 1993 the UN established the Black Sea Environment Programme, and in 2001 the Global Environmental Facility Strategic Partnership on the Black Sea and Danube Basin was launched by the World Bank, UNDP and United Nations Environment Programme (UNEP) (Aydin, 2004). Despite the interconnection between the different international actors, when exploring the spread of good governance in the area it is the BSEC and the EU that have been the most active and have dealt with the Black Sea as a region. Interestingly, all the organizations concentrate upon the use of 'soft' mechanisms. We will first turn our attention to the BSEC.

## The BSEC and the spread of governance reforms and institutional renewal

The BSEC came into existence in 1992 and brought together a diverse set of countries. It currently includes Caucasian countries such as Armenia, Azerbaijan and Georgia, which are also former Soviet Union countries, together with Russia, Moldova and Ukraine. It embraces Balkan countries such as Albania and Serbia as well as EU member states such as Greece, Bulgaria and Romania and EU candidate member states such as Turkey. Its activities include cooperation in a large number of areas such as energy, environmental protection, small and medium enterprises (SMEs) and tourism. In recent years, a boost has been given to cooperation in the area of institutional renewal and good governance (http://www.bsec-organization.org). In this section, the mechanisms used by the BSEC to promote institutional renewal and governance reforms are described in order to evaluate its push towards change and compare it with that of the EU.

The BSEC accepted governance and institutional renewal as a new area of cooperation among its member states in 2001 within the framework of the BSEC Economic Agenda for the Future. As was then pointed out, 'An economic agenda cannot be addressed in today's circumstances without the essential public institutions, as has been widely recognized by the major international organizations and many national governments. The international dimension, new economic actions and growth of competing interests demand reliable and trusted governance' (BSEC, 2001). This landmark document goes on to underline the aspects of good governance that can contribute to enhancing the multilateral cooperation that is promoted by the BSEC: legality, legitimacy and confidence in laws and institutions, effective partnerships, policy integration, responsible budgeting, investing in government capacity, anticipating crisis management and building key networks. It also makes clear that the BSEC is following the trend of other international organizations, discussed in the previous section.

The implementation of the Economic Agenda for the Future started with a seminar that took place in Taganrog, Russia, in 2002. It was an initiative of the International Centre for Black Sea Studies (ICBSS) in cooperation with the OECD and Transparency International, and it was decided that a series of workshops on the topic should follow (Interview 2, 7 August 2008). As a result, in 2003–2004 the BSEC, in cooperation with the ICBSS and the Friedrich Ebert Foundation, organized three workshops in Yerevan, Baku and Tbilisi. The workshop in Yerevan agreed on the importance and difficulty of reforms towards good governance and institutional renewal in BSEC member states, and suggested the formalization of cooperation as well as the use of the experience and best practices of OECD-Support for Improvement in Governance and Management (SIGMA) (BSEC, 2003a). The second workshop, which took place in Baku, focused on more specific aspects of policy reform and on policy sectors and decided that the third workshop should focus on specific projects (BSEC, 2003b). The idea of the formalization of a Working Group on Institutional Renewal and Good Governance was informally discussed for the first time (Interview 2, 7 August 2008). The Tbilisi workshop discussed the conclusions and lessons learned to date and agreed on the priorities of a roadmap of actions for the future. The possibility of the formation of a permanent working group on institutional renewal and governance improvement was elaborated and recorded (BSEC, 2004). In 2005, a final workshop took place in Athens under the auspices of the Hellenic Chairmanship-in-Office of the BSEC and the ICBSS, where the proposal of a permanent working group was strongly supported by the participants. A draft Joint Declaration was prepared for the Ministerial meeting that was planned for February of the same year (BSEC, 2005a).

The meeting of the BSEC Ministers in charge of Public Administration and the Ministers of Justice in Athens in February 2005 adopted the 'Joint Declaration on Good Governance and Institutional Renewal' (BSEC, 2005b). In the document, which constitutes the basis for intergovernmental cooperation in the field of good governance and endorses the BSEC Working Group on Institutional Renewal and Good Governance, the ministers collectively acknowledged that '... transparent, responsible, accountable and participatory government, responsive to the needs and aspirations of the people, is the foundation on which good governance rests and that such a foundation is a *sine qua non* for the full realization of economic and social development' (BSEC, 2005b). Since then, the BSEC Working Group on Institutional Renewal and Good Governance, under its Greek presidency, has taken an active role in promoting good governance principles and practices in BSEC member states through studies, discussions and best practice exchanges, which can all be described as 'soft' mechanisms of change.

Three specific instruments of the Working Group can be highlighted as the most important to date. The first was the organization of a workshop in Athens in June of 2006 on the 'Improvement of the Relationships between State and Society'. The second was the 'Study on Institutional Renewal and Good Governance in BSEC member states' that was commissioned from the ICBSS and was the first attempt to outline the current situation in respect of public administration reforms in the member states. The third was a 'Pilot Project on the Implementation of Better Regulation Principles on SMEs' Start-ups', launched in 2007. This project moved the cooperation to a more advanced technical level where four countries (Azerbaijan, Moldova, Turkey and Romania) initially stated their willingness to participate, but it was soon abandoned because of lack of capacity at the domestic level. The funding for all the activities up to 2009 came from the Hellenic Ministry of the Interior, which had been the country coordinator since the establishment of the Working Group (Interview 2, 7 August 2008). It is of no little importance that the drive towards a good governance agenda came from an old EU member state that was also a founding member of the BSEC. In 2009, Ukraine took over the coordination of the group and the Working Group became a loose forum for the exchange of information and ideas.

To summarize, what we have shown is that principles and practices of good governance have spread through the activities of a variety of international organizations, mainly through the use of 'soft' mechanisms. Nevertheless, it is mainly the BSEC, if compared with other international and regional organizations, that deals with the Black Sea as a region. Additionally, the BSEC has been fairly active in the field of good governance and has been building synergies with international organizations (i.e., OECD) and experienced countries (i.e., Greece). In the next section, the role of the EU in regard to the promotion of good governance in the Black Sea region is discussed.

## The EU and the promotion of governance reforms in the Black Sea area

Two aspects of EU policy are of interest for our analysis: the promotion of governance reforms by the EU and its policy towards the Black Sea region. The promotion of so-called good governance is part of the EU's foreign policy. The mainstreaming of the concept has been the work of the Directorate General Development of the European Commission, and it has been enriched by the enlargement process (Börzel et al., 2008). The European Neighbourhood Policy (ENP) has been the main tool for the promotion of what the EU understands as good governance (in line with the definitions of other major international organizations). It serves the goals of both development and of enlargement and is part of the external governance of the EU.

Börzel et al. (2008) describe four steps in the external governance of the EU towards the Black Sea. The first step came directly after the recognition of the successor states of the Soviet Union and the introduction of the Technical Assistance for the Commonwealth of Independent States (TACIS) programme for the provision of financial and technical assistance. The second step took place in 1997 with the formalization of nine bilateral Partnership and Cooperation Agreements. The third step was triggered by the Eastern enlargement and consists of the ENP. Of particular interest are the Action Plans of the ex-Soviet Union countries that copy the accession partnerships of the EU's enlargement process. In 2007, the fourth step was initiated with the replacement of TACIS by the European Neighbourhood and Partners Instrument (ENPI), which relies on the principle of co-financing and cooperation partnerships.

In May 2007 the EU launched the 'Black Sea Synergy (BSS) – a New Regional Cooperation Initiative' targeted more towards strengthening cooperation between the EU and the Black Sea Region. Ten priority areas were outlined, among them 'Democracy, respect for human rights and good governance'. The EU claimed that its actions were complementary to other regional organizations such as the BSEC, supporting their work in the field, sharing experience and providing training (European Commission, 2007). Japaridze et al. (2010) argue that the BSS enhanced BSEC–EU interaction and, even more importantly, secured a 'silent' consensus from Russia. It was the first time that the EU had considered the Black Sea as a distinct policy area. It brought together all the political actors of the region and it promoted the idea of regional cooperation not only between the EU and the region but also within the region.

At the same time, bilateral efforts were also encouraged (European Commission, 2008a). Yannis (2008: 4) rightly points out that 'the Black Sea Synergy is a concrete initiative aiming to reinforce the process of Europeanization in the region', although the process is not as straightforward as in South and Central East Europe where there was an EU membership perspective.

Not long after the BSS was launched, in May of 2009, the EU initiated the Eastern Partnership (EaP) which, although it concerns the same region, does not include Russia and Turkey because, it was argued, both of these countries have a different status in their relationship with the EU. Turkey is an accession country and Russia is a strategic partner. Similarly, the BSEC is not a partner in the same way as it was in the BSS. For example, it is not mentioned as a platform of implementation of multilateral initiatives. Indeed, the EaP is considered to be more flexible because it includes 5 (+1) countries and it allows for bilateral projects based on the principle of 'more for more', which is a variant of the conditionality principle and promises 'more' for the countries that perform better. The relationship of BSS with the EaP has already been questioned. The European Commission (2008b) in a Working Document claims that 'there is substantial complementarity between the EaP and the Black Sea Synergy and other regional and international initiatives'.

Even though the EaP is still young, four thematic platforms for multilateral cooperation have been developed. The first platform is termed 'democracy, good governance and stability', which shows that the issue of governance remains one of the priorities of the EU (European Commission, 2009a). The good governance platform had its first meeting in June of 2009, when its core objectives were defined (democracy and human rights, justice, freedom and security, and security and stability). A work programme for the period 2009–2011 was elaborated and activities were planned. The three aspects of democratic governance that were prioritized were, first, improved functioning of the judiciary; second, public administration reform; and third, the fight against corruption (European Commission, 2009b). All three topics were analysed, but it is still early days for an assessment of their implementation or for speculation about the willingness of the parties involved to take the cooperation further. What can be claimed is that 'soft' mechanisms of Europeanization are preferred and they are not very different to the mechanisms used by regional organizations such as the BSEC. The difference is the capacity and the prestige of the EU, as well as the expectation of increased funding that may accelerate the pace of the transfer. The adoption of the 'more for more' principle by the EaP reinforces these beliefs.

## Analysis and conclusions

In this section, the methodological, theoretical and empirical arguments presented in the chapter are brought together. The main question concerned the three rival alternative hypotheses about possible sources of domestic change in the Black Sea area. The question itself limited our search to exogenous and not to domestic factors. In order to answer whether the EU and thus Europeanization processes, the BSEC or a combination of organizations is responsible for change, we turned our attention to mechanisms of change. Thus, the research strategy applied in this chapter consisted of two steps for the better exploration of causality in Europeanization: first, the design of rival hypotheses, in order to avoid simplified answers in regard to the importance of Europeanization; and second, the empirical study of mechanisms of change in order to investigate what is really happening on the ground.

The literature on the mechanisms of Europeanization was used as the starting point for the comparison of the instruments adopted by the BSEC and the EU for the promotion of good governance. Turning to the case study, a number of international organizations (e.g., World Bank, UNDP) that are active, at least at a bilateral level, were observed. The only two organizations that demonstrably considered the Black Sea as a region and organized initiatives for the promotion of good governance were the BSEC and the EU. Interaction between the EU and BSEC has proved to be a common feature through the years, as has interaction with other international organizations such as the UNDP. This means that no major disagreement exists between the different international actors in the region over the significance of spreading good governance. Thus, the third hypothesis, which sees international and regional organizations and the EU as complementary in their role in pushing good governance in the Black Sea area, is the closest to reality.

When one looks more closely, there is a degree of harmony between the mechanisms used by the BSEC and the EU. Both organizations use 'soft' mechanisms of change, with a special preference for framing domestic beliefs and expectations, aiming to change the discourse in favour of good governance. Changing domestic opportunity structures requires more funding, something that has been limited in the case of the BSEC, given that the good governance working group activities have been solely funded by the Greek government. In the case of the EU, it is possible that more resources will be allocated to the 'good governance platform', which will allow for the use of harder mechanisms. Institutional compliance is relevant only for Black Sea countries that are members of the EU (e.g., Bulgaria and Romania) or for accession countries (e.g., Turkey) that do not participate in the EaP. Nevertheless, institutional reform may take place in the other countries as a result of the 'more for more' EU strategy. It is difficult even to imagine BSEC using mechanisms such as institutional compliance, given that it is an intergovernmental organization with limited funding and capacity. Last but not least, there is an agreement between BSEC and the EU on the definition of good governance and on the areas where cooperation should start. Both of the organizations emphasize the importance of democratic governance, accountability and participation. Administrative reform is an area that was prioritized by both, with BSEC already having implemented a few initial activities.

To return to the initial question of the book on how to address causality in European studies, this chapter has shown that a research design based on rival hypotheses and mechanisms of change can help us to be more rigorous when claiming causality. The fact that the EU, as well as other regional and international organizations, has been shown to cause the spread of good governance in the Black Sea region shows that causality in European studies is often complex and conjunctional, and thus sophisticated research designs are necessary in order to avoid verifying self-fulfilling prophesies. One way forward could be to combine the European and global levels of analysis in our search for causality (i.e., Bache et al., Chapter 4 in this volume). The prominence of 'soft' mechanisms of change reminds us that often, in order to establish causality between phenomena, we need to focus on discourse and discursive change, which means that methodological tools less associated with causality claims are necessary (i.e., Lynggaard, Chapter 5 in this volume). In conclusion, it would be interesting to apply what we have discovered about the Europeanization of non-member states into member states and see whether a more rigorous research design challenges our established assumptions of causality in European studies.

### Note

1. I would like to thank the participants in the seminar at the Politics Department, University of Sheffield, in January 2009 and the participants in the two workshops at the University of Exeter in 2010 for comments on early drafts of this chapter. Last but not least, I would like to thank the two editors of the book for their insightful comments and remarks throughout the process.

# Bibliography

Aydin, M. (2004), *Europe's Next Shore: The Black Sea Region after EU Enlargement*, Occasional Paper no. 53, Paris: European Union Institute for Security Studies.

Börzel, T., Pamuk, Y. and Stahn, A. (2008), 'The European Union and the Promotion of Good Governance in its Near Abroad- One Size Fits All?' paper presented at the *104th APSA Annual Meeting* in Boston, Massachusetts, 28–31 August.

BSEC (2001), *Agenda for the Future 2001*, available at www.bsec.org.

BSEC (2003a), *Summary Proceedings for the Workshop 'Getting the Act Together: Strengthening International Relations' Capacities in the BSEC Countries'*, Yerevan, 19–20 March 2003.

BSEC (2003b), *Summary Proceedings for the Workshop 'Getting the Act Together: Strengthening International Relations' Capacities in the BSEC Countries'*, Baku, 22–23 September 2003.

BSEC (2004), *Summary Proceedings for the Workshop 'Getting the Act Together: Strengthening International Relations' Capacities in the BSEC Countries'*, Tbilisi, 7–8 October 2004.

BSEC (2005a), *Workshop on 'Institutional Renewal and Good Governance in the BSEC Countries'*, Athens, 9–10 February 2005.

BSEC (2005b), *Joint Declaration on Good Governance and Institutional Renewal*, available at www.bsec.org.

Doornbos, M. (2001), ' "Good Governance": The Rise and Decline of a Policy Metaphor?', *Journal of Development Studies*, 37 (6): 93–108.

European Commission (2007), *Communication from the Commission to the Council and the European Parliament: Black Sea Synergy – A New Regional Cooperation Initiative*, http://ec.europa.eu/world/enp/pdf/com07_160_en.pdf.

European Commission (2008a), *Communication from the Commission to the Council and the European Parliament: Report on the First Year of Implementation of the Black Sea Synergy*, http://ec.europa.eu/external_relations/blacksea/doc/com08_391_en.pdf.

European Commission (2008b), Commission Staff Working Document accompanying the *Communication of the Commission to the European Parliament and the Council, Eastern Partnership*, Brussels, SEC (2008) 2974/3, COM (2008) 823.

European Commission (2009a), *Eastern Partnership Multilateral Platforms*.

European Commission (2009b), *Eastern Partnership: Platform 1 'Democracy, Good Governance and Stability', Core Objectives and Work Programme 2009–2011*.

Featherstone, K. and Papadimitriou, D. (2008), *The Limits of Europeanization: Reform Capacity and Policy Conflict in Greece*, Hampshire: Palgrave Macmillan.

Freyburg, T., Lavenex, S., Schimmelfennig, F., Skripka, T. and Wetzel, A. (2009), 'EU Promotion of Democratic Governance in the Neighbourhood', *Journal of European Public Policy*, 16 (6): 916–934.

Goetz, K. (2001), 'Making Sense of Post-Communist Central Administration: Modernization, Europeanization or Latinization?', *Journal of European Public Policy*, 8 (6): 1032–1051.

Grabbe, H. (2001), 'How does Europeanization affect CEE Governance? Conditionality, Diffusion and Diversity', *Journal of European Public Policy*, 8 (6): 1013–1031.

Grabbe, H. and Sedelmeier, U (2010), 'The Future Shape of the European Union', in M. Egan, N. Nugent and W. Paterson (eds.), *Research Agendas in EU Studies*, Hampshire: Palgrave Macmillan, pp. 375–397.

Huntington, S. (1991), *The Third Wave: Democratization in the Late Twentieth Century*, Norman: University of Oklahoma Press.

Japaridze, T., Manoli, P., Triantaphyllou, D. and Tsantoulis, Y. (2010), 'The EU's Ambivalent Relationship with the BSEC: Reflecting on the Past, Mapping out the Future', *ICBSS Policy Brief*, 20, Athens: ICBSS.

Knill, C. (2001), *The Europeanization of National Administrations*, Cambridge: Cambridge University Press.

Ladi, S. (2005), 'Europeanization and Environmental Policy Change', *Policy and Society*, 24 (2): 1–15.

Ladi, S. and Ruso-Dragoumis, E. (2007), *Study on Institutional Renewal and Good Governance in BSEC Member States*, Athens: International Centre for Black Sea Studies.

Lavenex, S. (2004), 'EU External Governance in "Wider Europe" ', *Journal of European Public Policy*, 11 (4): 680–700.

Olsen, J. (2002), 'The Many Faces of Europeanization', *Journal of Common Market Studies*, 40 (5): 921–952.

Papadimitriou, D. and Phinnemore, D. (2003), 'Exporting Europeanization to the Wider Europe: The Twinning Exercise and Administrative Reform in the Candidate Countries and Beyond', *Southeast European and Black Sea Studies*, 3 (2): 1–22.

Sciarini, P., Fischer, A. and Nicolet, S. (2004), 'How Europe Hits Home: Evidence from the Swiss Case', *Journal of European Public Policy*, 11 (3): 353–378.

Uvin, P. and Biagiotti, I. (1996), 'Global Governance and the 'New' Political Conditionality', *Global Governance*, 2 (3): 377–400.

Weiss, T. (2000), 'Governance, Good Governance and Global Governance: Conceptual and Actual Challenges', *Third World Quarterly*, 21 (5): 795–814.

Yannis, A. (2008), 'The European Union and the Black Sea Region: The New Eastern Frontiers and Europeanization', *Policy Brief*, 7, Athens: ICBSS.

## Web resources

Black Sea Economic Cooperation Organization, http://www.bsec-organization.org

International Monetary Fund, http://www.imf.org

Organization for Economic Co-operation and Development, http://oecd.org

United Nations Development Programme, http://www.undp.org

United States Agency for International Development, http://www.usaid.gov

The World Bank, http://www.worldbank.org

## Interviews

Ambassador Japaridze, Tedo, Alternate Director General ICBSS, ICBSS, Athens, 1/8/2008.

Dais, Panayiotis and Psarakis, Antonis, Co-ordinators from the Hellenic Ministry of the Interior, Hellenic Ministry of the Interior, Athens, 7/8/08.

# 13
## Being Clear Enough to Be Wrong: Europeanization Refuted and Defended

*Kyriakos Moumoutzis*

The purpose of this chapter is to demonstrate that it is possible to formulate, empirically test and *refute* explanations that conceptualize foreign policy change as the outcome of Europeanization,[1] thus establishing that the latter can indeed be useful for the study of foreign policy when it is embedded in carefully designed research projects. The first section of the chapter establishes that change in Greek policy towards Turkey during the second half of the 1990s constitutes a potential case of Europeanization, formulates three alternative explanations of change in Greek policy and specifies their observable implications for three dimensions of the policymaking process: the definition of the policy problem, the alternative courses of action considered and the manner in which the latter were assessed. The second section briefly presents the evidence drawn from process tracing the observable implications of the three alternative explanations for the three dimensions of the policymaking process mentioned above, which refutes both explanations that attribute causal significance to the European Union (EU). The concluding section discusses the implications for the design of empirical research on the Europeanization of EU member states' foreign policies.

### Designing research on the Europeanization of foreign policy

*Case selection.* Several studies have discussed the 'Europeanization' of Greek foreign policy (Economides, 2005; Ioakimidis, 2000; Kavakas, 2000; Tsakonas, 2010), and it has been argued that change in Greek policy towards Turkey during the second half of the 1990s constitutes its 'clearest manifestation' (Economides, 2005: 482). Indeed, while since its accession to the European Communities Greece had opposed progress in Turkey's relations with the Community/EU, at the 1999 Helsinki European Council Greece consented to the EU upgrading Turkey to candidate country status. The formulation of Greece's so-called 'Helsinki strategy' constitutes *a potential case of Europeanization* because the content of policy change is consistent with theoretically predicted outcomes of Europeanization (see Box 13.1).

---

**Box 13.1   Key ideas**

**What are we trying to establish and how?**
The purpose of empirical research on the Europeanization of national foreign policy is to establish the causal significance of the EU for its member states' foreign policies. The implementation of the research strategy presented here requires the following steps:

- Case selection: Identify a case of foreign policy change that constitutes a potential case of Europeanization. Has change rendered national policy more consistent with the prescriptions of established EU norms and practices?
- Alternative explanations: Formulate both explanations that attribute causal significance to the EU and explanations that attribute causal significance to other sources of foreign policy. What other variables may have produced policy change, and through what processes?
- Process tracing: Specify the observable implications of alternative explanations for policymakers' definition of the policy problem, the alternative courses of action they considered and the manner in which they were assessed.

  - Did national policymakers and their EU counterparts reach a shared definition of the situation?
  - Did national policymakers identify and consider an 'EU way of doing things' as an alternative course of action?
  - Did they assess it as a more effective or more appropriate alternative?

---

In this sense, the formulation of the Helsinki strategy can be conceptualized as the outcome of the incorporation of *EU enlargement conditionality* or the practice of 'reinforcement by reward' (Schimmelfennig et al.,

2003) into Greek policy towards Turkey. While some might consider enlargement as an atypical EU external policy, it remains one of the most successful and therefore it would not be surprising if certain national foreign policymakers considered incorporating EU enlargement policy instruments and practices into their own policies (on enlargement as part of the EU's external policies, see also Exadaktylos, Chapter 11 in this volume). According to the practice of reinforcement by reward, the EU offers the reward of membership and creates a link between payment of the reward and compliance with certain conditions. If the target government complies, the reward is paid. If the target government fails to comply, payment of the reward is withheld, but the EU 'does not intervene either coercively or supportively' (Schimmelfenning et al., 2003: 497). In contrast, until the Helsinki strategy was formulated, Greek governments had unilaterally withheld the offer of EU membership in an attempt to force Turkey to accept Greek positions on Greco-Turkish problems related to the Aegean. The Helsinki strategy involved considerable 'multilateralisation' (Economides, 2005) because the offer of EU membership can only be made collectively and therefore the incorporation of the procedural norm of collective decision making into Greek policy was necessary.

Change in Greek policy constitutes a least-likely potential case of Europeanization. As has been pointed out, 'it is impossible ( ... ) to advocate a policy (on Greco-Turkish relations) different from the one that is accepted as national policy without a significant electoral cost or the fear of being criticized as a traitor' (Kavakas, 2000: 150). In this sense, Greek foreign policymakers were unlikely voluntarily to incorporate EU practices that challenged the legacy of Greek policy towards Turkey, as they were severely constrained by vehement domestic opposition to foreign policy reform. Consequently, if the evidence confirms an explanation that conceptualizes change in policy on such a uniquely sensitive national issue introduced by such a severely constrained government as the outcome of Europeanization, the explanation will have passed a strong test and the findings will be generalizable across cases of Europeanization of policy on equally or less delicate issues pursued by governments operating under similar or fewer constraints. If the evidence refutes both explanations that conceptualize change in Greek policy as the outcome of Europeanization, these explanations will have a more limited range of applicability but, crucially, research design will have proved sufficiently effective to allow researchers to be 'clear enough to be wrong' and the usefulness of Europeanization for the empirical study of foreign policy will have been confirmed.

*Europeanization through socialization.* Constructivist explanations of Europeanization emphasize international socialization during EU-level interactions (Economides, 2005: 472; Rieker, 2006a, 2006b; Tonra, 2001; Wong, 2006; for different explanations in the literature, see Chapter 1 in this volume). The latter results in an incorporation of EU foreign policy norms and practices into national foreign policy that is driven by the logic of appropriateness. When social action is driven by this logic, actors try to answer questions such as what kind of situation this is, what kind of person I am and what does a person such as I do in a situation such as this. (March and Olsen, 2004: 4). National foreign policymakers redefine the situation they are facing as a result of socialization. They begin to identify violations of substantive EU foreign policy norms by third countries as a policy problem; they define third countries' compliance with these norms as their objective and select the relevant established EU foreign policy practices and procedures in order to achieve it.

In this sense, Greek foreign policymakers began to see Turkey as an applicant country with a rather weak democratic regime, where the rule of law was not observed and human rights, fundamental freedoms and the rights of minorities were being violated. Greek foreign policymakers identified themselves as officials of an EU member state and they identified reinforcement by reward as the established practice that determines what constitutes appropriate behaviour for EU member states when applicant countries violate substantive EU foreign policy norms. The policy previously pursued (preventing Turkey from developing its relations with the EU) was considered inappropriate because it contradicted established EU practice. Greek foreign policymakers chose to incorporate reinforcement by reward into their policy towards Turkey *because they felt that this was the appropriate course of action for an EU member state given the situation.*

*Europeanization through strategic calculation.* Alternatively, the incorporation of EU foreign policy practices and procedures into national foreign policy may be the result of strategic calculation.[2] According to such explanations, EU-level interactions do not result in a redefinition of the situation that national foreign policymakers are facing. The latter incorporates EU foreign policy practices and procedures into national policy because they have calculated that they might achieve *fixed policy objectives* more effectively. The causal significance of the EU lies in the fact that the establishment of EU foreign policy practices and procedures *alters the range of alternatives* available to national foreign policymakers.

In this sense, the establishment of EU enlargement conditionality altered the range of alternatives available to Greek foreign policymakers and provided them with the option of offering Turkey a conditional reward (EU membership). The 1996 Imia/Kardak crisis[3] demonstrated the failure of the Greek practice of withholding the offer of rewards to achieve Greek foreign policy objectives and established the need for policy change. As the crisis prompted a search for a more effective alternative, Greek foreign policymakers identified the discrepancy between Greek policy and established EU practice and chose to incorporate reinforcement by reward into their policy towards Turkey *because they calculated that it might be more effective* as it would offer Turkey greater incentive to comply with Greek demands.[4]

Several studies have emphasized the significance of reiterated EU-level interactions over long periods of time for socialization. As has been pointed out, however, this emphasis on the quantity rather than the quality of interactions is problematic. In cases where EU-level interactions are more accurately conceptualized as negotiations rather than deliberations, these interactions are unlikely to produce socialization effects regardless of their duration (Checkel, 2005: 807). It should be noted that while the quality rather than the quantity of interactions is emphasized here, none of the explanations of foreign policy change as the outcome of Europeanization presented above predict that change in national policy was an immediate response to changing EU-level dynamics. While EU enlargement conditionality was introduced in 1993, according to the explanation based on socialization it was not until several years later, and after reiterated EU-level interactions and deliberations on EU–Turkey relations, that Greek foreign policymakers decided to incorporate the practice of reinforcement by reward into their policy towards Turkey and, according to the explanation based on strategic calculation, the relevance of reinforcement by reward and the discrepancy between the latter and Greek policy was not identified or assessed until an exogenous shock demonstrated policy failure and resulted in a search for a more effective policy.

*Alternative explanations.* While Europeanization is usually defined as a process, it is often analysed as if it were merely an outcome. In this vein, it has been argued that the Helsinki strategy is consistent with 'Europeanization' in the sense of 'uploading' (Economides, 2005: 481–482; Tsakonas, 2010: 24–25). Uploading, however, describes only an empirically observable type of foreign policy action: the pursuit of EU-level foreign policy coordination. It does not indicate what the process that produced this action was. Uploading *might* be an outcome of

Europeanization. This is the case only when the establishment of EU practices leads national foreign policymakers to calculate that a collective decision on an issue that they had previously handled unilaterally might serve their interests best or when EU-level interactions convince national foreign policymakers that collective decision making on such an issue is appropriate. In both cases, developments that take place within the context of the EU cause uploading, and therefore the latter is consistent with Europeanization.

The decision to pursue EU-level foreign policy coordination on an issue previously handled unilaterally, however, may not be a response to EU-level dynamics. Processes of change may originate from domestic actors 'who impose (their) own vision of the basic redirection necessary in foreign policy' (Hermann, 1990: 11). Despite the fact that international relations scholarship has often 'neglected' the study of foreign policy change (Rosati et al., 1994), processes of leader-driven change can be identified and explained by existing theories. When our analyses fail to distinguish between Europeanization and alternative processes of (foreign) policy change that are not generated by EU dynamics, the causal significance of the EU is overestimated and the emergence of Europeanization as a *new* 'research agenda'[5] is inhibited.

As has been pointed out, this pitfall can be avoided by testing explanations that attribute causal significance to the EU against alternatives (Radaelli, 2004: 8). As indicated above, the emphasis on foreign policymakers and their particular characteristics and motivations – especially in cases where a predominant leader is the unit of decision[6] – has been a central element of foreign policy analysis since the 1950s (Hudson and Vore, 1995). More recently, it has been suggested that the causal significance of predominant leaders' characteristics varies depending on their *responsiveness to the policy context*. The less responsive a predominant leader, the more likely it is that their government's foreign policy actions will reflect the leader's own motivations rather than structural changes in the policy environment (Hermann et al., 2001). The least responsive predominant leaders are those who are motivated by a desire to pursue a set of ideas or resolve a specific problem, challenge constraints and are closed to information (Hermann, 2003; Hermann et al., 2001; Kaarbo, 1997; Stoessinger, 1985: xiii). When an unresponsive predominant leader enters the policymaking process with a set of preconceived ideas that contradict the policy legacy, they are likely to pursue policy actions that will result in policy change, as they will find it difficult to abandon their preconceived ideas, will exhibit a willingness to challenge constraints on their capacity to pursue them and will tend to disregard information that contradicts them. As the evidence presented below shows, the Helsinki strategy was indeed the outcome of Greek Prime Minister Costas Simitis' efforts to pursue his own vision for foreign policy reform. According to the latter, Greece should allow Turkey to develop its relations with the EU within a framework of EU rules for Turkey's behaviour towards Greece. Simitis believed that if Greece could have such rules established, the EU itself would see to it that its own rules were observed. The former Prime Minister remained unequivocally committed to the completion of this task, despite severe constraints on his government's capacity to do so and information that challenged that task's necessity.[7] As will be shown in the next section, while both the instrumental explanation of the Helsinki strategy as the outcome of Europeanization and the leader-driven change explanation predicted that Greek foreign policymakers' behaviour was driven by the logic of expected consequences, each predicted different cost–benefit calculations (see also Panke's contribution, Chapter 7 in this volume, on how one can empirically distinguish between alternative explanations that are based on the same logic of action by making detailed predictions regarding variation in actors' cost–benefit calculations).

*Process tracing.* It is possible empirically to distinguish between the above explanations by process tracing their observable implications for three dimensions of the policymaking process: (i) the policy problem that the Helsinki strategy was intended to address, (ii) the alternative courses of action that Greek foreign policymakers considered and (iii) the manner in which these were assessed (see also Lynggaard's contribution to this volume (Chapter 5) on the role of the empirical investigation of policy problems and solutions in discourse analysis). Process tracing is a method that allows researchers to trace a series of 'theoretically predicted intermediate steps' between the explanatory and the dependent variable (Checkel, 2006: 363). This method makes it possible to establish causality even in single cases of equifinality based on within-case observations (Bennett and Elman, 2006: 262; Cortell and Davis Jr, 2000: 84–86; Mahoney and Goertz, 2006: 236–237).

In this sense, empirical research started by establishing how national foreign policymakers defined the *policy problem* and whether the latter was redefined as a result of EU-level interactions.[8] According to the explanation based on socialization, Greek foreign policymakers began to identify Turkish *violations of substantive EU foreign policy* norms as a foreign policy problem and defined Turkey's compliance with these norms as their objective. According to the explanation based on strategic calculation, the 1996 crisis demonstrated policy failure and prompted a search for a more effective policy. In contrast, the leader-driven change explanation predicted that Simitis had concluded that Greek policy towards Turkey was ineffective and that he had selected the alternative he deemed optimal *prior to the crisis*. In order to determine whether the Prime Minister's role was causally significant, empirical research sought to determine whether his beliefs regarding the policy issue under investigation had been crystallized prior to his election, whether they were consistent with the policy previously pursued and whether they remained fixed during his premiership.

The next step was to identify the various courses of action that were considered as *alternative options* and determine whether they included established EU foreign policy practices. Both explanations that conceptualized change in Greek policy as the outcome of Europeanization predicted that Greek foreign policymakers considered the EU practice of *offering* applicant states *the reward of membership*, whilst making payment of the reward conditional upon the target country's compliance as a substitute for the Greek practice of *withholding the offer of EU membership* until Turkey complied with Greek demands. In contrast, the leader-driven change explanation predicted that Greek foreign policymakers distinguished between the policy previously pursued (*preventing progress in EU–Turkey relations*) and the policy for reform prescribed by Simitis' vision: *allowing progress within a framework of EU rules for Turkey's behaviour towards Greece and regardless of whether Turkey would be offered rewards*. The empirical investigation of the alternative courses of action that Greek foreign policymakers considered and the Prime Minister's reactions to those who opposed his preferred course of action made it possible to determine the Prime Minister's willingness to consider alternatives to the strategy that he preferred and his willingness to challenge constraints.

The final step was to establish whether national foreign policymakers considered the consequences (costs and benefits) of each alternative and, if so, what type of *costs and benefits* they calculated. According to the explanation based on socialization, the incorporation of EU enlargement conditionality into Greek policy towards Turkey was driven by a logic of appropriateness. By definition, behaviour based on this logic is *not driven by considerations of consequences* (March and Olsen, 2004: 3) and it is *consistent across issues and over time* (Cortell and Davis Jr., 2000: 71–72). According to the explanation based on strategic calculation, the Helsinki strategy was selected because it would offer Turkey *greater incentive to comply* with Greek demands. In contrast, the leader-driven change explanation predicted that the Helsinki strategy was selected because it would assign the *responsibility for ensuring Turkey's compliance* to the EU regardless of whether Turkey would be offered incentives to comply. By empirically investigating the manner in which Greek foreign policy-makers assessed the alternatives that they considered, it became possible to determine how the Prime Minister assessed information that contradicted his beliefs and evidence that suggested that his preferred course of action was ineffective. The following section briefly presents the most instructive pieces of evidence that refute both explanations that conceptualized policy change as the outcome of Europeanization and confirm the leader-driven change explanation.

## The findings

*The definition of the policy problem.* Simitis had publicly presented his own vision for foreign policy reform long before he was elected Prime Minister. In fact, with regard to the definition of the policy problem there is no variation during the period under investigation that requires explanation. The understanding of the situation – on which policy change was based – remained fixed throughout Simitis' premiership. He *intended to reduce what he saw as an excessive responsiveness of Greek policy* to Turkey's aggressiveness and other contextual factors (Simitis, 1992: 21). Strikingly enough, Simitis was suggesting that Greece's 'hyper-reactive' policy towards Turkey should be replaced by a policy on European integration (1995: 163). He believed that Greece should argue that Greco-Turkish problems were in fact 'Community problems' and pursue a multilateral policy towards Turkey that would establish Community rules for Turkey's behaviour towards Greece. If Greece could establish such rules, the Community would be responsible for ensuring Turkey's compliance with them (Simitis, 1992: 26–27, 1995: 162). The 1996 Imia/Kardak crisis was interpreted as evidence that confirmed his belief that the strategy he preferred was necessary (Simitis, 2005: 74–75, 86).

Simitis' attempts to pursue his vision for foreign policy reform found few supporters. Party members, members of parliament and cabinet members frequently criticized Greek policy towards Turkey (Featherstone, 2005: 226; Kazamias, 1997: 81, 85–87) and occasionally threatened to withdraw their support for the government. Even Foreign Minister Theodore Pangalos (1999, 2000) remained sceptical of deviations from Greece's traditional policy and continued to express the Pan-Hellenic Socialist Movement's (PASOK) traditional positions, according to which Greece should refrain from making 'unilateral good will gestures' because these would be interpreted as signs of weakness and result in further aggression. Similarly, non-governmental actors, such as the nationalist Head of the influential Greek Orthodox Church (Vasilakis, 2006: 307–308) and the media, whose coverage of Greco-Turkish relations assumed a similarly 'ultra-nationalist' character (Mitropoulos, 2003: 292–293), were critical of the government's policy, while policy change took place in the absence of epistemic communities that could have acted as agents of reform (Tsakonas, 2005: 429–430). Finally, shortly before the Helsinki summit 69 per cent of the Greek public remained opposed to the prospect of Turkey becoming a part of the EU (European Commission, 2000).

As the leader-driven change explanation predicted, Simitis' commitment to his preferred strategy remained unequivocal. Despite the fact that concerns were frequently voiced during cabinet meetings, few if any changes were introduced in Greek policy as a result. In fact, the Helsinki strategy was formulated by the Prime Minister himself in collaboration with his two most senior foreign policy advisors (Nicholas Themelis, Head of the Prime Minister's Office, and Christos Rozakis, previously briefly served as Undersecretary for Foreign Affairs, but held no official post at the time), in addition to Foreign Minister George Papandreou (who replaced Pangalos in early 1999) and Deputy Foreign Minister Yannos Kranidiotis (who was mostly responsible for Greek policy on the Cyprus problem). The strategy was subsequently, in Simitis' (2005: 93, 96) words, merely 'presented' to the cabinet. The foreign policymaking process was in fact fairly similar to that of the periods 1974–1981 and 1981–1989, when Prime Ministers Constantinos Karamanlis and Andreas Papandreou, respectively, were the key foreign policymakers assisted by Foreign Ministers and advisors, and who were often loyal personal friends (Ioakimidis, 2003: 111–115).

Greek foreign policymakers have indeed acknowledged the significance of Simitis' idiosyncratic vision and his commitment to it. It is often pointed out that Simitis was imbued with an entirely different understanding of what Greek policy towards Turkey ought to be, that he intended to pursue policy change as soon as he was elected Prime Minister, that he did so with a clear and firm sense of purpose and that the shift in Greek policy towards Turkey would not have been possible without his leadership.[9]

*The framing of alternatives.* Simitis' vision for foreign policy reform determined the alternative courses of action that Greek foreign policymakers considered and their assessment. As the leader-driven change explanation predicted, he assumed an active role in the implementation of his preferred policy as soon as he was elected Prime Minister, despite the fact that his government was severely constrained by the numerous actors mentioned above that opposed foreign policy reform. His efforts resulted *in a series of EU decisions* that established EU rules for Turkey's behaviour towards Greece and attributed a role in Greco-Turkish relations to the EU. First, on 15 July 1996 Greece managed to have an EU statement adopted that identified Greco-Turkish problems as problems that concerned the EU, and suggested that disputes such as the one over the Imia/Kardak islets should be submitted to the International Court of Justice. The EU was also assuming a role in Greco-Turkish relations as the Council was requesting the Presidency to invite Turkey to confirm that it was committed to the principles mentioned in the statement. In exchange Greece lifted its veto on EU financial assistance to Turkey within the context of Euro-Mediterranean cooperation. Second, having established the principle of judicial settlement of disputes as an EU rule applicable to Greco-Turkish relations, the Greek government wished to involve the EU further. The Greek government consented to a meeting of the EU-Turkey Association Council in 29 April 1997, when it was agreed that the member states' common position for the meeting would reiterate the content of the 15 July 1996 EU statement regarding the settlement of territorial disputes and that – in an unprecedented involvement of the EU in Greco-Turkish relations – the Dutch Presidency would accommodate exchanges between two groups of experts appointed by Greece and Turkey and instructed to make suggestions regarding procedural aspects of the resolution of Greco-Turkish problems. Finally, in December 1997 Greece managed to secure a decision that introduced EU rules for Turkey's behaviour towards it at the highest political level – that of the European Council – for the first time. Greece allowed the EU to address an offer to participate in the European Conference to Turkey, which was conditional on its commitment to the peaceful settlements of disputes, 'in particular through the jurisdiction of the International Court of Justice in the Hague' (Presidency Conclusions, 1997).

Simitis' preferred policy, however, did not have the desired effect. On the contrary, both EU–Turkey relations and Greco-Turkish relations deteriorated further. As the leader-driven change explanation predicted, this undesirable effect did not challenge Simitis' commitment to his preferred policy. The Helsinki strategy was formulated in June 1999 as an alternative that would constitute the *culmination of the shift* that Simitis had previously initiated, as Greece sought to establish *additional* EU rules for Turkey's behaviour towards it, including a specific timeframe for Turkey's compliance and provisions regarding the EU's response in case of non-compliance. The Greek government made it clear that vetoing the Turkish candidacy was still an alternative, which it would have to select if the EU refused to establish additional rules for Turkey's behaviour towards Greece.[10]

*The assessment of alternatives.* The role that the EU would assume in Greco-Turkish relations was considered the main benefit of the Helsinki strategy for Greece (Rozakis, 2005: 161; Simitis, 2005: 99).[11] Simitis believed that if rules for Turkey's behaviour towards Greece were established at the EU level, the EU would have to ensure that its own rules were observed. The EU's role in Greco-Turkish relations was seen as part of the EU's broader international role (Simitis, 1996).[12] Simitis' assessment of the EU foreign policy record shows that he acknowledged that the Union had enjoyed limited success as an international actor. As the leader-driven change explanation predicted, however, this information did not lead him to question the benefits of his preferred policy. According to Simitis, the rules that Greece managed to establish in Helsinki attributed to the EU not only the role of an agent responsible for monitoring Turkey's compliance, but also that of a 'guarantor', who would 'intervene' in order to ensure Turkey's compliance (1999, 2004, 2005: 99, 101). Indeed, according to the Presidency Conclusions, not only would the European Council monitor Turkey's compliance and consider the implications of non-compliance for Turkey's progress towards accession by the end of 2004, but it would also 'promote' the judicial settlement of disputes (Presidency Conclusions, 1999).

The evidence shows that neither of the explanations that conceptualized change in Greek policy as the outcome of Europeanization is convincing. First, in contrast to that predicted by the explanation based on socialization, Greek foreign policymakers did not begin to identify Turkish violations of substantive EU foreign policy norms as a problem for the first time during the period under investigation. Greece had criticized the Turkish regime long before the Helsinki strategy was formulated (Valinakis, 1989: 256). Turkey's weak democratic regime and human rights violations, however, were seen as further reasons why Turkey should not be allowed to develop its relations with the Community/EU further.[13] Consequently, the understanding of this particular aspect of the problem posed by Turkey remained constant, and therefore it cannot explain change in Greek policy.[14]

Second, there is no indication that Greek foreign policymakers became convinced of the inappropriateness of their policy within the context of the EU. In fact, it was argued that it was Greece's EU partners that had on certain occasions behaved inappropriately (Eleftherotypia, 1999; Papandreou, 1997). The most striking piece of evidence is the inconsistency of the Greek government's stance on the Turkish and the Cypriot candidacy. According to the explanation based on socialization, adherence to internalized behavioural rules should be expected to be consistent across issues and over time. While Greece insisted that Greco-Turkish problems should be resolved within a specific timeframe prior to the opening of accession negotiations with Turkey, it also insisted on an explicit commitment that Cyprus would join the EU regardless of the resolution of the Cyprus problem.[15]

Third, while some might argue that Simitis' vision for reform, which entails clear references to the EU, constitutes an observable implication of Europeanization, there is no evidence that its formation was the outcome of such a process. On the contrary, Simitis' preferred strategy and EU-level dynamics cannot be linked even at the analytical level. In sharp contrast to that predicted by the explanation based on strategic calculation, Simitis had already presented his vision for foreign policy reform *prior to the establishment of EU enlargement conditionality*, and therefore the latter could not have affected his calculations. Apart from the fact that this particular practice had not been established, leading European foreign policy analysts suggest that European foreign policy in general did not appear particularly promising at that time. The Gulf War and the disintegration of Yugoslavia had shown that 'the Community [was] not an effective international actor, in terms both of its capacity to produce collective decisions and its impact on events' (Hill, 1993: 306), and the recognition of the fiasco surrounding the former Yugoslav Republics had brought the very notion of a European foreign policy into 'disrepute' (Nuttall, 2000: 223). In 1992, nonetheless, Simitis had selected the Community as the preferable framework for the exercise of Greek policy towards Turkey.

Fourth, the benefits that Greek foreign policymakers calculated are not consistent with the EU's application of conditionality within the context of enlargement. Despite the fact that it was never made explicit how exactly the European Council would 'promote' the judicial settlement of disputes, this particular provision of the agreement attributed to the EU a proactive role in Greco-Turkish relations – precisely as Simitis' vision for reform prescribed – that contrasted sharply with the role entailed by reinforcement by reward.

Finally, in contrast to that predicted by both explanations that conceptualized change in Greek policy as the outcome of Europeanization,

Greek foreign policymakers failed to identify and therefore did not consider EU enlargement conditionality as a relevant established EU practice that might serve as a more effective or more appropriate alternative to the policy previously pursued.[16] Furthermore, while only the decision made in Helsinki is consistent with enlargement conditionality, all four EU decisions that Greece secured are consistent with Simitis' preferred policy. The decision made in Luxembourg offered Turkey a reward much less attractive than that entailed by enlargement conditionality, the 15 July 1996 agreement granted Turkey a reward that had already been offered and the 29 April 1997 agreement merely allowed a meeting of the EU-Turkey Association Council. All four decisions, however, established rules for Turkey's behaviour towards Greece and progressively increased the EU's involvement in Greco-Turkish relations.

## Conclusions

The evidence presented above refuting both explanations that conceptualized foreign policy change as the outcome of Europeanization is perhaps the most compelling indication that Europeanization can indeed be useful for the empirical study of foreign policy. It is, after all, possible to be 'clear enough to be wrong' when empirical research is designed carefully. First, researchers should make the logic of case selection much more explicit. The random search for some sort of EU impact on a member state's foreign policy over a long period of time runs the risk of both prejudging and overestimating the causal significance of the EU due to lack of empirical depth. Analysts should select empirical puzzles as the starting point of their research and establish why these puzzles constitute potential cases of Europeanization.

Second, researchers should formulate empirically testable explanations of Europeanization and test them against alternatives. The outcomes of Europeanization are not unique: alternative processes are capable of producing them. Potential cases of Europeanization are cases of equifinality. To establish the causal significance of the EU is to demonstrate that it is a more convincing cause than the alternatives one might consider.

While it is conceivable that there is evidence of Europeanization in other aspects of Greek foreign policy, the shift that culminated in the Helsinki strategy was not the outcome of such a process, but that of a process of leader-driven foreign policy change. The task Simitis was determined to complete was preconceived in the sense that it had been defined prior to his election as Prime Minister, and his participation in EU-level interactions during his premiership did not alter it. Similarly, leading EU foreign policy analysts suggest that at the time Simitis defined this task EU foreign policy dynamics offered little evidence that it was necessary. Clearly, if Europeanization is not a process whereby the EU causes change in national (foreign) policy, the concept is indeed redundant. As was shown above, processes of foreign policy change that originate from domestic actors who offer their own vision for the redirection of national foreign policy can be identified and explained by existing theories.

Finally, as has been pointed out, even though the use of 'some form of process tracing' (Haverland, 2008: 66) is fairly common, what constitutes 'good process tracing' (Checkel, 2006: 369) is yet to be determined. Detailed predictions regarding actors' understanding of the policy problem and the manner in which the latter influences the framing of alternatives and their assessment make it possible to distinguish between foreign policy change that constitutes a response to EU foreign policy dynamics or other external variables and that which is produced endogenously, when key foreign policymakers offer their own vision for foreign policy reform.

## Notes

1. Europeanization is a process of incorporation of EU norms, practices and procedures into the domestic level. For a detailed conceptual analysis of Europeanization, including an assessment of alternative conceptualizations, see Moumoutzis (2011).
2. For instrumental explanations of the Europeanization of national foreign policy, see Moumoutzis (2011).
3. In the aftermath of the Imia/Kardak crisis Turkey was claiming sovereignty over numerous islets in the Aegean, which Greece considered its own territory. The crisis was therefore interpreted as an escalation of – what is perceived in Greece as – Turkish aggression; see Simitis (2005: 58–74).
4. For external shocks that demonstrate policy failure as a powerful factor that drives (foreign) policy change, see Hermann (1990: 12).
5. For the term, see Featherstone and Radaelli (2003).
6. An individual – usually a head of state or government – who has and decides to exercise the authority to commit their country's resources; see Hermann and Hermann (1989).
7. A fourth explanation that attributed causal significance to shifts in Greece's relative power position and the economic implications of Greek policy was also tested. Due to space limitations and the fact that it was refuted, this explanation is not discussed here.

8. For this particular application of process tracing, see also Moumoutzis (2011).
9. Interviews with member of the Greek Cabinet (7 May 2008), high-ranking Greek government officials (13 March 2008, 2 April 2008 and 5 May 2008) and Greek Foreign Ministry officials (18 April 2008 and 27 May 2008).
10. Interviews with high-ranking Greek government official (2 April 2008) and advisors to Prime Minister Simitis (21 March 2008 and 14 July 2008).
11. Interview with advisor to Prime Minister Simitis (14 July 2008).
12. See also Simitis (1995: 135).
13. It is instructive to note that during the 1995 Cannes European Council, Greek Prime Minister Andreas Papandreou categorically rejected the proposal to invite the Turkish Prime Minister to attend the December 1995 summit in Madrid, citing not only Turkish policy towards Greece and Cyprus but also human rights violations. For Papandreou's statements, see Athens News Agency (1995).
14. As will be shown further, Greek foreign policymakers were not convinced that this course of action constituted an inappropriate response to this problem.
15. This particular provision of the agreement was the result of Greece's policy on the Cyprus problem. This policy is not discussed in great detail here, as Greece began to pursue it prior to Simitis' election as Prime Minister and it remained fairly uncontroversial during the period under investigation. For this policy, see Kranidiotis (2000) and Simitis (2005: 106–124).
16. Interviews with high-ranking Greek government officials (2 April 2008), high-ranking Foreign Ministry officials (15 May 2008 and 27 May 2008), advisor to Prime Minister Simitis (14 July 2008) and advisor to Foreign Minister Papandreou (12 May 2008).

# References

Athens News Agency (1995) Bulletin, No. 624, 28 June.

Bennett, A. and Elman, C. (2006) 'Complex Causal Relations and Case Study Methods: The Example of Path Dependence', *Political Analysis* 14 (3): 250–267.

Checkel, J.T. (2005) 'International Institutions and Socialisation in Europe: Introduction and Framework', *International Organization* 59 (4): 801–826.

Checkel, J.T. (2006) 'Tracing Causal Mechanisms', *International Studies Review* 8 (2): 362–370.

Cortell, A.P. and Davis Jr., J.W. (2000) 'Understanding the Domestic Impact of International Norms: A Research Agenda', *The International Studies Review* 2 (1): 65–87.

Economides, S. (2005) 'The Europeanisation of Greek Foreign Policy', *West European Politics* 28 (2): 471–491.

Eleftherotypia (1999) 'Simitis' Displeasure with Partners', 15 January.

European Commission (2000) Eurobarometer: Public Opinion in the European Union, Report Number 52.

Featherstone, K. (2005) 'Introduction: "Modernisation" and Structural Constraints of Greek Politics', *West European Politics* 28 (2): 223–241.

Featherstone, K. and Radaelli, C.M. (2003) 'A Conversant Research Agenda' in K. Featherstone and C.M. Radaelli (eds.) *The Politics of Europeanisation*, Oxford: Oxford University Press, pp. 331–341.

Haverland, M. (2008) 'Methodology' in P. Graziano and M.P. Vink (eds.) *Europeanisation: New Research Agendas*, Basingstoke: Palgrave Macmillan, pp. 59–72.

Hermann, C.F. (1990) 'Changing Course: When Governments Choose to Redirect Foreign Policy', *International Studies Quarterly* 34 (1): 3–21.

Hermann, M.G. (2003) 'Assessing Leadership Style: Trait Analysis' in Jerrold M. Post (ed.) *The Psychological Assessment of Political Leaders: With Profiles of Saddam Hussein and Bill Clinton*, Ann Arbor, MI: University of Michigan Press, pp. 178–212.

Hermann, M.G. and Hermann, C.F. (1989) 'Who Makes Foreign Policy Decisions and How: An Empirical Inquiry', *International Studies Quarterly* 33 (4): 361–387.

Hermann, M.G., Preston, T., Korany, B. and Shaw, T.M. (2001) 'Who Leads Matters: The Effects of Powerful Individuals', *International Studies Review* 3 (2): 83–131.

Hill, C. (1993) 'The Capability-Expectations Gap or Conceptualising Europe's International Role', *Journal of Common Market Studies* 31 (3): 305–328.

Hudson, V.M. and Vore, C.S. (1995) 'Foreign Policy Analysis Yesterday, Today and Tomorrow', *Mershon International Studies Review* 39 (2): 209–238.

Ioakimidis, P. (2000) 'The Europeanisation of Greece's Foreign Policy: Progress and Problems' in A. Mitsos and E. Mossialos (eds.) *Contemporary Greece and Europe*, Ashgate: Aldershot, pp. 359–372.

Ioakimidis, P. (2003) 'The Model of Foreign Policy Making in Greece: Individuals Versus Institutions' in P.I. Tsakonas (ed.) *Contemporary Greek Foreign Policy* [in Greek], Athens: Sideris, pp. 91–136.

Kaarbo, J. (1997) 'Prime Minister Leadership Styles in Foreign Policy Decision-Making: A Framework for Research', *Political Psychology* 18 (3): 553–581.

Kavakas, D. (2000) 'Greece' in I. Manners and R.G. Whitman (eds.) *The Foreign Policies of European Union Member States*, Manchester: Manchester University Press, pp. 144–161.

Kazamias, A. (1997) 'The Quest for Modernisation in Greek Foreign Policy and Its Limitations', *Mediterranean Politics* 2 (2): 71–94.

Kranidiotis, Y. (2000) *Greek Foreign Policy: Thoughts and Concerns at the Threshold of the 21st Century* [in Greek]. Athens: Sideris.

Mahoney, J. and Goertz, G. (2006) 'A Tale of Two Cultures: Contrasting Quantitative and Qualitative Research', *Political Analysis* 14 (3): 227–249.

March, J.G. and Olsen, J.P. (2004) 'The Logic of Appropriateness', *ARENA Working Papers*, 04/09.

Mitropoulos, D. (2003) 'Foreign Policy and Greek Media: Subordination, Emancipation and Apathy' in P.I. Tsakonas (ed.) *Contemporary Greek Foreign Policy* [in Greek], Athens: Sideris, pp. 275–295.

Moumoutzis, K. (2011) 'Still Fashionable Yet Useless? Addressing Problems with Research on the Europeanisation of Foreign Policy', *Journal of Common Market Studies* 49 (3): 607–629.

Nuttall, S.J. (2000) *European Foreign Policy*. Oxford: Oxford University Press.

Pangalos, T. (1999) 'EU Financial Assistance to Turkey', *Ta Nea*, 30 August.

Pangalos, T. (2000) Interview with Y. Papadopoulos, *Apogevmatini*, 24 January.

Papandreou, G.A. (1997) 'After Luxembourg', *To Vima*, 21 December.

Presidency Conclusions (1997) Luxembourg European Council, 12–13 December.

Presidency Conclusions (1999) Helsinki European Council, 10–11 December.

Radaelli, C.M. (2004) 'Europeanisation: Solution or Problem?', *European Integration Online Papers* 8 (16).

Rieker, P. (2006a) *Europeanisation of National Security Identity: The EU and the Changing Security Identities of the Nordic States*. London: Routledge.

Rieker, P. (2006b) 'From Common Defence to Comprehensive Security: Towards the Europeanisation of French Foreign and Security Policy?', *Security Dialogue* 37 (4): 509–528.

Rosati, J.A., Sampson III, M.W. and Hagan, J.D. (1994) 'The Study of Change in Foreign Policy' in J.A. Rosati, J.D. Hagan and M.W. Sampson III (eds.) *Foreign Policy Restructuring: How Governments Respond to Global Change*, Columbia, SC: University of South Carolina Press, pp. 3–21.

Rozakis, C.L. (2005) 'International Law and its Function in Greco-Turkish Relations (1974/2004)' in C. Arvanitopoulos and M. Koppa (eds.) *30 Years of Greek Foreign Policy 1974–2004* [in Greek], Athens: Livani, pp. 155–162.

Schimmelfenning, F., Engert, S. and Knobel, H. (2003) 'Costs, Commitment and Compliance: The Impact of EU Democratic Conditionality on Latvia, Slovakia and Turkey', *Journal of Common Market Studies* 41 (3): 495–518.

Simitis, C. (1992) *Nationalistic Populism or National Strategy?* [in Greek]. Athens: Gnosi.

Simitis, C. (1995) *For a Powerful Society, For a Powerful Greece* [in Greek]. Athens: Plethron.

Simitis, C. (1996) Speech in Parliament, Athens, 9 December.

Simitis, C. (1999) Speech in Parliament, Athens, 15 December.

Simitis, C. (2004) 'The End of a Strategy', Ta Nea, 23 April.

Simitis, C. (2005) *Policy for a Creative Greece 1996–2004* [in Greek]. Athens: Polis.

Stoessinger, J.G. (1985) *Crusaders and Pragmatists: Movers of Modern American Foreign Policy*. New York: Norton.

Tonra, B. (2001) *The Europeanisation of National Foreign Policy: Dutch, Danish and Irish Foreign Policy in the European Union*. Ashgate: Aldershot.

Tsakonas, P. (2005) 'Theory and Practice in Greek Foreign Policy', *Southeast European and Black Sea Studies* 5 (3): 427–437.

Tsakonas, P. (2010) *The Incomplete Breakthrough in Greek-Turkish Relations: Grasping Greece's Socialisation Strategy*. Basingstoke: Palgrave Macmillan.

Valinakis, Y. (1989) *Introduction to Greek Foreign Policy 1949–1988* [in Greek]. Thesaloniki: Paratiritis.

Vasilakis, M. (2006) *The Scourge of God* [in Greek]. Athens: Gnoseis.

Wong, R. (2006) *The Europeanisation of French Foreign Policy: France and the EU in East Asia*. Basingstoke: Palgrave Macmillan.

# 14
# Lessons Learned: Beyond Causality

*Claudio M. Radaelli and Theofanis Exadaktylos*

The ratification of the Treaty of Lisbon, the current financial outlook and sustainability concerns raise the key question of the effects of integration, more so than the origin or the nature of the process itself. The issue is exactly how, where and through which mechanisms and in combination with what other agents or parallel processes of change these transformative effects come about.

To that extent, making conditional propositions is more useful than the idea of making predictions through classic theories of European integration. Since there is no homogeneous response to European Union (EU) pressures by the member states, the issue is not one of convergence, modernization or harmonization, but rather one of measuring variation. This is evident when we consider the contemporary persistence of various forms of political organization of the economy across Europe, but also international policy diffusion beyond the EU. Resiliency on the one hand and sources of change external to the EU on the other make it difficult to establish which portion of the variation is attributed to EU causes and which part is accounted for by other factors.

There is now a substantial literature on processes and outcomes of Europeanization. Yet, scholars working in this field are still struggling with fundamental issues of research design. Our volume is informed by epistemological pluralism and the contemporary debates on designing social scientific research, addressing causality from different perspectives. Our aim at the beginning of our project was to draw on strong but diverse foundations in research traditions to deal with concrete, substantive problems of causal analysis of Europeanization effects. Consequently, we have sought to embed empirical research within a dimension of 'research design' awareness and to examine how we can answer substantive questions about public policy, legislation, cities, foreign policy and political parties, in relation to the literature on causality in the social sciences.

Let us recall the five questions introduced in Chapter 1 and take stock of the contributions to our project:

- What are the notions of causal explanation adopted by scholars in this field and how do they relate to different concepts of Europeanization?
- How do different research traditions handle causality in this field?
- What are the research design issues arising out of different strategies?
- What is the proper role of process-tracing techniques?
- How do individual case studies handle explanation and how do they generate the variation that is essential to deal with causal explanation?

*Notions of causal explanation:* The springboard for this discussion is of course the relationship between independent and dependent variables. The contributions to the volume seem to converge on the following points about causation, such as (i) a constellation of contributing causes, (ii) a plurality of outcomes and (iii) a set of triggering intervening variables and/or different mechanisms.

In terms of conceptions of causality, Exadaktylos and Radaelli have exposed the variability within the field in relation to the definition of Europeanization. Essentially, different authors are after different things when they attend to measuring Europeanization and its effects, although the literature is at least consolidating on some prevalent notions of causality. Töller has zoomed in on measuring Europeanization as quantitative effect of the EU on national legislation. Even in this narrower sense, causality presents its own set of challenges – but there are ways to cope with them. At the other extreme, Bache et al. and Lynggaard take bold steps in embedding the notion of causation in issues of epistemology and ontology. From their perspective, we can only talk of different types of causation and different understandings of what a cause is and what it 'does'. Their chapters have made these types and understandings explicit and amenable to social scientific enquiry.

In temporal analyses of change, complex notions of causality result from processes taking place simultaneously at the national and international levels – variably appraised in this volume (Ladrech; Exadaktylos; and Ladi on non-linearity and the conjunctional attributes of causation). All contributors have discussed research designs that, given a certain, explicit notion of causation (probabilistic, deterministic or counterfactual, see Radaelli, Chapter 1), make empirical analysis feasible and compatible with intersubjective standards of quality within the social sciences. Lynggaard and Bache et al. have also considered the link between concepts and empirical design from the angle of traditions that are more interested in understanding than in explaining and measuring. This brings us to the second question.

*Research traditions:* The contributions to this volume portray a very interesting ongoing debate in the field. Not only have we found the classic distinction between quantitative and qualitative research, but also among critical, discursive and (varieties of) neo-positivist accounts. Admittedly, there is an inclination towards qualitative research in Europeanization (Chapter 2), but in a subtle way Töller has shown that despite the rigour of quantitative research, a qualitative refinement of variables and mechanisms (at the stages of concept formation and operationalization) is essential. This idea of a constructive analytical dialogue has been taken up by Bache et al., who have argued that Europeanization would actually benefit from a combination of methods, adding however that bridge-building across (especially) contending approaches without any kind of meta-theoretical roadmap would be counterproductive. Bridge-building does not mean that 'anything goes': Lynggaard has segmented causality with reference to distinct discourse-analytical methods, arguing that this tradition is not a monolith. Some discursive approaches are amenable to measurement and stand up to classic quality criteria such as reliability, internal validity and external validity. Others are more anti-foundational. Saurugger has looked at bridge-building from a different perspective, seeking to make sense of the interplay of institutional and actor-based.

Most of our contributors have incorporated some notion of long-term causality, touching on path-dependent approaches to the causality chain (with important caveats). Thus, with their caveats and limitations of course, diachronic studies do have potential for uncovering complex processes (Martinsen and Exadaktylos). Long-term processes often interact with short-term processes such as a single episode or a land-marking decision, calling for sensible re-calibration of research design (Moumoutzis).

*Research design issues:* One important theme in this collection is justification for case selection: why do we look at one case instead of another? Another is the need for explicit theoretical frameworks with observable implications. The chapters have proposed a wide range of methodological solutions. In quantitative terms we would benefit from previous comparative manifesto research (Töller). Discursive designs would benefit from content analysis of documents and methods that distinguish between discourse as variable, strategic context or strategic choice (Lynggaard). The advantages of document analysis then are availability, accessibility, reliability and long-term coverage for longitudinal studies. Qualitative studies would also benefit from replicability – there are no easy answers to this problem, but today qualitative scholars can improve by inserting in their footnotes links to primary sources (including links to scanned copies of documents, archives and other repositories of primary information). As mentioned, case selection is a delicate issue in this field. Research design in qualitative case studies is quite challenging, since we are inclined to choose cases that are seemingly consistent with outcomes of Europeanization predicted by theory. The starting point should be to identify and establish why certain cases constitute potential cases of Europeanization (Moumoutzis).

Another topic that cropped up on several occasions throughout the chapters concerns the potential of various types of Europeanization research for mechanism-based analysis. Mechanisms are an essential feature of explanation. Although a plurality of mechanisms has been identified by our authors, it is fair to observe that for most of the contributors mechanisms do not represent an alternative to variable-based explanations – our reading of the majority of chapters is that they are complementary (see also the trend in the literature, in Chapter 2). Beyond this general remark, Europeanization scholars contribute to the literature on mechanisms by exploring specific types of mechanisms, such as coordination, non-compliance and implementation. Saurugger in particular shows how the causal analysis of non-compliance sheds light on more general mechanisms of implementation that may apply to other types of policy and contexts, outside the domain of the EU policy process. For Martinsen, the interaction of intervening variables and mechanisms is affected by rule specificity, means of regulation and time – by doing this, she provides general lessons on how to develop general scope conditions and how mechanisms affect other features of the policy process. Ladi has made the important point that, when designing rival hypotheses, we have to explicitly theorize types of mechanisms, rather than finding ad hoc pseudo-mechanistic explanations when we engage with process tracing. This leads us to the next question, about process-tracing techniques.

*The role of process tracing:* Clearly, there is enthusiasm for this technique among our contributors. We do not argue that process tracing is the only way forward, though. It is obvious that without rigour this technique turns explanation into description.

Process tracing can be organized by categories or 'big boxes' that have to be opened and investigated, such as actors, decisions and policy instruments, to mention a few (Exadaktylos). For Panke, process tracing can be an effective tool for testing hypotheses especially in small-$n$ research if within-case strategies are incorporated. Process tracing benefits immensely from explicit theorization, or at least a conceptual map of research questions, otherwise we end up with a map of reality that is as messy as reality itself.

*From case studies to causality:* Our missing link here is: how do individual case studies handle explanation and in what ways can they generate the variation necessary to lead to causal explanation? According to Exadaktylos, we have to both identify (theoretically and empirically) and single out the EU effect. For this purpose we select specific policy episodes and interrogate each of them in terms of direction of causation (from the EU to the member states being our hypothesized direction, but also remaining open to other possible directions). In the same vein, Ladrech builds on the question of Europeanization of party politics, with the intention of examining the exact causes and direction of EU-related party change. The methodological challenge in his field is precisely how to separate out EU-influenced change from other endogenous opportunistic and strategic changes. Multi-method approaches to establishing causality (qualitative and quantitative) are necessary, both in the study of party politics as well as in other fields such as the analysis of legislation. We submit that the explanatory-cumulative leverage of the single case study benefits from its integration in a multi-method framework – although, in terms of theoretical leverage, even the single case study can shed light on a mechanism that has not yet been theorized or prove the existence of a phenomenon.

Case studies face another layer of problems when we try to explain the absence of change. Saurugger has looked into the puzzle of how we establish causality in cases of no change (i.e., inertia or even retrenchment). Martinsen has provided suggestions for handling less likely cases of Europeanization, such as health care, where Europeanization may be gradual or delayed due to explicit causal factors of our unit of analysis. This is also a concern for Panke, especially when exploring mechanisms of shifting from non-compliance to compliance. Finally, Dossi has provided a template for inserting case studies within a broader framework of modes of Europeanization, beyond legalistic approaches and into theoretical policy analysis.

Reflecting on traditions, our project covered four important traditions. These are the qualitative tradition based on a small number of comparable cases (as shown by Panke, with the option of within-case observations); discourse-analytic approaches; the critical realist framework; and quantitative methods (in this volume chiefly represented by legislative studies, although the field of party politics is also rich in quantitative methods). In turn, the traditions can be divided into those with more emphasis on data set observations and those eminently concerned with causal-process observations. The former is the classic statistical notion of observation. In contrast, a causal-process observation is 'an insight or piece of data that provides information about context, process, or mechanism, and that contributes distinctive leverage in causal inference' (Seawright and Collier, 2004: 277). The causal-process observation is often portrayed metaphorically as 'smoking gun' observation, that is, evidence that confirms causal inference in qualitative research.

In our volume, we have approached both types of observations (with causal-process observations dominating the chapters with process-tracing methods), noting however that it is not easy to pin down exactly what the 'smoking gun' properties of causal-process observations may be in causal sequences. More generally on traditions, the boundaries between qualitative and quantitative research are often blurred – not only because, as we shall see in a moment, there is the option of multi-method or mixed-method research, but also because statements like 'Denmark is less Europeanized than Sweden' are about quantity (i.e., 'less' and 'more'), although they may be supported by qualitative research. It is indeed common to observe qualitative researchers making quantitative statements about Europeanization.

To conclude on the traditions represented in the volume, we observe that they are partially overlapping with the classic fourfold characterization of the field of political science, based on qualitative, quantitative, set-theoretic and interpretivist approaches. Although critical realism and interpretivism have crossed roads several times in the history of these approaches, the latter includes methods such as ethnography that have not been discussed here. As for set-theoretic approaches to causality and methods, this is actually a limitation of our project. Qualitative comparative analysis (QCA) and related techniques (Rihoux and Ragin, 2009) are now popular in political science. Beyond the technique, QCA raises important issues concerning causality, such as equifinality and the identification of different combinations of variables that are jointly sufficient or necessary for a certain outcome. The causal logic behind QCA is different from the logic of regression-inspired studies. Some elements of this causal logic feature in some small-*n* qualitative studies, but it is exemplified by methods embracing Boolean algebra and typically used for medium-*n* studies; for an example of QCA methods applied to Europeanization, see Klüver (2010).

This brings us to other limitations of the project. To begin with, the full range of qualitative methodologies for establishing causality has not been explored, given that most of our qualitative contributors have preferred to discuss process tracing rather than other qualitative techniques. The weaponry of quantitative techniques has barely been scratched, and we have not dealt with the classic problems of establishing causality in diffusion studies. As mentioned in Chapter 1, diffusion studies are concerned with establishing whether a pattern common to *n* units is the result of emulation or transfer from one unit to the others, or the outcome of independent responses to a common contextual situation or problem, or arises out of top-down Europeanization. This is a variation on the empirical challenge of spatial interdependence known as Galton's problem (Franzese and Hays, 2008: 574, n. 5).

Further, we have not linked empirical appraisals of causality to normative judgements about Europeanization. Although empirical causal inference and normative issues are separate, there is an obvious bridge between establishing causality about the role of the EU in domestic policy and propositions about the effects of Europeanization on legitimacy and what is left for democratic politics at the domestic level.

These limitations and caveats are a useful springboard for putting forward propositions about the direction of future research. We expect causality to remain prominent in this field. However, we will probably see (and we definitively need) a more diverse approach to causal inference and causality in general. QCA and related techniques are well suited to exploring the logic of causality in novel ways, possibly addressing medium-*n* samples, such as the core EU-15 'old' member states, or the current member states (a number too large for the traditional small-*n* comparisons and too limited for statistical analyses unless data are also available for a long-time sequence).

Following a trend in mainstream political science, research on Europeanization could usefully draw from the new generation of multi-method and mixed-method approaches – see Lieberman (2005) on mixing qualitative and quantitative methods; for an overview of professional associations and organizations fostering this type of research in political science, see Collier and Elman (2008). Perhaps with a hint of rhetorical exaggeration, a methodologist like Andrew Bennett noted in the context of a high-profile workshop of the National Science Foundation in the USA (Lamont and White, 2009) that '[t]here is tremendous interest in political science, especially among graduate students, in engaging in multi-method research. There is almost nothing written on how to combine research methods, however, and there are disciplinary/cultural barriers as well as technical challenges in doing so' (Bennett, 2009: 92).

Be it as it may, our experience in the UK is that at best we train Politics doctoral students and postdoctoral researchers in mixing qualitative and quantitative methods (mostly following the strategy suggested by Lieberman, 2005), but we have barely mapped the wider territory of multi-method approaches that go beyond the combination of quantitative and qualitative techniques. In this vein, Bache et al.'s chapter echoes Bennett's concern that when we travel across methods we also switch to different ontologies and epistemologies. These may or may not be 'cultural barriers' in the sense of Bennett, but – this is an essential input provided by Lynggaard's chapter on strategies for discourse analysis – beyond a certain threshold, methods embedded in very different research traditions (with their own quality standards) become somewhat incommensurable (Marsh and Furlong, 2002). Traditions, however, can hinder progress if their supporters assume that a given tradition is inherently superior to the others in solving all problems of causality – for example by arguing that a given tradition has the 'right' definition of causality, from which originate the 'best' approaches to establishing causality.

Fortunately, incommensurability can be overcome when we handle substantive research questions. Granted that there are genuine different ontological and epistemological assumptions (Marsh and Furlong, 2002), for some research puzzles researchers should embrace a kind of analytic eclecticism (Sil and Katzenstein, 2010) in Europeanization research. This is a strategy to recombine theoretical as well as substantive features of scholarship emanating from separate research traditions. The strategy is attractive. It goes beyond the meta-theoretical and ontological obstacles to use causal explanations drawn from different traditions to get to grips with substantive research problems. It is also distinct from the simple operation of applying more than one method to address causation. Indeed, a project can be analytic-eclectic even by using a single method, provided that it blends concepts, mechanisms and interpretations drawn from more than one paradigm or tradition.

Eclectic researchers can effectively overcome the paradigm-bound approach. In fact, analytic eclecticism accepts pragmatically that there are various types of causal mechanisms that operate at different levels, 'revealing hidden connections among elements of seemingly incommensurable paradigm-bound theories, with an eye to generating novel insights that bear on policy debates and practical dilemmas' (Sil and Katzenstein, 2010: 2, 43–48, on the pragmatic philosophical presuppositions of this approach). Essentially, this approach 'seeks to extricate, translate, and selectively integrate analytic elements – concepts, logics, mechanisms, and interpretations – of theories or narratives that have been developed within separate paradigms but that address related aspects of substantive problems that have both scholarly and practical significance' (Sil and Katzenstein, 2010: 10). Interestingly, Sil and Katzenstein include in their eclectic analysis of key authors some well-known European Studies specialists, such as Cornelia Woll, Nicolas Jabko and Frank Schimmelfennig. The door for this type of eclectic exploration in Europeanizaton research, therefore, is already ajar; it just needs to be pushed a bit.

Finally, we have addressed causality in this volume with two issues in mind: that is, how to establish cause–effect relationships in different types of research projects and how to use causal conjectures in testing theories. One challenge for future research is to carry on with *theory testing*, but also to address *theory development* (Mahoney, 2010). Although some chapters in the book have hinted at how quality standards for establishing causality contribute to the development of theories, this is clearly the next big question. How does Europeanization contribute to the development of political science theories and models of political behaviour? This is particularly important if we believe that Europeanization as such is not a theory, and hence there is no need to perfect a special, *sui generis* theory of Europeanization, but a component of more general theories of public policy, politics and institutions (Featherstone and Radaelli, 2003). It is in relation to these theories that the contribution of Europeanization as framework for causal analysis will have to be assessed by future research endeavours. This collection has shown that there are contributions to theory development in terms of process tracing, mechanisms, patterns of compliance, implementation and eclectic qualitative analysis, but future projects could usefully explore the theory-building potential of quantitative studies with the aim of integrating the overall theoretical results of Europeanization research into 'normal' theories of politics (Hassenteufel and Surel, 2000).

# References

Bennett, A. (2009) 'Overview of organizational efforts on qualitative methods in political science'. In M. Lamont and P. White (Eds.) *Workshop on Interdisciplinary Standards for Systematic Qualitative Research* (Washington, DC: National Science Foundation): 90–93.

Collier, D. and C. Elman (2008) 'Qualitative and multi-method research: Organizations, publication, and reflections on integration'. In J.M. Box-Steffensmeier, H. Brady and D. Collier (Eds.) *The Oxford Handbook of Political Methodology* (Oxford: Oxford University Press): 779–795.

Featherstone, K. and C.M. Radaelli (Eds.) (2003) *The Politics of Europeanization* (Oxford: Oxford University Press).

Franzese, R.J. and J. Hays (2008) 'Empirical models of spatial interdependence'. In J.M. Box-Steffensmeier, H. Brady and D. Collier (Eds.) *The Oxford Handbook of Political Methodology* (Oxford: Oxford University Press): 570–604.

Hassenteufel, P. and Y. Surel (2000) 'Des politiques publiques comme les autres? Construction de l'objet et outils d'analyse des politiques européennes', *Politique Européene*, 1: 8–24.

Klüver, H. (2010) 'Europeanization of lobbying activities: When national interest groups spill over to the European level', *Journal of European Integration*, 32(2): 175–191.

Lamont, M. and P. White (2009) *Workshop on Interdisciplinary Standards for Systematic Qualitative Research* (Washington, DC: National Science Foundation), available at http://www.nsf.gov/sbe/ses/soc/ISSQR_workshop_rpt.pdf.

Lieberman, E. S. (2005) 'Nested analysis as a mixed-method strategy for comparative research', *American Political Science Review*, 99(3): 435–451.

Mahoney, J. (2010) 'After KKV: The new methodology of qualitative research', *World Politics*, 62(1): 120–147.

Marsh, D. and P. Furlong (2002) 'A skin not a sweater: Ontology and epistemology in political science'. In D. Marsh and G. Stoker (Eds.) *Theory and Methods in Political Science*, 2nd edition (Basingstoke: Palgrave Macmillan): 17–44.

Rihoux, B. and C. Ragin (Eds.) (2009) *Configurational Comparative Methods: Qualitative Comparative Analysis and Related Techniques* (London: Sage).

Seawright, J. and D. Collier (2004) 'Glossary'. In H.E. Brady and D. Collier (Eds.) *Rethinking Social Inquiry: Diverse Tools and Shared Standards* (Oxford: Rowman & Littlefield).

Sil, R. and P. Katzenstein (2010) *Beyond Paradigms: Analytic Eclecticism in the Study of World Politics* (Basingstoke: Palgrave Macmillan).

# Index